D1391684

1968

INTRODUCTION TO ST AUGUSTINE
THE CITY OF GOD

FIDELIS SERVUS ET PRUDENS QUEM
CONSTITUIT DOMINUS SUPER FAMILIAM
SUAM UT DET ILLIS IN TEMPORE
TRITICI MENSURAM

*Luc. xii. 42. The Communio of the Feast
of St Augustine, 28 August*

Mentitur qui te totum legisse fatetur;
  Aut quis cuncta tua lector habere potest?
Namque voluminibus mille, Augustine, refulges;
  Testantur libri quod loquor ipse tui.
Quamvis multorum placeat praesentia libris,
  Si Augustinus adest, sufficit ipse tibi.

Lines placed by St Isidore over the
shelves containing St Augustine's works
in the library at Seville.

INTRODUCTION TO ST AUGUSTINE

THE CITY OF GOD

being
selections from the De Civitate Dei
including most of the XIXth book
with text, translation and
running commentary
by

R. H. BARROW

FABER AND FABER LIMITED
24 Russell Square
London

First published in mcml
by Faber and Faber Limited
24 Russell Square London W.C.1
Printed in Great Britain by
R. MacLehose and Company Limited
The University Press Glasgow

CARISSIMIS MEIS

GRATI ANIMI PIGNUS

Contents

9

Preface

This volume contains selections from the *de civitate Dei* of St Augustine, Latin text and English translation, with an analysis of the argument and a running commentary. The selections are taken from Books i, ii, v, xii, xiv, xv, xviii; they lead up to the nineteenth book, of which nearly the whole is included.

The main purposes in publishing this selection are:

(1) to bring within the reach of a wider public than hitherto one of the great books of the world, great not only in its range and depth, but in its historical influence, yet a work which in its original fullness is so long and discursive as to deter modern readers.

(2) to encourage a wider horizon in the teaching and learning of classics so as to include Christian writers whose debt to classics was great; and to link up once again the study of classics and the study of divinity. At present classical and Christian literature, and their teaching and learning, tend to be separated—to the great loss of both. Classical studies thus lack a conclusion, and Christian studies lack a foundation. The classical student would gain from becoming aware of the criticism passed upon classical ways of thought by the Christian writers trained upon classical literature and philosophy; the student of Christianity would understand more fully the background of thought in early Christian literature and would be more fitted for the task of interpretation. The medieval historian would start with knowledge of the roots of the Middle Ages.

(3) to reaffirm the importance of a particular method of study, the method (*a*) of reading the actual words of an author rather than reading about him, (*b*) of reading those words in the light of the author's own day and not in the light of interpretations put upon them by later ages. For the running commentary assumes a reading of the text, and the text is approached from the standpoint of its own day and not from the Middle Ages, as is the general custom. Yet a work of the fifth century A.D. would be of no appeal, except to a curious few, if it did not deal with topics of live interest in the twentieth century. It is one purpose of the commentary to leave the reader with a sense of the relevance of the *de civitate Dei* to the conditions of modern times.

The Latin text is the text of Dombart-Kalb 1928, and for permission to print it I am indebted to the publishers B. G. Teubner. The translation

is not chiefly concerned to give a close rendering of the original, but to convey St Augustine's meaning to those who do not read Latin; very occasionally the English contains a few words of explanation which are not in the Latin.

With the generosity which his friends well know Professor N. H. Baynes was kind enough to read the translation and the commentary in typescript, and I owe to him many suggestions, though it must not be assumed that he always agrees with the views expressed. To Lady Helen Asquith I am grateful for reading the proofs and for help in compiling the Index.

R. H. B.

TABLE OF EXTRACTS FROM BOOKS I, V, XII, XIV, XV AND XVIII AND OF OMISSIONS FROM BOOK XIX

13

SOME DATES

	A.D.
Birth of St Augustine	354
Reign of Valentinian I	364–375
Reign of Valentinian II	375–392
Reign of Gratian	375–383
Reign of Theodosius I	379–395
Reign of Honorius	395–423
contra Academicos, de ordine	386
Soliloquia	387
de vera religione	389–391
Claudian	flor. 395–408
The Confessions	*c.* 400
de doctrina Christiana	397–427
de Trinitate	400–416
de catechizandis rudibus	*c.* 400
Death of Stilicho	408
First siege of Rome by Alaric	408
Second siege of Rome by Alaric	409
Attalus Emperor	
Third siege and capture of Rome	410
de urbis excidio	
Goths enter Gaul	412
de civitate Dei begun	413
Orosius at Hippo	414
Reign of Valentinian III	425–455
de civitate Dei finished	426?
Vandals cross to Africa	428
Siege of Hippo	430
Death of St Augustine	430

INTRODUCTION

Introduction

(A) ST AUGUSTINE'S OWN ACCOUNT
OF THE *DE CIVITATE DEI*

St Augustine's own account of the *de civitate Dei* is given in chapter lxix of the second book of the *Retractationes*.

'In the meantime Rome was overwhelmed by the invasion of the Goths under their king Alaric and by the tide of the great calamity which followed. The worshippers of the false gods in all their diversity, whom we call by a name now well established "pagans", tried to attribute the overthrow of Rome to the Christian religion and excelled themselves in the bitterness and malignity of the blasphemy which they now began to utter against the true God. Blazing with zeal for the household of God[1] I started to write the books of the *de civitate Dei* to combat their blasphemies and errors. This work detained me for several years, since many problems interrupted me, the solution of which I did not think it right to postpone, and therefore they had first claim on my time. However, this ambitious work, *de civitate Dei*, was at last concluded in twenty-two books.

The first five books refute the argument that human prosperity depends upon the worship of those numerous gods whom the pagans have long been accustomed to worship, and that all the evils which we see around us spring into being and abound because that worship is now forbidden.

The next five books are directed against those who admit that mortal men have never been and never will be free from such evils, which vary in degree from place to place and from time to time and with different individuals; but who argue that the worship of many gods and the sacrifices which accompany that worship are a valuable investment against the life after death. In these ten books, then, those two sets of empty fancies are refuted.

The second part of this work, occupying twelve books, is devoted expressly to meeting the criticism that we have refuted other people's position but have not declared our own; nevertheless, even in the first ten books we declare our beliefs when there is need, and also in the following twelve books we refute the views of our opponents.

[1] John ii. 17.

Of the twelve books which make up the latter part the first four contain an account of the two cities, the city of God and the city of this world. The second four books describe their growth or progress; the third, and last, four are concerned with their proper ends.

And so the whole twenty-two books, though treating of both cities, take their title from the better of the two cities and are therefore called *de civitate Dei....*[1]

This work begins with the words, "The most glorious city of God."'

Thus the first ten books are on the whole negative and destructive in character, demolishing the arguments of the pagans. The remaining books are positive and constructive. The bare scheme, therefore, is as follows:

NEGATIVE	Books i–v	the evils of this world cannot be attributed to the ban which Christianity lays upon pagan cults.
	Books vi–x	pagan cults are valueless as an investment against the future life.
POSITIVE	Books xi–xiv	the rise of the city of God and the earthly city.
	Books xv–xviii	their growth.
	Books xix–xxii	their proper 'ends'.

But it would be a mistake to regard the first ten books as wholly negative in character. Their general trend may be destructive, but they contain very much constructive criticism and statement.

The *Retractationes*, written in A.D. 427, is a remarkable document. When St Augustine was nearly 74 years old—for 'the task ought not to be put off any longer'—he set himself to review ninety-three of his own works. The review of each follows the same plan; first, he describes the circumstances which led him to write the book, and then he restates passages which might easily be interpreted by his opponents in a sense contrary to his intention, or corrects mistatements and errors or deliberately withdraws what he had said. 'When I said . . ., I ought to have said . . .'; 'the passage must not be interpreted to mean . . .'; 'the expression seems most unfitting'; 'the statement was made without due care'; 'I had not pursued the enquiry carefully enough'; 'the statement is true enough, but it leaves unanswered the question whether . . .'; 'I now strongly disapprove of my argument . . .'; 'Why I said . . . I cannot remember'. These are typical sentences quoted at random. To the student of St Augustine the *Retractationes* is invaluable for the brief account of the

[1] In the passage omitted, A. corrects two errors of detail which his work contains, the first a point about Abraham's sacrifice, the second about Samuel.

historical setting of each work no less than for the corrections themselves. But the book is also most striking evidence of the character of the man; for no reader can miss the passion for truth, the eagerness that his case should be clearly presented and no weapons left in his opponents' hands, the readiness to correct and condemn himself, the humility of one who showed himself to the very end of a laborious life to be a good fighter, a candid self-critic and a humble disciple.

St Augustine's first reaction to the capture of Rome by Alaric is shown in the sermon known as 'On the destruction of the City' (*de urbis excidio*). He compares the capture of Rome with the destruction of Sodom, but immediately points the difference. There are two categories of just men, he argues—those who are just by divine standards, those who are just by human standards. Of the first there are none: even Daniel, an example of righteousness, confessed his sins. It is true that God scourges the just and the unjust, the 'just' according to human standards. But He does not destroy the just, even though He may slay them; they are preserved for ever. But Sodom He did destroy, for there were no just men; Rome He has not destroyed; Rome was spared from utter destruction for the sake of its just men; many escaped and many were spared. The destruction of buildings is not the destruction of a state, which consists of men rather than of walls. Rome was chastised and corrected rather than consumed. God was merciful: tribulation is salutary.

Within a short time St Augustine began the *dcD*,[1] as the *Retractationes* records, probably in A.D. 413, or shortly before. It was published in parts between A.D. 417 and 426; it was finished when St Augustine was 71 years old.

The extent of the destruction caused by Alaric should not be estimated too severely; the evidence of the sermon and of passages in the early books of the *dcD* make it clear that not much damage was done and that there was no massacre. Alaric himself was an Arian Christian and gave orders that life should be spared. For the invasion of Italy was not undertaken by Alaric out of hatred of the Roman Empire. Soon after the death of Theodosius in A.D. 395 he had become King of the Visigoths, a German people which, as a result of Hun pressure from the North-east, had eventually wrested from the Emperor permission to settle in lower Moesia (Bulgaria). For some fifteen years he had striven to attain power within the imperial administration, and, after invading Greece, was made 'Master of Soldiers' in Illyricum. He now turned his attention to the Western Empire, but an anti-German movement culminating in a slaughter of barbarians in Italy made it clear that he could expect neither land for his followers nor a position of authority for himself. He determined to seize

---

[1] In the following pages the abbreviation *dcD* will be used for *de civitate Dei*.

both, and eventually captured Rome in August, A.D. 410. Soon afterwards he died. Yet he was ambitious for power not in order to overthrow Rome, for like all barbarians he regarded the Roman Empire as necessary and desirable, but to claim for his people a share in its privileges.

After his death his brother Ataulf, who regarded the Goths almost as the servants of the Roman Empire, led his people into France and eventually into Spain. Here in A.D. 416 Wallia, successor to Ataulf, was employed by the Romans to keep in check the Vandals and Alans in Spain; in this task he had some success, driving them down into the south of the peninsula. The Visigoths were recalled and given settlements in Aquitaine.

But the Vandals had not been finally disposed of by Wallia. They had originally been pushed out of the Theiss valley as an indirect consequence of the Hun migration; they crossed the Rhine frontier in A.D. 406, found their way into France and thence into Spain, A.D. 409. For twenty years they laid waste this province, suffering only temporary check by Wallia; and in A.D. 428 Gaiseric became King and led his forces across the straits of Gibraltar into Africa. After initial success he was defeated and was forced into making a treaty under which the Vandals were recognised as *foederati*, that is, Roman subjects bound by treaty to Rome. But he was only biding his time; in a few years he captured Carthage and in A.D. 442 he extorted from Rome recognition as sovereign ruler of most of Roman Africa, and no longer a Roman subject. It was during this invasion that St Augustine died, with the Vandals round the walls of Hippo.

(B) NOTES ON SOME WORDS USED IN THE TEXT AND TRANSLATION

Before reading any part of the *dcD* it is important to understand some of the implications of certain words which constantly recur. The notes which follow do not profess to give a history of the word, but attempt to bring out some of the meanings which are vital to the *dcD*—since any English translation necessarily misses some of these meanings and is liable to import others foreign to the Latin.

City, Civitas

Four meanings may be distinguished:

(*a*) A body of citizens (*cives*); citizens regarded collectively as members of a political organisation; the stress here lies on 'citizen', not on 'political organisation'.

(*b*) The town or the area in which a body of *cives* lives.

(c) Community, state, unit of political association.

At the lowest the word implies some kind of cohesion, however loose, and some kind of order and government, however elementary: Caesar and Tacitus use the word for the Gallic and German tribes. At the highest level it implies a highly developed 'state' with an elaborated system of law and government and an advanced civilisation. In this sense a *civitas* may be a city-state with or without dependent cities or tracts of territory. Here the stress is on 'political organisation'.

(d) The status of being a citizen, citizenship, involving duties and rights. The status excludes those outside it, as, for example, foreigners and partially enfranchised people.

Without entering fully into what St Augustine means by *civitas Dei* we may say that sense (b) is entirely absent from the word; sense (a) is certainly present, but the organisation is not political; sense (c) is present, but the law is not political law, but religious and moral law; organisation is not external but internal. The *civitas Dei* has its own highly developed rules, but they are rules of its own. Sense (d) is present, but the status is conferred not by birth and decree, but by will and grace; citizenship is a state rather than a status. In so far as some are members of the *civitas Dei* and some are not, the *civitas Dei* is necessarily exclusive.

The traditional translation of *civitas* is 'city', and it is best to preserve it, since any other rendering is open to greater objection. It is so clear that *civitas Dei* does not mean a city made with bricks and stones and built in a particular place that the word can be made to carry the implication which the reader puts into it. It is a convenient blank which the reader will fill up as he reads. In some places the idea of fellow-citizen will be uppermost, in others the idea of government; elsewhere status or community or exclusion may be the implication of the word.

St Augustine calls the city a *civitas*, not a *respublica*. Yet, when Cicero wrote a treatise on 'the State' in imitation of Plato's on the 'Politeia', he called it *de republica* and the Latin translation of Plato's 'Politeia' is *respublica*, and the English is republic. In Roman political theory *respublica* is the technical word for the state; it has no implication of republic in the modern sense. It is, in fact, *res publica*, the public thing, whether the state be a monarchy or tyranny or democracy. Thus *respublica* is the word used when the Romans spoke of the 'theory of the state' or of an ideal 'state', and St Augustine had good knowledge of Cicero's *de re publica*, as will be seen in the nineteenth book. But he calls his work *de civitate*. He could not have called it *de republica*, for *respublica* implies the organisation of the material and human assets, the *res publica* of a community. *De republica* as a title means the theory of how best to organise these assets, and *respublica* as a title would mean the description of a 'state' in which these assets were

best organised[1]; with none of these ideas is St Augustine primarily concerned. What *de republica Dei* would mean it is hard to say.

From the title, then, it may be inferred that St Augustine does not intend to theorise on the ideal state in the sense of a Utopia; in fact, he proposes to treat of a partly actual state or rather *civitas*, showing its origin, tracing its development and defining its proper 'ends'. His work, therefore, is historical in the sense that it deals with what has been and is and will be.

But when he adds 'of God' he selects the city which is his concern from other cities, though in actual fact he classes all that is not *civitas Dei* under one heading as *civitas terrena*—'earthly city'. To select implies a standard or a theory of selection, a particular way of looking at the data and a principle of selecting some of the data and rejecting others. In the *dcD* history, the data, is looked at from the point of view of a theory, the principle on which the selection is made. The *dcD*, therefore, is philosophical as well as historical in nature; it is a philosophical criticism of history. So much the title shows.

This consideration of the title is not affected by the undoubted fact that St Augustine found the phrase ready to hand in the lxxxviith Psalm—'Glorious things are spoken of thee, city of God'—and found the idea of a heavenly citizenship in the Epistles of St Paul. But these matters are reserved for separate consideration.[2]

Fellowship, Societas

Socius is a partner; *societas* is either several partners or the relationship of partners. In ordinary social relationships *socius* may be a friend or intimate acquaintance, but some special relationship is often implied as the ground of the relationship. In business, *socii* are members of the same business company or syndicate; in politics, *socii* are allies joined to one another by special treaties for a common end. *Societas* in the abstract means any relationship of human beings brought together by a common purpose; the family, as persons regarded collectively, is a *societas*; their relationship is also *societas*. In the political sphere *societas* is the relationship of allies. The root meaning, therefore, is fellowship. The English 'society' is narrower in meaning than the Latin word; it fits some of its contexts but not all. For example, *societas* is applied to the family, but 'society' is not easily used in this context. The relationship of members of a state or country or culture to one another may be called, from one aspect, social relations, and 'society' is usual to denote such relations. On

---

[1] See, e.g. Cicero *de officiis* ii. 21, 73, where Cicero states that the function of society is to assert and maintain the rights of property.
[2] See page 140.

the other hand *societas hominum* is normal Latin for the relationship of all human beings to the rest; here English usually has to amplify the word 'society' by turning it into 'world society' or substituting some such phrase as 'the brotherhood of man'. In short, *societas* can be applied equally readily to a group of friends, a city, a nation, the human race, or the 'company of the faithful' on earth and in heaven. 'Society' in English is more restricted and tends to suggest social relations or 'social problems', the relations of members of a political or cultural or economic group; it is narrower in scope and introduces ideas often foreign to the Latin. In the translation, 'fellowship' has invariably been used; in some places it may sound somewhat unusual, but it is the rendering which suits most contexts and it preserves in all contexts the root idea which is essential to St Augustine's thought.

Ends, Fines

The following senses may be distinguished:

(*a*) *Finis* is properly that which sets a limit or marks a boundary. If a line is in process of being drawn, its limit is marked by its end; if an area is in process of being covered, the area is marked off by the limits or boundaries which the covering material imposes on itself or which are imposed on it. The *fines* mark the covered area from the uncovered area. Thus *finis* might be used to denote the end of a journey; *fines* is frequently used for the boundaries of an estate or a country.

(*b*) These notions are readily transferred from their literal 'spatial' sense to the sphere of thought and action. 'End', then, means 'end in view'. The end of a race is in sense (*a*) above the tape; in another sense it is the winning of the race, or the glory or the cup. Hence *finis* means 'purpose'.

(*c*) In moral philosophy *finis* is the technical word for the moral end, the pursuit of which determines that a particular line of conduct shall be adopted rather than another; one moral philosophy is distinguished from another by the *fines* which it proposes as ends to be pursued as the goal of moral action. Cicero's *de finibus* is a review of moral philosophies considered in the light of the ends proposed by them. The ends thus become the standards of comparison by which philosophies are judged in relation to one another.

(*d*) The realisation of a purpose, or the reaching of the goal, carries with it, from one point of view, the end or termination of a process; thus *finis* may imply consummation; from another point of view consummation is not a termination but a beginning. In a way, therefore, this sense of *finis* comes round again to sense (*a*).

St Augustine announces his intention of considering the 'ends' of the city of God. All these senses of *finis* are present in varying degree of relevancy in the passages which treat of the 'ends of the city of God'. The city has its purposes, its standards, its moral and spiritual objectives; they set a goal; they prescribe limits of thought and aspiration and action; they mark off, like boundaries, those who share the purposes of the city from those who do not; they reach their realisation and their consummation, which mark the end of one process and the beginning of another which is without end. They are different from the 'ends' of other states and therefore they serve as a basis of comparison. Other states, represented by but not identical with the *civitas terrena*, have their 'ends', which fulfil for them the same functions as the ends of the city of God fulfil for it.

In the translation the word 'end' has been used; it is the most satisfactory rendering because the various senses of *finis* are most easily read into it.

Justice, Righteousness, Iustitia

This is one of the most difficult words to translate, and a discussion of its meaning would involve a lengthy review of Hebrew and Greek and Roman thought on morals and politics and religion and law. For the present purpose it must suffice to separate some of the strands of meaning which make up the meaning of *iustitia* in the *dcD*.

In Hebrew thought the just man or the righteous man is the man who stands in right relationship to God. 'Noah was a righteous man . . . Noah walked with God'.[1] St Augustine can refer, without any further identification, to *iusti patres nostri*, and be understood to mean the patriarchs, who were righteous men.[2] Now, in different minds and in different stages of Hebrew religion, 'righteousness' varies according to the conception of what was necessary to keep the right relationship with God. In the Prophets all emphasis is placed on certain moral and religious qualities of mind; when the 'law' exercises its greatest influence, observance of the law is a necessary part of the keeping of the right relations.

By the age of St Augustine the word 'righteous' of Hebrew thought had been translated into Greek as *dikaios* and into Latin as *iustus*; and, as is to be expected, both words carried with them special interpretations from Latin and Greek thought. *Dikaiosunē* had been one of the most discussed and most powerful words of Greek philosophy. The thought of Plato had a profound influence upon St Augustine, and in Plato *dikaiosunē* had been primarily a moral notion; it meant the observance of 'the right' by each individual in a society, leading to the goodness of each member and of the

---

[1] Gen. vi. 9.   [2] *dcD* xix. 16 ad init.

society as a whole; the result would be righteousness in all spheres of relationship. Within its pervasive influence no particular sphere is to be isolated as the particular residence of justice; the field of legal relations is certainly covered and therefore *dikaiosunē* has its narrow meaning of legal justice, but it is only a fragment of the much vaster area covered by the word, which is essentially moral, even religious, in character. The sub-title of the *Republic* of Plato is 'concerning righteousness'; the ideal state was perfect because it was the embodiment of righteousness; the individual embodied righteousness, the state embodied it collectively. For individual and for state righteousness consisted in right relations; in the individual the soul and its desires, the body and its desires, must all be in the right relationship to each other (hence the importance of psychology to Plato); in the state each one individual must be in right relation to each other; and these right relations were dependent on a system of order, assigning to each part of the soul its place, to each member of the state his place.

In Latin thought *iustitia* carries with it very different notions, and particularly the notion of the law (*ius*) of the state. 'Law' covers the relationship of citizens to each other within the political system; if it extends to religion, for example, it does so in so far as religion is regarded as of political significance. If to the state *ius* is 'law', to the individual it is 'right' or 'rights' offered and safeguarded to him by law. *Iustitia* therefore always has the notion of assigning to the individual his rights with due regard also to the rights of others; the distributive element of justice therefore is always present. The definition of *iustitia* in the Digest of Justinian is as follows: 'justice is the constant and persistent will to assign to each individual his rights.' This 'will' has a moral quality, for its sanction is not to be found in *ius* itself, but in something which is higher than *ius* and is moral; *iustitia* therefore in spite of its derivation embraces the morality on which law is founded. Thus it is the most suitable word in Latin for *dikaiosunē* and St Augustine found it ready to hand in the Latin rendering of the *dikaiosunē* of St Paul's Epistles and of the Hebrew word for righteousness.

At the same time there is a sense in which law is always behind *iustitia*, but it is the law of order, the order which is at the back of all creation because the Creator is an *Ordinator* imposing on all things in Heaven, in the Universe and in the earth His own order. Thus *iustitia* is wider than the right relations of man to man; it includes the Universe and the right relations of men, angels and God; the rightness of the relations is due to the 'order' of God.

In the translation *iustitia* has been rendered as 'justice' or as 'righteousness' as seemed most appropriate. But it is essential to remember that the original word is the same.

TEXT AND TRANSLATION

S. Aurelius Augustinus
BISHOP
ON THE CITY OF GOD
DIRECTED AGAINST THE PAGANS

Preface

I. (preface)

The most glorious city of God—to defend that city against those who prefer their own gods to its Creator is the task which I have undertaken in this book, begun in fulfilment of my promise to you, my dearest son Marcellinus. I defend it in its two aspects—as it exists in its present temporal pilgrimage among the pagans, drawing its life from faith,[1] and as it exists in the permanence of that eternal abiding-place which it now awaits in patience,[2] till justice be turned into judgement,[3] and which it will fully obtain one day in final victory and in perfected peace. It is a great and difficult task, but God is my helper.[4]

For I know what efforts are needed to persuade the proud of the virtue of humility. It is humility which overtops all earthly heights, which are temporary, unstable, and tottering to their fall, and lifts us to an altitude which is not claimed as a right by human arrogance but is the free gift of divine grace. For in the Scriptures of His chosen people the king and founder of this city which we now undertake to describe revealed the meaning of His divine law, wherein it is declared, 'God resists the proud, but gives grace to the humble'.[5] This prerogative belongs to God; but the soul which is puffed up with pride also claims it as his own and loves to hear among his praises that 'he spares the conquered and breaks the proud in war'.[6] For this reason I cannot pass over in silence the earthly city which, thirsting for dominion, is itself dominated by lust for dominion, even though its peoples are slaves; about this city I must say, as opportunity affords, whatever is demanded by the plan of the work which I have undertaken.

---

[1] Hab. ii. 4; Rom. i. 17.   [2] Rom. viii. 25.   [3] Ps. xciv. 15.
[4] Ps. lxii. 9.   [5] Prov. iii. 34; Jam. iv. 6; 1 Pet. v. 5.   [6] Verg. *Aen.* vi. 853.

S. Aurelii Augustini
EPISCOPI
DE CIVITATE DEI
CONTRA PAGANOS

LIBER I

PRAEFATIO

Gloriosissimam civitatem Dei sive in hoc temporum cursu, cum inter impios peregrinatur ex fide vivens, sive in illa stabilitate sedis aeternae, quam nunc expectat per patientiam, *quoadusque iustitia convertatur in iudicium*, deinceps adeptura per excellentiam victoria ultima et pace perfecta, hoc opere instituto et mea ad te promissione debito defendere adversus eos, qui conditori eius deos suos praeferunt, fili carissime Marcelline, suscepi, magnum opus et arduum, sed Deus adiutor noster est. Nam scio quibus viribus opus sit, ut persuadeatur superbis quanta sit virtus humilitatis, qua fit ut omnia terrena cacumina temporali mobilitate nutantia non humano usurpata fastu, sed divina gratia donata celsitudo transcendat. Rex enim et conditor civitatis huius, de qua loqui instituimus, in scriptura populi sui sententiam divinae legis aperuit, qua dictum est: *Deus superbis resistit, humilibus autem dat gratiam.* Hoc vero, quod Dei est, superbae quoque animae spiritus inflatus adfectat amatque sibi in laudibus dici:

Parcere subiectis et debellare superbos.

Unde etiam de terrena civitate, quae cum dominari adpetit, etsi populi serviant, ipsa ei dominandi libido dominatur, non est praetereundum silentio quidquid dicere suscepti huius operis ratio postulat et facultas datur.

THE ORIGIN OF THE TWO CITIES

EXTRACT 2 THE DIVISION AMONG THE ANGELS

XII.1 (part)

The good and the bad angels are at variance with one another in desiring opposite things. This variance, however, is not due to any difference in their original natures, since God, who of His goodness is the author and stablisher of all that has being, created them both; it is due rather to their difference of will and desire, and on this point it would be wrong to have any doubt. The good angels persist in desiring that good which is available to all to share and which God Himself is to them, and so they continue in the eternity and the truth and the love which belong to Him. The bad angels rejoice rather in their own power, as though of their own resources they could provide themselves with their own good; from that pre-eminent good in which it is open to all to find their happiness they have slipped down to the level of their own selfish desires. They exalt themselves and become proud instead of relying on the eternity which would lift them to the heights; they invent their clever inanities instead of holding fast to the truth which is assured; they are moved by partisanship for their own cause instead of by love which makes no distinction: hence their arrogance, their falsehood, their malignity. And so the good angels are happy because they cling to God; and on the same showing we must assume that the bad angels are not happy for the opposite reason, which is not clinging to God.

EXTRACT 3   ITS CAUSE

XII.6 (part)

The sure and certain cause of the happiness of the good angels is found in their readiness to cling to God who is the absolute being; the unhappiness of the bad angels, if you seek its cause, justly comes about because they have turned away from Him who is the absolute being and have turned to themselves who are not absolute beings. This is behaviour which vitiates their nature and which we can call nothing but pride; for 'the beginning of all sin is pride'.[1] They refused to safeguard their strength for His service; and instead of having a fuller being, which they could have had if they had clung to Him who is the absolute being, they preferred themselves to

---

[1] Ecclus. x. 13.

LIBER XII
Caput i

. . Angelorum bonorum et malorum inter se contrarios adpetitus non
naturis principiisque diversis, cum Deus omnium substantiarum bonus
auctor et conditor utrosque creaverit, sed voluntatibus et cupiditatibus
extitisse dubitare fas non est, dum alii constanter in communi omnibus
bono, quod ipse illis Deus est, atque in eius aeternitate veritate caritate
persistunt; alii sua potestate potius delectati, velut bonum suum sibi ipsi
essent, a superiore communi omnium beatifico bono ad propria defluxer-
unt et habentes elationis fastum pro excelsissima aeternitate, vanitatis
astutiam pro certissima veritate, studia partium pro individua caritate
superbi fallaces invidi effecti sunt. Beatitudinis igitur illorum causa est
adhaerere Deo; quocirca istorum miseriae causa ex contrario est intel-
legenda, quod est non adhaerere Deo. . .

LIBER XII
Caput 6

Proinde causa beatitudinis angelorum bonorum ea verissima reperitur,
quod ei adhaerent qui summe est. Cum vero causa miseriae malorum
angelorum quaeritur, ea merito occurrit, quod ab illo, qui summe est,
aversi ad se ipsos conversi sunt, qui non summe sunt; et hoc vitium quid
aliud quam superbia nuncupetur? *Initium* quippe *omnis peccati superbia.*
Noluerunt ergo ad illum custodire fortitudinem suam, et qui magis essent,
si ei qui summe est adhaererent, se illi praeferendo id quod minus est
praetulerunt. Hic primus defectus et prima inopia primumque vitium eius
naturae, quae ita creata est, ut nec summe esset, et tamen ad beatitudinem
habendam eo, qui summe est, frui posset, a quo aversa non quidem nulla,

31

Him and so preferred that which is less. This was the original falling-away, the original failure of strength, the original flaw which appeared in natures whose creation presupposed that they should become, not indeed absolute beings themselves but, capable of enjoying Him who is the absolute being and should find their happiness therein; if however they turned away from Him, they would not be extinguished and become nothing, but would have a less full being than they might have had and therefore would be unhappy. If you press the matter further and ask what was the efficient cause of this evil will [that is, the cause which brought it about], you find no cause. For there is nothing outside the will which actually makes the will evil, for the evil will of itself brings about any act which is evil. Hence the evil will is the efficient cause of the evil act, and the efficient cause of the evil will is just nothing.

EXTRACT 4
XII.7 (part)

A 'DEFICIENT' RATHER THAN 'EFFICIENT' CAUSE

Let no one therefore search for the efficient cause of the evil will, for there is no efficient cause but rather a deficient cause. [The cause is not something which produces effect, but is defect.] There is no process of effecting anything, but a process of defection or default. For to default from that which is the absolute being to that which is less is to begin to have a will which is evil. Since, as I have said, the cause of that defection is not an efficient cause but a deficient cause, to wish to find out the cause is like wishing to see darkness or to hear silence. Both darkness and silence are known to us, the one purely through the eyes, the other through the ears; yet we know them, not because of the presence of any realities, but rather because of the absence of realities. No one therefore should try to know from me what I know I do not know—unless indeed it is to learn not to know something which he must eventually know to be beyond knowledge.

EXTRACT 5 (a)
XIV.11 (part)

THE FALL OF MAN

God made man morally upright, as the Scripture says, and therefore He made him possessed of a good will; for he would not have been upright if he had not been possessed of a will which was good. The good will is the work of God, and by God man was created in possession of it. The first evil will (for evil will was antecedent in man to all evil acts) was rather

sed tamen minus esset atque ob hoc misera fieret. Huius porro malae
voluntatis causa efficiens si quaeratur, nihil invenitur. Quid est enim quod
facit voluntatem malam, cum ipsa faciat opus malum? Ac per hoc mala
voluntas efficiens est operis mali, malae autem voluntatis efficiens nihil
est. . .

LIBER XII

Caput 7

Nemo igitur quaerat efficientem causam malae voluntatis; non enim est
efficiens sed deficiens, quia nec illa effectio sed defectio. Deficere namque
ab eo, quod summe est, ad id, quod minus est, hoc est incipere habere
voluntatem malam. Causas porro defectionum istarum, cum efficientes
non sint, ut dixi, sed deficientes, velle invenire tale est, ac si quisquam velit
videre tenebras vel audire silentium, quod tamen utrumque nobis notum
est, neque illud nisi per oculos, neque hoc nisi per aures, non sane in
specie, sed in speciei privatione. Nemo ergo ex me scire quaerat, quod me
nescire scio, nisi forte ut nescire discat, quod sciri non posse sciendum
est. . .

LIBER XIV

Caput 11

. . Fecit itaque Deus, sicut scriptum est, hominem rectum ac per hoc
voluntatis bonae. Non enim rectus esset bonam non habens voluntatem.
Bona igitur voluntas opus est Dei; cum ea quippe ab illo factus est homo.
Mala vero voluntas prima, quoniam omnia opera mala praecessit in
homine, defectus potius fuit quidam ab opere Dei ad sua opera quam opus

c   33

a defection from the original act of God towards acts of his own than any positive act. And so the evilness of evil acts lay in their being done according to man's way and not according to God's way; hence the evil will itself—or man in so far as his will was evil—produced those acts as a bad tree produces bad fruit. Now the bad will is not according to nature but is contrary to nature, for it is nature spoilt; nevertheless it is a part of the nature which it has spoilt, for it cannot exist except in a nature. But the nature in which it exists is the nature which the Creator created out of nothing, not the nature which He originated out of Himself—(as He originated the Word by which all things are made). God moulded man from the dust of the earth, but the earth and all bodily shapes upon the earth were made absolutely from nothing; similarly the soul was made from nothing and God gave it to the body when He made man. . . Evil is done away with, not by removing some nature which had been added nor by removing some part of such nature, but by healing the nature which had been spoilt and by making straight what had become twisted. And so the will is really free in its choice at the moment when it is not in bondage to that which spoils it, that is, to sin. Such a will is the gift of God to man; if the gift is lost because the will spoils itself, it can be restored only by Him who had the power to give it. Hence the Truth says, 'If the Son has made you free, then in truth will you be free,'[1] which is the same as saying 'If the Son has made you safe and whole, then indeed will you be safe and whole'. He derives His character as one who makes us free from the same principle from which He derives His character as one who saves us.

EXTRACT 5(*b*) HUMILITY IN THE CITY OF GOD

XIV.13 (part)

It is a good thing to keep the heart lifted up, not towards oneself, which is a sign of pride, but to the Lord, which is the sign of obedience which can belong to none but the humble. In some wonderful way there is something in humility which can lift up the heart, and there is something in self-exaltation which can depress the heart. It may seem paradoxical that the movement of self-exaltation should be downwards and of humility upwards. But humility founded on religion subordinates the heart to what is higher and there is nothing higher than God; that is why humility which subordinates it to God lifts it up. On the other hand self-exaltation, which bases itself on a spoiling of our nature, for that very reason scorns such subordination and lapses from Him who is above all; and therefore it will

[1] John viii. 36.

34

ullum, et ideo mala opera, quia secundum se, non secundum Deum; ut
eorum operum tamquam fructuum malorum voluntas ipsa esset velut
arbor mala aut ipse homo in quantum malae voluntatis. Porro mala voluntas quamvis non sit secundum naturam, sed contra naturam, quia vitium
est, tamen eius naturae est, cuius est vitium, quod nisi in natura non potest
esse; sed in ea, quam creavit ex nihilo, non quam genuit Creator de semet
ipso, sicut genuit Verbum, per quod facta sunt omnia; quia, etsi de terrae
pulvere Deus finxit hominem, eadem terra omnisque terrena materies
omnino de nihilo est, animamque de nihilo factam dedit corpori, cum
factus est homo. . . . Detrahitur porro malum non aliqua natura, quae
accesserat, vel ulla eius parte sublata, sed ea, quae vitiata ac depravata
fuerat, sanata atque correcta. Arbitrium igitur voluntatis tunc est vere
liberum, cum vitiis peccatisque non servit. Tale datum est a Deo; quod
amissum proprio vitio, nisi a quo dari potuit, reddi non potest. Unde
Veritas dicit: *Si vos Filius liberaverit, tunc vere liberi eritis.* Id ipsum est
autem, ac si diceret: 'Si vos Filius salvos fecerit, tunc vere salvi eritis.'
Inde quippe liberator, unde salvator. . .

LIBER XIV

CAPUT 13

. Bonum est enim sursum habere cor; non tamen ad se ipsum, quod est
superbiae, sed ad Dominum, quod est oboedientiae, quae nisi humilium
non potest esse. Est igitur aliquid humilitatis miro modo quod sursum
faciat cor, et est aliquid elationis quod deorsum faciat cor. Hoc quidem
quasi contrarium videtur, ut elatio sit deorsum et humilitas sursum. Sed
pia humilitas facit subditum superiori; nihil est autem superius Deo; et
ideo exaltat humilitas, quae facit subditum Deo. Elatio autem, quae in
vitio est, eo ipso respuit subiectionem et cadit ab illo, quo non est quic-

be lower. And so the Scripture is borne out which says 'Thou hast cast them down when they were being exalted'.[1] It does not say 'When they had been exalted', as though to imply that they were first exalted and then cast down; it means that they were cast down when they were in process of being exalted. To be self-exalted is itself to be cast down. Humility is highly extolled in the city of God and it is commended to the city of God which sojourns in this span of time; it is loudly proclaimed in its king, who is Christ. But the vice of self-exaltation, which is the antithesis of the virtue of humility, dominates Christ's adversary the devil, as the Scriptures show. This is the dividing line which most clearly distinguishes the two cities of which we are speaking; the one is the fellowship of faithful men, the other of unfaithful men, each fellowship with its appropriate angels; in the one the love of God is pre-eminent, in the other the love of self.

EXTRACT 6   THE LOVES OF THE TWO CITIES

XIV.28

And so the two cities have been fashioned by two loves, the earthly city by the love of self to the contempt of God, the heavenly city by the love of God to the contempt of self. In a word, the one glories in itself, the other in the Lord; the one looks for glory from men; to the other God, who is the witness of its good conscience, is its greatest glory. The one in its own glory lifts up its head; the other says to its God 'Thou art my glory and Thou art he who lifts up my head'.[2] Lust for domination dominates the one, as is shown by its rulers and the nations which it subjugates; in the other rulers and ruled alike serve one another in love, rulers taking thought for their subjects and their subjects rendering obedience to their rulers. The one loves its own earthly strength in its potentates; the other says to its God 'I will love thee, O Lord, my strength'.[3] Hence the wise men and philosophers of the one city lived by the standards of men; they either pursued the goods of their bodies or of their minds or the goods of both; or else, when they were able to know God, did not honour Him as God nor render thanks to Him; their speculations have come to nothing and their foolish hearts have been clouded over. They have said that they were wise (that is, they have exalted themselves in their own wisdom because they were dominated by pride) and so they have been made foolish. They have changed the glory of the incorruptible God into the likeness of the image of corruptible man or birds or beasts or reptiles (in praying to such images they either led the peoples or were led by them); and they have worshipped and served created things rather than the Creator who is

[1] Ps. lxxiii. 18.   [2] Ps. iii. 3.   [3] Ps. xviii. 1.

quam superius, et ex hoc erit inferius et fit quod scriptum est: *Deiecisti eos, cum extollerentur.* Non enim ait: 'Cum elati fuissent', ut prius extollerentur et postea deicerentur; sed cum extollerentur, tunc deiecti sunt. Ipsum quippe extolli iam deici est. Quapropter quod nunc in civitate Dei et civitati Dei in hoc peregrinanti saeculo maxime commendatur humilitas et in eius rege, qui est Christus, maxime praedicatur contrariumque huic virtuti elationis vitium in eius adversario, qui est diabolus, maxime dominari sacris litteris edocetur: profecto ista est magna differentia, qua civitas, unde loquimur, utraque discernitur, una scilicet societas piorum hominum, altera impiorum, singula quaeque cum angelis ad se pertinentibus, in quibus praecessit hac amor Dei, hac amor sui...

LIBER XIV

Caput 28

Fecerunt itaque civitates duas amores duo, terrenam scilicet amor sui usque ad contemptum Dei, caelestem vero amor Dei usque ad contemptum sui. Denique illa in se ipsa, haec in Domino gloriatur. Illa enim quaerit ab hominibus gloriam; huic autem Deus conscientiae testis maxima est gloria. Illa in gloria sua exaltat caput suum; haec dicit Deo suo: *Gloria mea et exaltans caput meum.* Illi in principibus eius vel in eis quas subiugat nationibus dominandi libido dominatur; in hac serviunt invicem in caritate et praepositi consulendo et subditi obtemperando. Illa in suis potentibus diligit virtutem suam; haec dicit Deo suo: *Diligam te, Domine, virtus mea.* Ideoque in illa sapientes eius secundum hominem viventes aut corporis aut animi sui bona aut utriusque sectati sunt, aut qui potuerunt cognoscere Deum, *non ut Deum honoraverunt aut gratias egerunt, sed evanuerunt in cogitationibus suis, et obscuratum est insipiens cor eorum; dicentes se esse sapientes* (id est dominante sibi superbia in sua sapientia sese extollentes) *stulti facti sunt et inmutaverunt gloriam incorruptibilis Dei in similitudinem imaginis corruptibilis hominis et volucrum et quadrupedum et serpentium* (ad huiusce modi enim simulacra adoranda vel duces populorum vel sectatores fuerunt), *et coluerunt atque servierunt creaturae potius quam Creatori, qui est*

37

blessed for ever.[1] But in the city of God there is no wisdom of men—only the wisdom of the religion which enjoins the right worship of the true God and which awaits its reward in the fellowship of the saints, angels as well as men, the reward being that God may be all in all.[2]

THE GROWTH OF THE CITIES

EXTRACT 7   THEIR FOUNDERS

XV.5 (part)

The first founder of the earthly city was Cain who killed his brother; in a fit of jealousy he slew his brother Abel, who was sojourning in this world as a citizen of the eternal city. It is therefore not surprising that, when years afterwards the city was being founded which was to be the head of the earthly city which we are discussing and was to rule so wide an empire, its lineaments were in some way true to the original pattern, or the archetype, as the Greeks call it. For in Rome too 'the new-built walls were wet with the blood of a murdered brother',[3] to use the words in which a poet has described the crime. That is the way in which Rome was founded, for Roman history testifies that Remus was slain by his brother Romulus; although both of them were citizens of the earthly city. Both pursued their own glory in the foundation of the Roman state; but, since there were two of them, each could not enjoy as much glory as he might have done if there had been only one. The one who gloried in his power would have had less power if it had been reduced by being shared with a brother, alive to be a partner in it. And so, that one might have all power, the other, his fellow, was removed; and by crime that empire grew greater but worse, whereas in innocence it would not have grown so large but would have been better.

But the brothers Cain and Abel did not share a common ambition for earthly success, and one was not jealous of the other because the power of the one (who in fact slew the other) would be diminished by a joint rule; for Abel did not seek any dominion in the city founded by his brother. Rather the jealousy of Cain was that diabolical jealousy which the evil feel towards the good, for no other reason than that they are evil and the good are good. For it cannot be said that goodness as a possession is diminished if it begins or continues to be shared. Goodness is a possession which enlarges itself in proportion as it gathers more people to share in it, each being united to the other in love. In short, to refuse to share goodness is to cease to have it as a possession; the fuller a man's love in goodness

[1] Rom. i. 21-25.   [2] 1 Cor. xv. 28.   [3] Lucan i. 95.

38

benedictus in saecula; in hac autem nulla est hominis sapientia nisi pietas, qua recte colitur verus Deus, id expectans praemium in societate sanctorum non solum hominum, verum etiam angelorum, *ut sit Deus omnia in omnibus.*

LIBER XV

Caput 5

Primus itaque fuit terrenae civitatis conditor fratricida; nam suum fratrem civem civitatis aeternae in hac terra peregrinantem invidentia victus occidit. Unde mirandum non est, quod tanto post in ea civitate condenda, quae fuerat huius terrenae civitatis, de qua loquimur, caput futura et tam multis gentibus regnatura, huic primo exemplo et, ut Graeci appellant, ἀρχετύπῳ quaedam sui generis imago respondit. Nam et illic, sicut ipsum facinus quidam poeta commemoravit illorum,

Fraterno primi maduerunt sanguine muri.

Sic enim condita est Roma, quando occisum Remum a fratre Romulo Romana testatur historia; nisi quod isti terrenae civitatis ambo cives erant. Ambo gloriam de Romanae rei publicae institutione quaerebant; sed ambo eam tantam, quantam si unus esset, habere non poterant. Qui enim volebat dominando gloriari, minus utique dominaretur, si eius potestas vivo consorte minueretur. Ut ergo totam dominationem haberet unus, ablatus est socius, et scelere crevit in peius, quod innocentia minus esset et melius. Hi autem fratres Cain et Abel non habebant ambo inter se similem rerum terrenarum cupiditatem, nec in hoc alter alteri invidit, quod eius dominatus fieret angustior, qui alterum occidit, si ambo dominarentur (Abel quippe non quaerebat dominationem in ea civitate, quae condebatur a fratre), sed invidentia illa diabolica, qua invident bonis mali, nulla alia causa, nisi quia illi boni sunt, illi mali. Nullo enim modo fit minor accedente seu permanente consorte possessio bonitatis, immo possessio bonitas, quam tanto latius, quanto concordius individua sociorum possidet caritas. Non habebit denique istam possessionem, qui eam noluerit habere communem, et tanto eam reperiet ampliorem, quanto amplius ibi

39

for those with whom he shares it, the wider he will find goodness to be. The episode of Romulus and Remus demonstrates how the earthly city is divided in hostility against itself; the story of Cain and Abel shows the hostility of the two cities to one another, the city of God and the city of men.

XVIII.47 (part)

THE CITY OF GOD BEFORE
CHRIST'S ADVENT

To crown the list of authorities whom I have quoted I can make mention of all those foreigners—that is, men not descended from Israel nor adopted by the Jews into their canon of sacred literature—who have come or will come to our knowledge as having prophesied about Christ in their writings. Not that they are necessary to us as authorities, even if they were not available; but we can reasonably believe that there have been men in other nations than the Jewish nation to whom the mystery of Christ has been revealed and who were constrained also to foretell it. They may have shared the same grace as ourselves; or they may not, in which case they were instructed by evil angels, who, as we know, confessed Christ when they saw Him face to face, though the Jews did not recognise Him. I do not think the Jews themselves would venture to maintain that no one except the Israelites belonged to God ever since the seed of Israel began to multiply after the rejection of Israel's elder brother. It is true in fact that there was no other people which could properly be called the people of God; but the Jews cannot deny that there were individual men belonging to other nations who belonged, by virtue of a heavenly and not an earthly fellowship, to the true Israelites, who are citizens of the fatherland which is above. If they deny this, it is easy to refute them by citing the saintly and venerable Job. He was not a native Israelite nor a proselyte (that is, a new-comer to the people of Israel), but was sprung from the Idumaean tribe, and in Idumaea he was born and there he died. The divine writings praise him so highly that, as far as goodness and devotion to God are concerned, he is without an equal in his own day.[1]. . I have no doubt that it was intended in the divine scheme of Providence that from the one example of Job we should know that in other nations also there may have existed men who have lived according to God and have pleased Him and therefore belong to the spiritual Jerusalem. But we must believe that this favour can have been granted only to those who received from God a revelation of the one Mediator of God and man, the man Christ Jesus. It was foretold to the saints of old that He would come in the

[1] Cf. Job i. 8.

potuerit amare consortem. Illud igitur, quod inter Remum et Romulum exortum est, quem ad modum adversus se ipsam terrena civitas dividatur, ostendit; quod autem inter Cain et Abel, inter duas ipsas civitates, Dei et hominum, inimicitias demonstravit...

LIBER XVIII

Caput 47

Quapropter quisquis alienigena, id est non ex Israel progenitus nec ab illo populo in canonem sacrarum litterarum receptus, legitur aliquid prophetasse de Christo, si in nostram notitiam venit aut venerit, ad cumulum a nobis commemorari potest; non quo necessarius sit, etiamsi desit, sed quia non incongrue creditur fuisse et in aliis gentibus homines, quibus hoc mysterium revelatum est, et qui haec etiam praedicere inpulsi sunt, sive participes eiusdem gratiae fuerint sive expertes, ŝed per malos angelos docti sint, quos etiam praesentem Christum, quem Iudaei non agnoscebant, scimus fuisse confessos. Nec ipsos Iudaeos existimo audere contendere neminem pertinuisse ad Deum praeter Israelitas, ex quo propago Israel esse coepit, reprobato eius fratre maiore. Populus enim re vera, qui proprie Dei populus diceretur, nullus alius fuit; homines autem quosdam non terrena, sed caelesti societate ad veros Israelitas supernae cives patriae pertinentes etiam in aliis gentibus fuisse negare non possunt; quia si negant, facillime convincuntur de sancto et mirabili viro Iob, qui nec indigena nec proselytus, id est advena populi Israel fuit, sed ex gente Idumaea genus ducens, ibi ortus, ibidem mortuus est; qui divino sic laudatur eloquio, ut, quod ad iustitiam pietatemque adtinet, nullus ei homo suorum temporum coaequetur... Divinitus autem provisum fuisse non dubito, ut ex hoc uno sciremus etiam per alias gentes esse potuisse, qui secundum Deum vixerunt eique placuerunt, pertinentes ad spiritalem Hierusalem. Quod nemini concessum fuisse credendum est, nisi cui divinitus revelatus est unus mediator Dei et hominum, homo Christus Iesus, qui venturus in carne sic antiquis sanctis praenuntiabatur, quem

flesh in just such manner as it was told to us that He had come, in order that through one and the same faith granted to us through Christ all who are destined for the city of God, for God's house and God's temple, may be led towards God. . .

THE CHURCH

XVIII.49 (part)

In this age of ill-will and in these evil days the Church by her present humility prepares her future exaltation. Urged on by fears, tormented by pains, harassed by toil, endangered by temptations she learns her wisdom, and, when she feels sober joy, she is made joyful only by hope. With the good are mingled many who are reprobate; both are gathered into the Gospel's drag-net; enclosed within its meshes they swim about together in this world, as it were in a sea, until they are drawn to the shore, where the evil are separated from the good and God dwells in the good as though in His temple and is 'all in all to them'.[1] Wherefore we recognise the fulfilment of the word which He spake in the Psalm, saying, 'I have declared and spoken of them, they have been multiplied beyond all counting'.[2] This is now being fulfilled, from the time when He spoke first through the mouth of His fore-runner John and then through His own mouth and declared 'Repent, for the Kingdom of Heaven has drawn near'.[3] He chose disciples whom He called also Apostles, men humbly born, without honour, unlearned, that, if they should be great or do great things, in them *He* might be great or do great things. Among them He had one disciple whom, though evil, He turned to good account, that He might fulfil through him the divine ordinance of His passion and might hold up to His Church an example of the way in which evil men should be borne. Having sowed the seed of His holy Gospel, as far as was right for Him by means of His bodily presence, He suffered, died and rose again. By His passion He showed what we must bear in the cause of truth, by His resurrection what we must hope for in eternity—I say nothing of that high sacrament in which His blood was shed for the remission of sins. For forty days He moved about on earth with His disciples, and in their sight He ascended to Heaven and ten days later He sent the Holy Spirit whom He had promised. When the Spirit came upon those who had believed, a wonderful and indeed necessary sign was given; each of those present spoke in the tongues of all nations; the sign meant that the Catholic Church would be one throughout all nations and would speak in all their tongues.

[1] 1 Cor. xv. 48.   [2] Ps. xl. 5.   [3] Mt. iii. 2; iv. 17.

ad modum nobis venisse nuntiatus est, ut una eademque per ipsum fides omnes in Dei civitatem, Dei domum, Dei templum praedestinatos perducat ad Deum. . .

LIBER XVIII

CAPUT 49

In hoc ergo saeculo maligno, in his diebus malis, ubi per humilitatem praesentem futuram comparat ecclesia celsitudinem et timorum stimulis dolorum tormentis, laborum molestiis, temptationum periculis eruditur sola spe gaudens, quando sanum gaudet, multi reprobi miscentur bonis et utrique tamquam in sagenam evangelicam colliguntur et in hoc mundo tamquam in mari utrique inclusi retibus indiscrete natant, donec perveniatur ad litus, ubi mali segregentur a bonis et in bonis tamquam in templo suo *sit Deus omnia in omnibus*. Proinde vocem nunc agnoscimus eius impleri, qui loquebatur in psalmo atque dicebat: *Adnuntiavi et locutus sum, multiplicati sunt super numerum*. Hoc fit nunc, ex quo primum per os praecursoris sui Iohannis, deinde per os proprium adnuntiavit et locutus est dicens: *Agite paenitentiam, adpropinquavit enim regnum caelorum*. Elegit discipulos, quos et apostolos nominavit, humiliter natos, inhonoratos, inlitteratos, ut, quidquid magnum essent et facerent, ipse in eis esset et faceret. Habuit inter eos unum, quo malo utens bene et suae passionis impleret dispositum et ecclesiae suae tolerandorum malorum praeberet exemplum. Seminato, quantum per eius oportebat praesentiam corporalem, sancto evangelio passus est, mortuus est, resurrexit, passione ostendens quid sustinere pro veritate, resurrectione quid sperare in aeternitate debeamus, excepta altitudine sacramenti, qua sanguis eius in remissionem fusus est peccatorum. Conversatus est in terra quadraginta dies cum discipulis suis atque ipsis videntibus ascendit in caelum et post dies decem misit promissum Spiritum sanctum; cuius venientis in eos qui crediderant tunc signum erat maximum et maxime necessarium, ut unusquisque eorum linguis omnium gentium loqueretur; ita significans unitatem catholicae ecclesiae per omnes gentes futuram ac sic linguis omnibus locuturam.

EXTRACT 10

XVIII.50 (part)

First the Church spread from Jerusalem and, when many in Judaea and
Samaria had believed, it travelled also into other nations, the Gospel being
proclaimed by those 'lights of the world' whom Christ had equipped with
its word and had kindled by His holy Spirit. For He had said to them 'Do
not fear those who kill the body but cannot kill the soul'[1]; and they
kept away the chill of fear by the warmth of their burning love. Finally,
both those who had seen and heard Him before the passion and after the
resurrection and those who succeeded the disciples at their death preached
the Gospel throughout the whole world in spite of dreadful persecutions
and tortures of all kinds and the deaths of martyrs. God bore witness to
the Gospel, granting signs and revelations and divers powers and the gifts
of the Holy Spirit. Hence the nations of the world believed upon Him
who was crucified for their redemption, and in Christian love they
venerated the blood of the martyrs which lately they had shed in devilish
frenzy. Even their kings whose decrees laid waste the Church found their
salvation in being subject to that name which they had tried by every
cruelty to abolish from the earth, and they began to persecute those false
gods in whose defence they had earlier persecuted the worshippers of the
true God.

EXTRACT 11

XVIII.51 (ad fin.)

And so in this age, in these evil days, starting not merely from the time
of the bodily presence of Christ and His Apostles on earth but actually
from the time of the first righteous man, Abel himself, slain by his wicked
brother, and thenceforth to the end of time, as a stranger upon the earth,
suffering the persecutions of the world and receiving the consolation of
God, the Church travels onwards.

EXTRACT 12   **SUMMARY**

XVIII.54 (part)

Let us at long last bring this book to an end; in it we have discussed and
demonstrated, as fully as seemed good to us, the manner in which the two

[1] Mt. x. 28.

44

LIBER XVIII

CAPUT 50

.. Primum se ab Hierusalem diffudit ecclesia, et cum in Iudaea atque
Samaria plurimi credidissent, et in alias gentes itum est, eis adnuntiantibus
evangelium, quos ipse, sicut luminaria, et aptaverat verbo et accenderat
Spiritu sancto. Dixerat enim eis: *Nolite timere eos, qui corpus occidunt,
animam autem non possunt occidere.* Qui ut frigidi timore non essent, igne
caritatis ardebant. Denique non solum per ipsos, qui eum et ante pas-
sionem et post resurrectionem viderant et audierant, verum etiam post
obitum eorum per posteros eorum inter horrendas persecutiones et varios
cruciatus ac funera martyrum praedicatum est toto orbe evangelium, con-
testante Deo signis et ostentis et variis virtutibus et Spiritus sancti
muneribus; ut populi gentium credentes in eum, qui pro eorum redemp-
tione crucifixus est, Christiano amore venerarentur sanguinem martyrum,
quem diabolico furore fuderunt, ipsique reges, quorum legibus vastabatur
ecclesia, ei nomini salubriter subderentur, quod de terra crudeliter auferre
conati sunt, et falsos deos inciperent persequi, quorum causa cultores Dei
veri fuerant antea persecuti.

LIBER XVIII

CAPUT 51

.. Sic in hoc saeculo, in his diebus malis non solum a tempore corporalis
praesentiae Christi et apostolorum eius, sed ab ipso Abel, quem primum
iustum impius frater occidit, et deinceps usque in huius saeculi finem inter
persecutiones mundi et consolationes Dei peregrinando procurrit ecclesia.

LIBER XVIII

CAPUT 54

.. Sed aliquando iam concludamus hunc librum, hoc usque disserentes et
quantum satis visum est demonstrantes, quisnam sit duarum civitatum,
caelestis atque terrenae, ab initio usque in finem permixtarum mortalis

cities, the heavenly and the earthly, progress together on earth, the one intermingled with the other from their beginning to their end. The earthly city, as we have seen, fashioned for itself false gods of its own wish, creating them from any source whatever or even deifying men to whom to offer worship and sacrifice. The other city which, though heavenly, sojourns on earth does not fashion false gods, but is itself created by the true God and is itself the true sacrifice offered to God. Nevertheless both cities alike make use of temporal goods and both alike are distressed by temporal evils; but they differ in faith, in hope and in love, until they shall be separated by a final judgement and each shall reap as its reward its own end, to which there is no end. It is with the ends of both cities that our future discourse must be concerned.

THE PROVIDENCE OF GOD AND THE ROMAN EMPIRE

EXTRACT 13
V.11

HISTORY IS NOT OUTSIDE
GOD'S PROVIDENCE

The all-high and true God with His Word and Holy Spirit (which are three and one), the one Almighty God, creator and maker of all spirit and all body, to share whose life creates happiness for men if they are happy through the truth and not through foolishness; who made man a creature possessed of reason and composed of spirit and body; who did not allow man when he sinned to go unpunished, yet did not leave him forsaken without mercy; who gave to good and bad men alike existence just as He gave it to stones, a life which could reproduce itself as to trees, a life of physical feeling as to beasts, a life of the mind as to angels and to no others; from whom comes every mode of being, every real thing, all order in creation; from whom is measurement and number and weight; from whom is all that exists in nature, whatever its species, whatever its rank in the scale of creation; from whom are the potentialities of things yet to be realised, the realisation of things once only potential, and the motion of development which enables what is potential to become real and what is real to create other potentiality; who gave even to flesh its birth, its beauty, its health, its power of procreation, its orderly arrangement of limbs, its physical well-being arising from harmony in its members; who gave even to the irrational spirit memory and feeling and desire and to the rational spirit all these and also mind and intelligence and will; who left without due orderly arrangement of its parts, and a kind of peace

46

excursus; quarum illa, quae terrena est, fecit sibi quos voluit vel unde-
cumque vel etiam ex hominibus falsos deos, quibus sacrificando serviret;
illa autem, quae caelestis peregrinatur in terra, falsos deos non facit, sed a
vero Deo ipsa fit, cuius verum sacrificium ipsa sit. Ambae tamen temporalibus vel bonis pariter utuntur vel malis pariter affliguntur, diversa
fide, diversa spe, diverso amore, donec ultimo iudicio separentur, et per-
cipiat unaquaeque suum finem, cuius nullus est finis; de quibus ambarum
finibus deinceps disserendum est.

LIBER V

Caput 11

Deus itaque summus et verus cum Verbo suo et Spiritu sancto, quae tria
unum sunt, Deus unus omnipotens, creator et factor omnis animae atque
omnis corporis, cuius sunt participatione felices, quicumque sunt veritate
non vanitate felices, qui fecit hominem rationale animal ex anima et corpore, qui eum peccantem nec inpunitum esse permisit nec sine misericordia dereliquit; qui bonis et malis essentiam etiam cum lapidibus, vitam
seminalem etiam cum arboribus, vitam sensualem etiam cum pecoribus,
vitam intellectualem cum solis angelis dedit; a quo est omnis modus
omnis species omnis ordo; a quo est mensura numerus pondus; a quo est
quidquid naturaliter est, cuiuscumque generis est, cuiuslibet aestimationis
est; a quo sunt semina formarum formae seminum motus seminum atque
formarum; qui dedit et carni originem pulchritudinem valetudinem, pro-
pagationis fecunditatem membrorum dispositionem salutem concordiae;
qui et animae inrationali dedit memoriam sensum adpetitum, rationali
autem insuper mentem intellegentiam voluntatem; qui non solum caelum

47

resulting therefrom, neither the sky nor the earth, neither angel nor man nor the organs of the smallest and meanest living creature nor the feather of the bird nor the flower of the field nor the leaf of the tree—it is beyond belief that such a God wished the kingdoms of men, their lordships and their servitudes, to be outside the laws of his Providence.

EXTRACT 14 (*a*)   ROMAN CHARACTER

V.12 (part)

Let us see then what element in the Roman character moved the true God to think fit to aid the increase of the Roman Empire; for in His power are all earthly empires. . . Roman history tells us, inviting our approval, that the early Romans (in spite of worshipping false gods and sacrificing victims to daemons, as did all nations except the Jews, instead of to God) were 'greedy of praise, generous in money-dealings, ambitious in pursuit of world-wide glory and of riches honourably acquired'.[1] Glory was their supreme passion; for this they wished to live, for this they did not hesitate to die. All other desires they curbed in order to give rein to this absorbing ambition. In short, they thought it inglorious to be a subject people and glorious to rule and to be an imperial power; and so they ardently desired their country, first, to be free and then to rule an empire; and to these ends they devoted all their effort. . .

EXTRACT 14 (*b*)

V.13

The famous Oriental empires had long been in existence when God willed that a Western empire should come into being which should be later in time but before all others in the glory of its wide dominions and its greatness. To subdue the evils which oppressed the many nations He chose to grant the empire to men of such quality as were the Romans. For the sake of honour and praise and glory the Romans subordinated everything to their country's good, demanding that in their country they should receive that glory; and they did not hesitate to prefer their country's welfare to their own, curbing desire for money and many other vices to satisfy that one vice of which we have spoken, namely love of praise. . .

[1] Sall. *Cat.* vii. 6.

et terram, nec solum angelum et hominem, sed nec exigui et contemptibilis animantis viscera nec avis pinnulam, nec herbae flosculum nec arboris folium sine suarum partium convenientia et quadam veluti pace dereliquit: nullo modo est credendus regna hominum eorumque dominationes et servitutes a suae providentiae legibus alienas esse voluisse.

LIBER V

Caput 12

Proinde videamus, quos Romanorum mores et quam ob causam Deus verus ad augendum imperium adiuvare dignatus est, in cuius potestate sunt etiam regna terrena... Veteres igitur primique Romani, quantum eorum docet et commendat historia, quamvis ut aliae gentes excepta una populi Hebraeorum deos falsos colerent et non Deo victimas, sed daemoniis immolarent, tamen 'laudis avidi, pecuniae liberales erant, gloriam ingentem, divitias honestas volebant'; hanc ardentissime dilexerunt, propter hanc vivere voluerunt, pro hac emori non dubitaverunt; ceteras cupiditates huius unius ingenti cupiditate presserunt. Ipsam denique patriam suam, quoniam servire videbatur inglorium, dominari vero atque imperare gloriosum, prius omni studio liberam, deinde dominam esse concupiverunt...

LIBER V

Caput 13

Quam ob rem cum diu fuissent regna Orientis inlustria, voluit Deus et Occidentale fieri, quod tempore esset posterius, sed imperii latitudine et magnitudine inlustrius, idque talibus potissimum concessit hominibus ad domanda gravia mala multarum gentium, qui causa honoris laudis et gloriae consuluerunt patriae, in qua ipsam gloriam requirebant, salutemque eius saluti suae praeponere non dubitaverunt, pro isto uno vitio, id est amore laudis, pecuniae cupiditatem et multa alia vitia conprimentes...

EXTRACT 15   THE LESSON FOR CHRISTIANS
V.14

Without hesitation we Christians had better resist this ambition for praise
rather than yield to it. For the more a man preserves himself free from this
uncleanness, the more like to God will he be. Even if it cannot be entirely
rooted out from the heart (for it does not cease to attract even those minds
which are making good progress), at any rate craving for glory should be
overcome by love of righteousness, in order that, wherever and whenever
things which are good and right lie neglected and unhonoured, even this
love of the praises of men may blush for shame and may give place to the
love of truth... [And so 'Let your works shine in the face of men'] not
'that you may be seen by men' (that is, with the intention of wishing to
turn their gaze upon you, for of yourselves you are nothing) but 'that
they may glorify your Father which is in Heaven',[1] in order that they may
turn to Him and become what you are. This is the example which the
martyrs followed who surpassed the Scaevolae and Curtii and Decii of
Roman History, not by bringing suffering upon themselves but by bearing
the sufferings inflicted upon them. They surpassed them too in true virtue
because their virtue was true religion, and they were countless in number.
The great men of Roman history were citizens of an earthly city. In all
their devotion to that city they set before themselves the aim of promoting
her safety. Their kingdom was not in Heaven but on earth, not in the life
eternal but in the departure of dying men and the replacement of them by
men soon to die. What else could they have loved except glory? By means
of glory they wished to enjoy even after death a kind of a life in the praises
of posterity.

EXTRACT 16   ROME HAS REAPED HER REWARD
V.15

To men of this kind God was not likely to grant eternal life in company
with His holy angels in His heavenly city. Entry to that fellowship is given
only by true religion which renders service and worship (called by the
Greeks λατρεία) only to the one true God. If however He had not
granted to them the earthly glory of a splendid empire (as He did), they
would not receive, you might argue, the just reward for their good
qualities, the virtues by which they strove to attain to such glory. Now
in reply to those who are seen to do good that they may win glory from

[1] Mt. v. 16.

LIBER V

CAPUT 14

Huic igitur cupiditati melius resistitur sine dubitatione quam ceditur. Tanto enim quisque est Deo similior, quanto est ab hac inmunditia mundior. Quae in hac vita etsi non funditus eradicatur ex corde, quia etiam bene proficientes animos temptare non cessat: saltem cupiditas gloriae superetur dilectione iustitiae, ut, si alicubi iacent quae apud quosque improbantur, si bona, si recta sunt, etiam ipse amor humanae laudis erubescat et cedat amori veritatis... Non ergo *ut videamini ab eis,* id est hac intentione, ut eos ad vos converti velitis, quia non per vos aliquid estis; sed *ut glorificent patrem vestrum, qui in caelis est,* ad quem conversi fiant quod estis. Hos secuti sunt martyres, qui Scaevolas et Curtios et Decios non sibi inferendo poenas, sed inlatas ferendo et virtute vera, quoniam vera pietate, et innumerabili multitudine superarunt. Sed cum illi essent in civitate terrena, quibus propositus erat omnium pro illa officiorum finis incolumitas eius et regnum non in caelo, sed in terra; non in vita aeterna, sed in decessione morientium et successione moriturorum: quid aliud amarent quam gloriam, qua volebant etiam post mortem tamquam vivere in ore laudantium?

LIBER V

CAPUT 15

Quibus ergo non erat daturus Deus vitam aeternam cum sanctis angelis suis in sua civitate caelesti, ad cuius societatem pietas vera perducit, quae non exhibet servitutem religionis, quam λατρείαν Graeci vocant, nisi uni vero Deo, si neque hanc eis terrenam gloriam excellentissimi imperii concederet: non redderetur merces bonis artibus eorum, id est virtutibus, quibus ad tantam gloriam pervenire nitebantur. De talibus enim, qui propter hoc boni aliquid facere videntur, ut glorificentur ab hominibus,

men the Lord says, 'Verily I say unto you they have reaped their reward'.[1] This was true of the Romans; in the interest of the common weal, that is of the commonwealth and its treasury, they disregarded their own wealth, they resisted avarice, they promoted the prosperity of their country by a policy of freedom, they yielded neither to sin, as defined by their laws, nor to selfish desires. They relied upon these qualities to lead them as by a veritable high road to honour, empire and glory. And they did obtain their glory in almost all nations; upon many nations they imposed the laws of their empire, and to-day their glory is written in the literature and history of most nations. They have no reason to complain of the righteous justice of the all-high and true God: they have reaped their reward.

EXTRACT 17   THE REWARD OF THE SAINTS
V.16

Very different is the reward of the saints who even here endure insult for the sake of the truth of God, which is hated by those who love this world. The city of God endures for ever; in it no-one is born because no-one dies, in it dwells true and plentiful happiness—happiness which is not regarded as a goddess (as among the Romans) but as the gift of God. From this city we have received a pledge of faith as long as we sojourn here and sigh after its beauty; in it the sun does not rise upon the good and the evil, but the sun of righteousness shines only upon the good; in it there will be no anxious effort to enrich the public treasury by restricting private wealth, for there the treasure is shared by all alike and it is the treasure of the truth. Wherefore there were two reasons why the Roman empire was expanded and won glory from men; first, that due reward might be given to its citizens who were of the character which I have described, secondly, that the citizens of the eternal city during their sojourn here might study with sober diligence the examples set before them in Roman history, and might perceive how much affection they owe to their heavenly country in order to win eternal life, if the earthly city has inspired such affection in its own citizens that they may win glory among men.

EXTRACT 18   ROMAN RULE: ITS EXAMPLE
V.17

You might ask what difference it makes under whose government a man lives—for his life lasts but a few days and then ceases and he is destined to

[1] Mt. vi. 2.

etiam Dominus ait: *Amen dico vobis, perceperunt mercedem suam.* Sic et isti
privatas res suas pro re communi, hoc est re publica, et pro eius aerario
contempserunt, avaritiae restiterunt, consuluerunt patriae consilio libero,
neque delicto secundum suas leges neque libidini obnoxii; his omnibus
artibus tamquam vera via nisi sunt ad honores imperium gloriam;
honorati sunt in omnibus fere gentibus, imperii sui leges inposuerunt
multis gentibus, hodieque litteris et historia gloriosi sunt paene in omnibus gentibus: non est quod de summi et veri Dei iustitia conquerantur;
perceperunt mercedem suam.

LIBER V

Caput 16

Merces autem sanctorum longe alia est etiam hic opprobria sustinentium
pro veritate Dei, quae mundi huius dilectoribus odiosa est. Illa civitas
sempiterna est; ibi nullus oritur, quia nullus moritur; ibi est vera et plena
felicitas, non dea, sed donum Dei; inde fidei pignus accepimus, quamdiu
peregrinantes eius pulchritudini suspiramus; ibi non oritur sol super bonos
et malos, sed sol iustitiae solos protegit bonos; ibi non erit magna industria
ditare publicum aerarium privatis rebus angustis, ubi thensaurus communis est veritatis. Proinde non solum ut talis merces talibus hominibus
redderetur Romanum imperium ad humanam gloriam dilatatum est;
verum etiam ut cives aeternae illius civitatis, quamdiu hic peregrinantur,
diligenter et sobrie illa intueantur exempla et videant quanta dilectio
debeatur supernae patriae propter vitam aeternam, si tantum a suis civibus
terrena dilecta est propter hominum gloriam.

LIBER V

Caput 17

Quantum enim pertinet ad hanc vitam mortalium, quae paucis diebus
ducitur et finitur, quid interest sub cuius imperio vivat homo moriturus,
si illi qui imperant ad impia et iniqua non cogant? Aut vero aliquid

die—provided that those who govern him do not compel him to acts of impiety or unrighteousness. But the Romans did no harm to the nations whom they conquered and brought under their own laws, except that they did these things at the cost of tremendous slaughter in wars. If only they could have imposed their laws by agreement, they would have brought about the same result more successfully (though then they would not have enjoyed the glory of triumph); and indeed they themselves actually lived under the laws which they imposed on the rest of the world. If this could have been done without invoking Mars and Bellona and without giving Victory a place in the picture (for there must be battles if there is to be a victor), then without doubt the Romans would have been on one and the same plane with the rest of the world. Particularly would this have been true if that most acceptable and equitable measure had been brought in earlier than in fact it was—I mean the extension of the fellowship of the state to all belonging to the Roman Empire so that they became Roman citizens and the privileges of the few were granted to all alike. But even so the landless populace would have depended for a livelihood on public funds[1]; it would have been more acceptable, surely, if under a system of good state administration the means of that livelihood had been provided by agreement rather than extorted from defeated peoples.

For I simply do not see what contribution can be made to wholeness and goodness of character by the actual rankings which men give themselves—I mean, one set of men being the victors, another the vanquished. All that is achieved is an empty pride in worldly reputation; the men who have been fired with insatiable desire for glory and have conducted flaming wars have already reaped their reward. They gain no other advantages; their estates are not free from land-duty, they have no access to knowledge which others have not. There are many senators in other lands who have never set eyes on Rome. Take away vain-glory and what are all men except just plain men? If this obstinate age were to permit honour to run with character, even so worldy reputation ought not to count for much; it is just smoke without substance. No. In dealing with this subject let us avail ourselves of the help which our Lord God has given us. Let us reflect upon the attractions despised and the sufferings borne, the cravings suppressed in the quest of worldly reputation by men who deserved to win it as the reward of all their high qualities. And then let us Christians draw a lesson even from this source and take it to heart and learn to stifle our own pride. It may be true that between the city in which it has been promised that we shall reign and the earthly city there is a great gulf—as wide as the distance between heaven and earth and likewise between

[1]And so would have been regarded as a privileged class supported by once 'defeated peoples', now technically equal.

nocuerunt Romani gentibus, quibus subiugatis inposuerunt leges suas, nisi quia id factum est ingenti strage bellorum? Quod si concorditer fieret, id ipsum fieret meliore successu; sed nulla esset gloria triumphantium. Neque enim et Romani non vivebant sub legibus suis, quas ceteris inponebant. Hoc si fieret sine Marte et Bellona, ut nec Victoria locum haberet, nemine vincente ubi nemo pugnaverat: nonne Romanis et ceteris gentibus una esset eademque condicio? praesertim si mox fieret, quod postea gratissime atque humanissime factum est, ut omnes ad Romanum imperium pertinentes societatem acciperent civitatis et Romani cives essent, ac sic esset omnium, quod erat ante paucorum; tantum quod plebs illa, quae suos agros non haberet, de publico viveret; qui pastus eius per bonos administratores rei publicae gratius a concordibus praestaretur quam victis extorqueretur.

Nam quid intersit ad incolumitatem bonosque mores, ipsas certe hominum dignitates, quod alii vicerunt, alii victi sunt, omnino non video, praeter illum gloriae humanae inanissimum fastum, in quo perceperunt mercedem suam, qui eius ingenti cupidine arserunt et ardentia bella gesserunt. Numquid enim illorum agri tributa non solvunt? Numquid eis licet discere, quod aliis non licet? Numquid non multi senatores sunt in aliis terris, qui Romam ne facie quidem norunt? Tolle iactantiam, et omnes homines quid sunt nisi homines? Quod si perversitas saeculi admitteret, ut honoratiores essent quique meliores: nec sic pro magno haberi debuit honor humanus, quia nullius est ponderis fumus. Sed utamur etiam in his rebus beneficio Domini Dei nostri; consideremus quanta contempserint, quae pertulerint, quas cupiditates subegerint pro humana gloria, qui eam tamquam mercedem talium virtutum accipere meruerunt, et valeat nobis etiam hoc ad opprimendam superbiam, ut, cum illa civitas, in qua nobis regnare promissum est, tantum ab hac distet, quantum distat caelum a terra, a temporali laetitia vita aeterna, ab inanibus

temporal felicity and everlasting life and between vapid praise and real substantial glory, between the fellowship of angels and the fellowship of mortals, between the light of the sun and moon and the light of Him who made the sun and moon. Yet the citizens of so glorious a country must not imagine that they have done anything wonderful if to obtain that land they have done a little good or suffered a few evils, when the Romans wrought such heroic deeds and endured such trials on behalf of an empire which they had already won. Why, there is even a faint shadowy resemblance between the Roman Empire and the heavenly city. The one gathers its citizens to the everlasting country by promising remission of sins; Romulus offered a place of refuge for the multitude from which Rome was later to be founded, and he attracted them by freeing them from punishment for all their former misdeeds of every kind.

EXTRACT 19
V.19 (*ad fin.*)

FURTHER JUSTIFICATION OF THE ROMAN EMPIRE

. . I have explained to the best of my ability the reason why the one true and righteous God aided the Romans, who were good if judged by the rough standards of the earthly city, to attain the glory of so great an empire. All the same there may be another reason which does not lie so much on the surface, since the varied merits which are to be found in the human race are known to God rather than to us. To all who are truly religious it is obvious that true religion—the true worship of the true God—is essential to true virtue, which cannot be true if it is directed towards worldly reputation. Yet they would hold that men who were not citizens of the everlasting city (called in our sacred literature the city of God) are of greater service to the earthly state if they have virtue as a possession without true religion than if they have no virtue at all. If however under the inspiration of true religion men lead good lives and possess also the skill to rule peoples, there can be no greater fortune for humanity than that under the mercy of God power should be in their hands. Such men attribute their high qualities, such as they can be in this life, to no source but the grace of God, knowing that He has given them in response to their wish, their belief and their prayer. At the same time they are aware how great are their short-comings in comparison with the perfection of the righteousness which is to be found in the fellowship of the holy angels, for which they strive to fit themselves. However much praise and credit may be given to the virtue which unaccompanied by true religion aims at worldly reputation, it is certainly not to be com-

laudibus solida gloria, a societate mortalium societas angelorum, a lumine solis et lunae lumen eius qui solem fecit et lunam, nihil sibi magnum fecisse videantur tantae patriae cives, si pro illa adipiscenda fecerint boni operis aliquid vel mala aliqua sustinuerint, cum illi pro hac terrena iam adepta tanta fecerint, tanta perpessi sint, praesertim quia remissio peccatorum, quae cives ad aeternam colligit patriam, habet aliquid, cui per umbram quandam simile fuit asylum illud Romuleum, quo multitudinem, qua illa civitas conderetur, quorumlibet delictorum congregavit inpunitas.

LIBER V

CAPUT 19

. . Quam ob rem, quamvis ut potui satis exposuerim, qua causa Deus unus verus et iustus Romanos secundum quandam formam terrenae civitatis bonos adiuverit ad tanti imperii gloriam consequendam: potest tamen et alia causa esse latentior propter diversa merita generis humani, Deo magis nota quam nobis, dum illud constet inter omnes veraciter pios, neminem sine vera pietate, id est veri Dei vero cultu, veram posse habere virtutem, nec eam veram esse, quando gloriae servit humanae; eos tamen, qui cives non sint civitatis aeternae, quae in sacris litteris nostris dicitur civitas Dei, utiliores esse terrenae civitati, quando habent virtutem vel ipsam, quam si nec ipsam. Illi autem, qui vera pietate praediti bene vivunt, si habent scientiam regendi populos, nihil est felicius rebus humanis, quam si Deo miserante habeant potestatem.   Tales autem homines virtutes suas, quantascumque in hac vita possunt habere, non tribuunt nisi gratiae Dei, quod eas volentibus credentibus petentibus dederit, simulque intellegunt, quantum sibi desit ad perfectionem iustitiae, qualis est in illorum sanctorum angelorum societate, cui se nituntur aptare. Quantumlibet autem laudetur atque praedicetur virtus, quae sine vera pietate servit hominum gloriae, nequaquam sanctorum exiguis initiis comparanda est, quorum spes posita est in gratia et misericordia veri Dei.

pared even with the earliest and slenderest efforts of the saints, whose hope is set in the grace and mercy of the true God.

EXTRACT 20

V.21 (part)

Therefore let us ascribe to none but the true God the power to grant kingdom and empire to men. God gives only to those who worship Him happiness in the kingdom of Heaven. Earthly kingdom He gives alike to those who do and to those who do not, according to His will who wills nothing unjust. I have stated a truth which He willed should be clear to us. None the less it is beyond me and it defeats the powers of us men to disclose what is hidden and to pass clear and transparent judgement upon the merits of this or that kingdom. And so the one true God who did not leave the human race without His guidance and help granted to the Romans an Empire when He willed it and as far-flung as He willed.

EXTRACT 21   THE CHARACTER OF THE
V.24   CHRISTIAN EMPEROR

We Christians do not account Christian Emperors happy and fortunate because their reigns have been longer than others' reigns, or because they have left their sons on the throne and have therefore died in contentment, or because they have conquered the foreign enemies of the state, or because they have been able to guard against and to crush the insurrections of disloyal subjects. These achievements and others like them are favours or consolations which relieve this life's worries; but they have been received and deservedly received by Emperors who worshipped pagan deities and did not belong, as do Christian Emperors, to the Kingdom of God. This impartial distribution really springs from God's mercy; for He does not wish those who believe in Him to long for such blessings as though they were the supreme goods bestowed by God, as otherwise they might think. No. We call Emperors happy and fortunate if their rule is just, if amid the chorus of praises lauding them to the skies and amid the cringing servility of excessive adulation they preserve their humility and remember that they are men; if they make their own power the handmaid to God's majesty for the widest extension of His worship; if they fear, love and serve Him; if they set their affection not upon their own kingdom but upon that kingdom in which they are not afraid to have co-regents; if they are slow to punish, swift to forgive; if they exert their power of punishing not as a

LIBER V

Caput 21

Quae cum ita sint, non tribuamus dandi regni atque imperii potestatem nisi Deo vero, qui dat felicitatem in regno caelorum solis piis; regnum vero terrenum et piis et impiis, sicut ei placet, cui nihil iniuste placet. Quamvis enim aliquid dixerimus, quod apertum nobis esse voluit: tamen multum est ad nos et valde superat vires nostras hominum occulta discutere et liquido examine merita diiudicare regnorum. Ille igitur unus verus Deus, qui nec iudicio nec adiutorio deserit genus humanum, quando voluit et quantum voluit Romanis regnum dedit; . .

LIBER V

Caput 24

Neque enim nos Christianos quosdam imperatores ideo felices dicimus, quia vel diutius imperarunt vel imperantes filios morte placida reliquerunt, vel hostes rei publicae domuerunt vel inimicos cives adversus se insurgentes et cavere et opprimere potuerunt. Haec et alia vitae huius aerumnosae vel munera vel solacia quidam etiam cultores daemonum accipere meruerunt, qui non pertinent ad regnum Dei, quo pertinent isti; et hoc ipsius misericordia factum est, ne ab illo ista qui in eum crederent velut summa bona desiderarent. Sed felices eos dicimus, si iuste imperant, si inter linguas sublimiter honorantium et obsequia nimis humiliter salutantium non extolluntur, et se homines esse meminerunt; si suam potestatem ad Dei cultum maxime dilatandum maiestati eius famulam faciunt; si Deum timent diligunt colunt; si plus amant illud regnum, ubi non timent habere consortes; si tardius vindicant, facile ignoscunt; si eandem vindictam pro necessitate regendae tuendaeque rei publicae, non pro saturandis inimicitiarum odiis exerunt; si eandem veniam non ad inpunitatem iniquitatis, sed ad spem correctionis indulgent; si, quod aspere

means of glutting their private hatreds and feuds, but as a necessity imposed upon them by their duty to govern and protect the state; if they yield to their inclination to grant pardon, desiring rather to bring about a change of heart than to let unrighteousness escape its punishment; if they offset the harsh decrees which they are often compelled to make with a mercy which is indulgent and a generosity which is lavish; if their extravagances are checked the more severely because they have the power to enlarge them without limit; if they choose to rule their own desires rather than any number of nations; if they do all these things not through eagerness for empty fame but through love of everlasting happiness; if through consciousness of their own sins they do not omit to offer to their own true God the sacrifice of their humility and their compassion and their prayers. Such are the Christian Emperors whom we call happy and fortunate—happy for the moment of this life through their hope, but destined to be happy in full reality when that for which we look shall have come to pass.

coguntur plerumque decernere, misericordiae lenitate et beneficiorum largitate compensant; si luxuria tanto eis est castigatior, quanto posset esse liberior; si malunt cupiditatibus pravis quam quibuslibet gentibus imperare et si haec omnia faciunt non propter ardorem inanis gloriae, sed propter caritatem felicitatis aeternae; si pro suis peccatis humilitatis et miserationis et orationis sacrificium Deo suo vero immolare non neglegunt. Tales Christianos imperatores dicimus esse felices interim spe, postea re ipsa futuros, cum id quod expectamus advenerit.

Book XIX

THE PROPER ENDS OF THE TWO CITIES
[See the Analysis on p. 177]

Chapter 1 HAPPINESS AND ENDS: VARRO'S REVIEW

I am aware that I must discuss at this point the proper ends of the city of God and of the earthly city.

But first I must set out, at such length as is consistent with bringing this work to the conclusion which I have planned, all those theories by which men have striven to make happiness for themselves amid the unhappiness of this life; in this way we can reveal in clear colours the contrast between pagan men's futile realities and our hope which God has given us and the reality which He will give us, namely true happiness. We shall point this contrast not only by invoking divine authority but also by the application of reason—such reason as can be used, since we are dealing with the unfaithful. The ends of good and evil have been the subject of many disputations conducted in various ways by philosophers among themselves; turning over this problem with the most concentrated attention they have endeavoured to find out what it is that renders a man happy. For the end of human good is that which makes everything else worth pursuing, while it itself is to be pursued for its own sake only; the end of evil is that which makes everything else an object to be avoided, while it itself is to be avoided for its own sake only. And so we define the end of good to be as follows: it is not something by which the good is consumed so that it ceases to exist but something by which the good is perfected so as to reach fullness; and the end of evil is not something by which evil ceases to be, but something by which evil is carried to the extreme point in doing harm. These ends are the 'supreme good' and the 'supreme evil'. In this age of empty fancies philosophers have laboured much, as I have said, to discover these ends and to obtain the good and to avoid evil in this life; but, though they have been led astray in various ways, nature has drawn a line and has not allowed them to deviate from the track of the truth more than is consistent with placing these ends either in the mind, as some do, or in the body, as others, or in both, as yet others. Availing himself of this threefold classification of 'schools' Marcus Varro

LIBER XIX

Caput i

Quoniam de civitatis utriusque, terrenae scilicet et caelestis, debitis finibus deinceps mihi video disputandum: prius exponenda sunt, quantum operis huius terminandi ratio patitur, argumenta mortalium, quibus sibi ipsi beatitudinem facere in huius vitae infelicitate moliti sunt, ut ab eorum rebus vanis spes nostra quid differat, quam Deus nobis dedit, et res ipsa, hoc est vera beatitudo, quam dabit, non tantum auctoritate divina, sed adhibita etiam ratione, qualem propter infideles possumus adhibere, clarescat. De finibus enim bonorum et malorum multa et multipliciter inter se philosophi disputarunt; quam quaestionem maxima intentione versantes invenire conati sunt, quid efficiat hominem beatum. Illud enim est finis boni nostri, propter quod appetenda sunt cetera, ipsum autem propter se ipsum; et illud finis mali, propter quod vitanda sunt cetera, ipsum autem propter se ipsum. Finem boni ergo nunc dicimus, non quo consumatur, ut non sit, sed quo perficiatur, ut plenum sit; et finem mali, non quo esse desinat, sed quo usque nocendo perducat. Fines itaque isti sunt summum bonum et summum malum. De quibus inveniendis atque in hac vita summo bono adipiscendo, vitando autem summo malo, multum, sicut dixi, laboraverunt, qui studium sapientiae in saeculi huius vanitate professi sunt; nec tamen eos, quamvis diversis errantes modis, naturae limes in tantum ab itinere veritatis deviare permisit, ut non alii in animo, alii in corpore, alii in utroque fines bonorum ponerent et malorum. Ex qua tripertita velut generalium distributione sectarum Marcus Varro

reviewed and examined with great care and acumen in his book on philosophy a wide variety of doctrines. So varied were they that by applying certain 'differentiae' he easily arrived at two hundred and eighty-eight schools, not ever actually in existence, but theoretically possible. . . .

Chapter 1 cont. [SUMMARY OF CHAPTERS 1, 2 and 3:
and 2   VARRO'S REVIEW]

From this point to the end of Chapter 4 there follows a long summary of a part of Varro's book on philosophy. The full text is not necessary for the understanding of the remainder of the nineteenth book; but, since St Augustine uses Varro's summary as the basis for his own treatment of the ends of the two cities, an outline of Varro's classification must be given.

Varro finds that there are two hundred and eighty-eight possible theories about the nature of the 'supreme good', though that does not mean that they have all been held. Philosophers have held that there are certain objectives which men pursue of their own natural wish uninfluenced by the doctrine or training given by a 'school' or a teacher or a system. Four such objectives have been put forward; they are

(i) pleasure (*voluptas*).

(ii) quiet, freedom from pain and discomfort (*quies*, ἀταραξία).

(iii) pleasure and quiet in combination (Epicurus combines them as *voluptas*).

(iv) *prima naturae*, those universal and primary goods which are taken for granted when the body and the mind function unhampered; e.g. the goods of a body working properly unhampered by disease, the goods of intellectual activity operating according to the capacity of individual natural gifts.

Virtue is not any of these; it comes from teaching and training (*doctrina*). But according to different schools virtue may stand in different relations to any of these ends. For example, virtue may be relative to any of them, that is to say, virtue may be sought as a means to one of these ends as further ends, e.g. pleasure; or virtue may be the end, pleasure, quiet and the rest being related as ends, or means, to virtue; or virtue and the other ends may be independently desirable, each in themselves being intrinsically ends.

Thus, if there is a choice of four ends and if virtue may stand in relation to each of them in three different ways, there are (theoretically) twelve different positions which it would be possible for a philosopher to take up.

To these twelve positions we may apply another 'differentia'; is an end to be pursued on purely individual and personal grounds or on social grounds? Ought a man to wish the end for himself only or for others also, his *socii* who share a 'social' life with him? Hence there are now twenty-four possible positions.

Further 'differentiae' are now applied.

(i) Are these positions defended and maintained

(*a*) with sure and certain knowledge, as, e.g. when the Stoics assert that man's good, which gives him happiness, consists solely in the virtue of the mind, or

(*b*) with probable and uncertain knowledge, that is, with consciousness that knowledge can be only approximate or a good guess, as the New Academics say?

Thus, differences in the 'theory of knowledge' held by the enquirer may lead

in libro de philosophia tam multam dogmatum varietatem diligenter et subtiliter scrutatus advertit, ut ad ducentas octoginta et octo sectas, non quae iam essent, sed quae esse possent, adhibens quasdam differentias facillime perveniret...

to different answers to the original questions. And so the positions are now multiplied by two, making forty-eight.

(ii) The next 'differentia' is unimportant; are we to follow the manner of life of the general run of philosophers or to adopt the special dress and life of the Cynics? Nevertheless this 'differentia' raises the total to ninety-six!

(iii) Finally, it may be asked whether the pursuit of whatever end is adopted

(a) needs the whole of one's time, undisturbed by another occupation, such as business or administration or government, or

(b) should be undertaken amid the activities of ordinary occupations, or

(c) needs a life which will offer some freedom for the special pursuit of the 'end', while at the same time allowing ordinary occupations to be followed.

Thus, the previous figure ninety-six is now multiplied by three, making two hundred and eighty-eight possible positions.

Having classified theories of good and evil in this way, Varro passes to criticism; eventually he adopts as his own position that of the older Academics. St Augustine says it would be tedious to set out the whole argument, but it cannot be wholly omitted. This is the method of criticism adopted by Varro.

He regards as invalid all those 'differentiae' which are not strictly concerned with the 'end' of the good; for no real distinction can be drawn between moral philosophies which, though differing in other respects, do not differ as regards the nature of the end. Thus,

(a) the question of social life is irrelevant; it makes no difference to the nature of the end whether it is pursued by the individual or whether the individual also wishes his friend to share it; this is a question not of the ultimate nature of the good, but merely whether you share the good with your fellows and rejoice in their good as though it were your own, or whether you do not.

(b) questions involving the 'theory of knowledge' are irrelevant; they are concerned not with the nature of the good but with the truth. The moral philosopher who is not convinced that the truth can be known and the philosopher who is convinced that it can be known may agree as to the nature of the good, though differing as to the degree to which it can be known with certainty.

(c) questions of external manner of life, dress and so on are no criterion; there have been Cynics who conformed in this respect, but differed from each other as to the nature of the good.

(d) questions relating to the 'active' or 'contemplative' life are irrelevant; they concern not the nature of the good but the difficulty or ease with which it is pursued in differing circumstances. Happiness awaits successful pursuit of the good; it does not depend upon a cultured ease or a busy public life or both in turns.

And so, having removed these differences, Varro is reduced to his original

twelve, namely, pleasure, 'quiet', pleasure and 'quiet' combined, the 'primary goods', each regarded as capable of (i) being subordinated to virtue (ii) taking precedence over virtue (iii) being joined with virtue, each retaining, with virtue, its own independent status as an end to be desired in itself.

But Varro has not yet finished with his twelve; of his original four—pleasure, quiet, both combined, the primary goods—he rules out the first three, not because he regards them as unsound, but because they are contained in the fourth.

Left with the primary goods and their three possible relations to virtue, Varro arrives at three positions, of which he chooses one; for, as St Augustine says, true reason will allow you to hold only one, but whether it is to be selected from these three is another matter. The three positions are:

(i) the primary goods are to be pursued as a means to virtue which is the final or absolute end,

(ii) virtue is to be pursued as a means to the primary goods,

(iii) both virtue and the primary goods are to be pursued independently as being each desirable in its own right.

Chapter 3

Varro tries to demonstrate which of the three positions should be chosen. He starts by asking what is the nature of man. Man is made up of body and spirit, and spirit is superior to body. But he may be made up of body and spirit in three different ways:

(*a*) Man may be wholly spirit, the spirit being in relation to the body as the horseman is to the horse (the horseman is not horse plus man, but man, wholly man, in relation to a horse).

(*b*) Man may be wholly body, the body being in a certain relation to the spirit, as the wine-cup is to the wine in it.

(*c*) Man may be wholly composed of body and spirit together, just as we can speak of a pair of horses, regarding them as inseparable as making up a pair, but can also speak of them separately if contrasting them with each other.

[*Continued on p. 67*

Chapter 4   THE REPLY OF THE CITY OF GOD

If it be enquired what the city of God replies when asked about the separate points of the foregoing chapters and in particular about the 'ends' of good and evil, it will reply that eternal life is the supreme good and eternal death the supreme evil; we must live our lives aright to gain the one and to avoid the other. It is written, 'The righteous man lives by faith'.[1] We do not see our good; hence we must seek it by believing, nor does the power of living aright come to us of ourselves, unless we believe and pray and receive the aid of Him who gives us faith so that by it we

[1] Hab. ii. 4; Gal. iii. 11.

Varro chooses the third of these alternatives. Therefore the supreme good which will give a man happiness is compounded of the goods both of the body and of the spirit. The primary goods are to be pursued for their own sake; likewise virtue, which teaching and training add as a guide to the art of living, is to be pursued for its own sake as the greatest good of the spirit. Virtue uses the goods offered by the primary goods and uses also her own goods, and using them aright nature wins happiness for a man.

This life of happiness is a social life; it starts in the family and reaches out to the city, the world and its human fellowship, and thence to the Universe and the fellowship of gods who are friendly to the (pagan) saint (gods whom the Christian calls angels). As for the other 'differentiae', certainty of knowledge is undoubtedly attainable; methods of outward life are of no account, and a life compounded of time for reflection and time for action is the best. Such is St Augustine's account of Varro's discussion.

Caput 4

Si ergo quaeratur a nobis, quid civitas Dei de his singulis interrogata respondeat ac primum de finibus bonorum malorumque quid sentiat: respondebit aeternam vitam esse summum bonum, aeternam vero mortem summum malum; propter illam proinde adipiscendam istamque vitandam recte nobis esse vivendum. Propter quod scriptum est: *Iustus ex fide vivit*; quoniam neque bonum nostrum iam videmus, unde oportet ut credendo quaeramus, neque ipsum recte vivere nobis ex nobis est, nisi credentes adiuvet et orantes qui et ipsam fidem dedit, qua nos ab illo adiuvandos esse credamus. Illi autem, qui in ista vita fines bonorum et malorum esse

may believe that He will give us His aid. It was an amazing folly which led philosophers to wish to be happy in this life and to achieve happiness out of their own resources—philosophers who believed that the ends of good and evil lay in the life of this world, whether they put the supreme good in the body or the mind or both or, to specify more accurately, in pleasures or virtue or both, or in quiet or virtue or both, or in pleasure and quiet combined or in virtue or in both, or in the satisfaction of primary goods or in virtue or in both. Truth mocked at them through the prophet, who said 'The Lord knows the thoughts of men', or, as St. Paul quoted the testimony, 'The Lord knows the thoughts of the wise, that they are vain'.[1]

The argument of this chapter continues as follows in summary:

All other ends are vain, and the happiness given by them is illusory. Who can explain evil? The primary goods are subject to chance. The pagan saint can suffer pains which are the reverse of pleasurable—unrest, which is the reverse of peace, weakness, deformity, weariness, lethargy, madness. The primary goods of the body are often perverted thus. Again, the primary goods of the mind are liable to go wrong; for example, feeling and understanding are such primary goods, but deafness, blindness, insanity, demoniac possession may pervert them and even the pagan saint is liable to such catastrophes. These primary goods are in themselves neutral; they may be directed to good or evil and they themselves can be destroyed by evil.

As for virtue, which is not one of the primary goods since it is acquired during life by training and teaching, it is the cause of perpetual conflict in the personality of a man. In particular, it is the task of self-control (temperantia, σωφροσύνη) to bridle the carnal desires to prevent them dragging with them a consenting mind. And so to be perfected by virtue means to get rid of the conflict and to be free from it. On the absence of conflict depends happiness. But even the pagan saint is not above and beyond this conflict. All that Christians can do is to rely on the help of God to enable them not to be defeated and thus to sin willingly. The conflict is part of this life; therefore we should not delude ourselves into thinking that we have reached happiness.

In the same way the virtue of prudence is concerned with the choice between good and evil; it cannot ignore evil. Justice, which is concerned with rendering to each its due, must concern itself with the rendering of what is due to the spirit by the flesh and of what is due to God by the spirit; this is a task at which man is perpetually labouring; he cannot take rest as though the task were completed. Final happiness therefore is beyond him, for he is not yet saved from the weaknesses which make it incumbent upon him to shoulder this task. Again, fortitude admits that there are evils to be borne; the pagan saint may say that evil does not exist and that he can therefore be happy on the rack; but there comes a time when he considers himself justified in ending his life. It is a curious happiness which invokes the aid of death to put an end to itself. Cato's suicide shows that he could not bear Caesar's triumph; where was his fortitude? and why did he leave a life which on his own Stoic principles could nevertheless be happy? It must have been because it was not happy; in other words Stoicism is compelled to admit the reality of evil.

The Peripatetics and older Academicians admit the reality of evil, but assert

[1] Ps. xciv. 11; 1 Cor. iii. 20.

putaverunt, sive in corpore sive in animo sive in utroque ponentes summum bonum, atque, ut id explicatius eloquar, sive in voluptate sive in
virtute sive in utraque, sive in quiete sive in virtute sive in utraque, sive in
voluptate simul et quiete sive in virtute sive in utrisque, sive in primis
naturae sive in virtute sive in utrisque, hic beati esse et a se ipsis beatificari
mira vanitate voluerunt. Inrisit hos Veritas per prophetam dicentem:
Dominus novit cogitationes hominum vel, sicut hoc testimonium posuit
apostolus Paulus: *Dominus novit cogitationes sapientium, quoniam vanae
sunt.* . .

that, though it may be so great as to justify suicide, a man's life may none the less be happy. To be forbidden to seek release in death would be a misery to him, and this suggests that his life is a misery, and to abbreviate misery by death does not turn misery into happiness. They had much better admit the reality of evil which compels a man to do violence to the natural impulse of self-preservation and to kill himself—behaviour which reverses the meaning of fortitude and makes it so illogical as to include the surrender implied by suicide.

Men had better recognise that the final realisation of the supreme good is impossible in a world in which the very virtues testify to the reality of evil. They testify all the more powerfully in proportion as they face the truth; when they recognise God (*pietas*), they are true, and, if they are truthful, they must admit the reality of evil. To be saved from evil in this life is impossible, and safety is necessary to happiness. All we can have in this life is the hope of safety and happiness in a future life; this hope saves us and makes us happy, but it is a hope for the future, and in it virtues, as practised in this life, are enabled to face the truth and do not bury their heads in the sand. 'For by hope were we saved; but hope that is seen is not hope; for what a man seeeth why doth he yet hope for it? But if we hope for that which we see not, then do we with patience wait for it'. 'With patience'—thus the Stoic *patientia*, which was seen to be self-contradictory and illusory, in the light of this hope can become a true virtue. 'To be saved from evil by hope—and this lies in a future life—is itself the final happiness for man. Such happiness the pagan philosophers cannot see and therefore cannot believe; they try to invent for themselves an entirely spurious happiness with a virtue which departs further from the truth as it becomes more arrogant.'[1]

Chapter 5   THE LIFE OF FELLOWSHIP

But, when the philosophers demand that the pagan saint should live a life of fellowship, we should be much more ready to applaud them. For how would that city of God—the description of which has now brought us into the nineteenth book of this work—how would that city originate and find a beginning or march forward in its course or attain its proper 'ends' if the life of its saints were not a life of fellowship? Nevertheless in this careworn mortal life the fellowship of men abounds in evils, and no one could reckon up their number or assess their magnitude. Let the pagan philosophers listen to the man in one of their comedies who uttered his own feelings and those of all his fellows, when he said: 'I married a wife: and what unhappiness I found there; sons were born to me, an added anxiety!'[2] Remember too how the same comic play-wright, Terence, describes the ills which befall those who are in love; 'slights and suspicions, feuds, open war, and then peace again'.[3] These have everywhere filled up human life to the brim, often appearing even in the purest friendships. Don't you agree that they fill up human life everywhere? We feel slights and suspicions, feuds and war to be certainly evils; on the other hand we feel the blessings of peace to be uncertain, for we are ignorant of the

[1] xix. 4 ad fin.   [2] Ter. *Ad.* 867 sq.   [3] id. *Eun.* 59 sqq.

70

Caput 5

Quod autem socialem vitam volunt esse sapientis, nos multo amplius adprobamus. Nam unde ista Dei civitas, de qua huius operis ecce iam undevicensimum librum versamus in manibus, vel inchoaretur exortu vel progrederetur excursu vel adprehenderet debitos fines, si non esset socialis vita sanctorum? Sed in huius mortalitatis aerumna quot et quantis abundet malis humana societas, quis enumerare valeat? quis aestimare sufficiat? Audiant apud comicos suos hominem cum sensu atque consensu omnium hominum dicere:

> *Duxi uxorem; quam ibi miseriam vidi! Nati filii,*
> *Alia cura.*

Quid itidem illa, quae in amore vitia commemorat idem Terentius, 'iniuriae suspiciones, inimicitiae bellum, pax rursum': nonne res humanas ubique impleverunt? nonne et in amicorum honestis amoribus plerumque contingunt? nonne his usquequaque plenae sunt res humanae, ubi iniurias suspiciones, inimicitias bellum mala certa sentimus; pacem vero incertum

hearts of those with whom we wish to keep peace, and, even if we could know them to-day, we should be quite in the dark about their attitude to-morrow. Again, you would expect those who live within the walls of the same house usually to be friendly or to feel a duty to be friendly to one another; yet no one can derive any feeling of confidence from such conditions. For often secret intrigues give rise to serious evils, which are all the more bitter in contrast with the sweets of the peace which was thought to be real, though in fact it was due to most clever pretence. Everyone recognises the truth of this and is therefore moved to give mournful assent to the passage in Cicero: 'no intrigues are more difficult to detect than those which are covered up by the pretence of affection or hidden under the cloak of family relationship. For you could easily take precautions to avoid a declared enemy; but the hidden evil which lurks in the heart of your home not only is there—bad as that is—but it over-whelms you before you could look round and search it out.'[1] The Scripture says that 'a man's foes shall be those of his own household'.[2] The reason why this saying so pierces the heart is that, whereas a man can be brave enough to endure with composure the plots aimed against him under cover of friendship, or watchful enough to foresee them and guard against them, the good man is bound to suffer anguish from the treacher-ous hurt done to him by those whom he discovers to be wicked; and it makes no difference whether they always were evilly disposed to him and pretended to be the opposite or whether they have changed from a good to an evil disposition. If then the household, in which most men find shelter from these evils that beset the human race, offers no security, what are we to say about the city? For the larger the city the more crowded are its law-courts with civil and criminal cases; and, though open insurrection and civil war, which are always the cause of upheaval and more often than not of bloodshed, may not openly break out and cities may at times be spared their actual horrors, yet the threat of them is always overhanging.

Chapter 6

Consider now the nature of the judgements which men pass upon men in the law courts; for, however profound and enduring the peace which cities may enjoy, there are bound to be such judgements. How pitiable they are, how utterly regrettable! One set of men passes judgement upon others whose consciences they are unable to see. This explains why they are forced to examine innocent witnesses under torture, in order that they may seek the truth in a matter which concerns them not at all. Again, even

[1] Verr. ii. 1, 15.   [2] Mt. x. 36.

bonum, quoniam corda eorum, cum quibus eam tenere volumus, igno-
ramus, et si hodie nosse possemus, qualia cras futura essent utique nescire-
mus. Qui porro inter se amiciores solent esse vel debent, quam qui una
etiam continentur domo? Et tamen quis inde securus est, cum tanta saepe
mala ex eorum occultis insidiis extiterint, tanto amariora, quanto pax
dulcior fuit, quae vera putata est, cum astutissime fingeretur? Propter
quod omnium pectora sic adtingit, ut cogat in gemitum, quod ait Tullius:
'Nullae sunt occultiores insidiae quam hae, quae latent in simulatione
officii aut in aliquo necessitudinis nomine. Nam eum, qui palam est adversarius, facile cavendo vitare possis; hoc vero occultum intestinum ac
domesticum malum non solum existit, verum etiam opprimit, antequam
prospicere atque explorare potueris.' Propter quod etiam divina vox illa:
Et inimici hominis domestici eius cum magno dolore cordis auditur, quia,
etsi quisque tam fortis sit, ut aequo animo perferat, vel tam vigilans, ut
provido consilio caveat, quae adversus eum molitur amicitia simulata,
eorum tamen hominum perfidorum malo, cum eos esse pessimos experi-
tur, si ipse bonus est, graviter excrucietur necesse est, sive semper mali
fuerint et se bonos finxerint, sive in istam malitiam ex bonitate mutati sint.
Si ergo domus, commune perfugium in his malis humani generis, tuta non
est, quid civitas, quae quanto maior est, tanto forum eius litibus et civilibus
et criminalibus plenius, etiamsi quiescant non solum turbulentae, verum
saepius et cruentae seditiones ac bella civilia, a quorum eventis sunt aliquando liberae civitates, a periculis numquam?

Caput 6

Quid ipsa iudicia hominum de hominibus, quae civitatibus in quantalibet
pace manentibus deesse non possunt, qualia putamus esse, quam misera,
quam dolenda? Quando quidem hi iudicant, qui conscientias eorum, de
quibus iudicant, cernere nequeunt. Unde saepe coguntur tormentis inno-
centium testium ad alienam causam pertinentem quaerere veritatem. Quid

in his own trial a suspect may be tortured and put on the rack during the inquiry into his guilt; and, though he is innocent, he pays for a hypothetical crime with the most definite penalties, not because his guilt is detected, but because his innocence is not established. And so the ignorance of the judge often spells catastrophe for the innocent. But the position may develop into something quite intolerable which demands our anguished grief and the outpouring, if it were possible, of rivers of tears. I mean that a judge, to avoid condemning to death in his ignorance an innocent man, tortures the prisoner before him, and then it results from the tragedy of his ignorance that he actually puts to death a tortured and innocent man whom he has tortured in order to avoid putting to death an innocent man. For, if the prisoner has elected to follow the wisdom of pagan philosophers and to escape from life rather than submit any longer to his torture, he actually pleads guilty to a crime which he has not committed. And so the prisoner is condemned and put to death; the judge is still in ignorance whether he has caused the death of an innocent or a guilty man, though he tortured him to avoid putting to death in his ignorance an innocent man. In short, he tortured him, though innocent, to discover the truth, and with the truth undiscovered he caused his death. If the life of fellowship is shrouded in such darkness as this, you may well ask whether the learned judge will sit or whether his courage will not fail him. Of course he will sit. For human fellowship, which he thinks it wrong to leave in the lurch, places its compulsion upon him and drags him off to fulfil his duty to the end. He does not feel it a wrong that innocent witnesses are tortured in causes which are not theirs, or that those who are themselves in the dock are often so overcome by the anguish of their pain that they make a false confession of guilt, and so are punished, though innocent, after being tortured as innocent—or that, even if they are not punished by death, they frequently die in the midst of their torture or as a result of it. There are men who prosecute through anxiety, perhaps, to benefit human fellowship by seeing that crimes do not go unpunished; they may fail to prove their charges, however true, because the witnesses lie or the prisoner bears up heroically under torture and does not confess. Yet the judge does not scruple to condemn these self-appointed prosecutors,[1] even though he does not know whether the charges are true or not. He does not regard all these glaring evils as sins. For, as a learned judge, he does not commit them from a wish to do hurt; he labours under the constraint which his ignorance imposes upon him. Yet in spite of his ignorance he is constrained to pass judgement because human fellowship compels him to pass it. Here you have without disguise that tragedy of the man of which we are speaking, even if we do not suggest

[1] As ancient law might enjoin.

74

cum in sua causa quisque torquetur et, cum quaeritur utrum sit nocens, cruciatur et innocens luit pro incerto scelere certissimas poenas, non quia illud commisisse detegitur, sed quia non commisisse nescitur? Ac per hoc ignorantia iudicis plerumque est calamitas innocentis. Et quod est intolerabilius magisque plangendum rigandumque, si fieri possit, fontibus lacrimarum, cum propterea iudex torqueat accusatum, ne occidat nesciens innocentem, fit per ignorantiae miseriam, ut et tortum et innocentem occidat, quem ne innocentem occideret torserat. Si enim secundum istorum sapientiam elegerit ex hac vita fugere quam diutius illa sustinere tormenta: quod non commisit, commisisse se dicit. Quo damnato et occiso, utrum nocentem an innocentem iudex occiderit, adhuc nescit, quem ne innocentem nesciens occideret torsit; ac per hoc innocentem et ut sciret torsit, et dum nesciret occidit. In his tenebris vitae socialis sedebit iudex ille sapiens an non audebit? Sedebit plane. Constringit enim eum et ad hoc officium pertrahit humana societas, quam deserere nefas ducit. Hoc enim nefas esse non ducit, quod testes innocentes in causis torquentur alienis; quod hi, qui arguuntur, vi doloris plerumque superati et de se falsa confessi etiam puniuntur innocentes, cum iam torti fuerint innocentes; quod, etsi non morte puniantur, in ipsis vel ex ipsis tormentis plerumque moriuntur; quod aliquando et ipsi, qui arguunt, humanae societati fortasse, ne crimina inpunita sint, prodesse cupientes et mentientibus testibus reoque ipso contra tormenta durante inmaniter nec fatente probare quod obiciunt non valentes, quamvis vera obiecerint, a iudice nesciente damnantur. Haec tot et tanta mala non deputat esse peccata; non enim haec facit sapiens iudex nocendi voluntate, sed necessitate nesciendi, et tamen, quia cogit humana societas, necessitate etiam iudicandi. Haec est ergo quam dicimus miseria certe hominis, etsi non malitia sapientis. An vero

evil in him as a learned judge. Constrained to be in ignorance and yet to pass judgement, he tortures the guiltless; and is he then not satisfied with escaping prosecution for this, but actually asks to be happy on top of it all? He shows greater power of reflection, as well as his worth as a man, when he recognises the tragedy of the constraint which is upon him and hates it in himself; and, if his learning springs from piety, he cries aloud to God, 'Deliver me from my constraints'.[1]

Chapter 7

After the *civitas* or the city comes the world, in which the pagan philosophers find the third stage of human fellowship; they begin with the home, pass to the city and then they move on and come to the world, which, inasmuch as it is larger than the others, is all the more full of dangers, just as flood waters are all the more dangerous as they pile up. Here difference of language is the first cause of estrangement between man and man. If two men, neither of whom knows the other's language, meet each other and are compelled by some constraint not to pass by each other, but to be together, they do not find it as easy, though they are both men, to enter into fellowship with each other as would dumb animals, even of different species. They cannot share their feelings with one another, and so their inability to speak the same language prevents their natural kinship availing to bring them into fellowship—so marked is this, that a man would rather be in the company of his dog than in the company of a foreigner.

To this you will reply that an imperial city, besides imposing its yoke upon the nations which it subdues, takes great pains to impose also its language; this it does through the peace which results from fellowship with it and which ensures that there shall be no dearth, but rather a plentiful supply of interpreters. This is all true; but at what a cost is this end achieved—repeated and gigantic wars, massacres and a vast outpouring of human blood. When these are over, the same ills and all their tragedy are not done with. For apart from the wars with hostile foreign nations, which, as history shows, inevitably occur, the mere vastness of an empire produces war of worse kind—I mean wars between partners in the empire and civil wars which convulse mankind with far greater suffering than others; and this is true equally of actual war in order at last to suppress the rebels and of dread that there will be further outbreaks. As for the many and manifold catastrophes, the stern and stark constraints which follow in the wake of such evils, if I wished to describe them in fit terms—in

[1] Ps. xxv. 17.

necessitate nesciendi atque iudicandi torquet insontes, punit insontes, et parum est illi, quod non est reus, si non sit insuper et beatus? Quanto consideratius et homine dignius agnoscit in ista necessitate miseriam eamque odit in se et, si pie sapit, clamat ad Deum: *De necessitatibus meis erue me!*

Caput 7

Post civitatem vel urbem sequitur orbis terrae, in quo tertium gradum ponunt societatis humanae, incipientes a domo atque inde ad urbem, deinde ad orbem progrediendo venientes; qui utique, sicut aquarum congeries, quanto maior est, tanto periculis plenior. In quo primum linguarum diversitas hominem alienat ab homine. Nam si duo sibimet invicem fiant obviam neque praeterire, sed simul esse aliqua necessitate cogantur, quorum neuter linguam novit alterius: facilius sibi muta animalia, etiam diversi generis, quam illi, cum sint homines ambo, sociantur. Quando enim quae sentiunt inter se communicare non possunt, propter solam diversitatem linguae nihil prodest ad consociandos homines tanta similitudo naturae, ita ut libentius homo sit cum cane suo quam cum homine alieno. At enim opera data est, ut imperiosa civitas non solum iugum, verum etiam linguam suam domitis gentibus per pacem societatis inponeret, per quam non deesset, immo et abundaret etiam interpretum copia. Verum est; sed hoc quam multis et quam grandibus bellis, quanta strage hominum, quanta effusione humani sanguinis comparatum est? Quibus transactis, non est tamen eorundem malorum finita miseria. Quamvis enim non defuerint neque desint hostes exterae nationes, contra quas semper bella gesta sunt et geruntur: tamen etiam ipsa imperii latitudo peperit peioris generis bella, socialia scilicet et civilia, quibus miserabilius quatitur humanum genus, sive cum belligeratur, ut aliquando conquiescant, sive cum timetur, ne rursus exsurgant. Quorum malorum multas et multiplices clades, duras et diras necessitates si ut dignum est eloqui velim,

20

reality I could certainly not do justice to them—I should write a long essay, indeed an essay without end.

But the wise ruler of pagan philosophy, I shall be told, is likely to wage only just wars. What nonsense! If he remembers that he is a man with human feelings, it will cause him all the more grief that the wars that he has become constrained to wage are just wars. For, if the wars were not just, he would not have to wage them; and so for the wise ruler there would be no wars at all. For it is the wickedness of the enemy that lays upon him the necessity of waging just wars, and this wickedness must assuredly cause grief to him as a man because it is the wickedness of man, even though it should not give rise to the constraint of going to war. Whosoever feels grief when he reflects upon these evils, must admit misery, for they are great and terrifying and cruel; but whosoever allows them to go on or contemplates them without any feeling of grief is all the more a miserable figure; for he thinks himself happy because he has lost all human feeling.

Chapter 8

Let us suppose, however, that we are not dealing with a case of ignorance bordering upon madness, which drives a man to mistake enemy for friend or friend for enemy; though as a matter of fact such cases are frequent in the miserable setting of this life. Surely amid the abundant errors and worries which beset this human fellowship of ours we derive comfort from the sincere trust of true and good friends and from our love for them and theirs for us. Yet the more such friends we have, and the more they are scattered, the more widely spread is our fear lest any evil should befall them from the vast piles of evil accumulated in this world. Not only does it worry us that they may be struck down by famine or war or disease or carried off as prisoners, or that in conditions of slavery they may suffer such horrors as it is beyond us to imagine; we are afraid also that they may change and become treacherous and evilly disposed and wicked, and this fear is much more bitter than the other. When our fears are realised—the more friends we have, the more often it happens—and when news is brought to us of our friends' behaviour, no one can describe, unless from similar experience, the burning emotions with which our hearts are on fire. We should prefer to hear that they were dead, though even this we could not hear without pain; for we cannot help feeling sorrow at the death of those whose lives gave us the joy and solace of friendship. If you forbid us such sorrow, you must forbid us also the friendly intercourse, you must put a ban on all friendly feeling or put an axe to its root, you must shatter

78

quamquam nequaquam sicut res postulat possim: quis erit prolixae disputationis modus? Sed sapiens, inquiunt, iusta bella gesturus est. Quasi non, si se hominem meminit, multo magis dolebit iustorum necessitatem sibi extitisse bellorum, quia nisi iusta essent, ei gerenda non essent, ac per hoc sapienti nulla bella essent. Iniquitas enim partis adversae iusta bella ingerit gerenda sapienti; quae iniquitas utique homini est dolenda, quia hominum est, etsi nulla ex ea bellandi necessitas nasceretur. Haec itaque mala tam magna, tam horrenda, tam saeva quisquis cum dolore considerat, miseriam fateatur; quisquis autem vel patitur ea sine animi dolore vel cogitat, multo utique miserius ideo se putat beatum, quia et humanum perdidit sensum.

Caput 8

Si autem non contingat quaedam ignorantia similis dementiae, quae tamen in huius vitae misera condicione saepe contingit, ut credatur vel amicus esse, qui inimicus est, vel inimicus, qui amicus est: quid nos consolatur in hac humana societate erroribus aerumnisque plenissima nisi fides non ficta et mutua dilectio verorum et bonorum amicorum? Quos quanto plures et in locis pluribus habemus, tanto longius latiusque metuimus, ne quid eis contingat mali de tantis malorum aggeribus huius saeculi. Non enim tantummodo solliciti sumus, ne fame, ne bellis, ne morbis, ne captivitatibus affligantur, ne in eadem servitute talia patiantur, qualia nec cogitare sufficimus; verum etiam, ubi timor est multo amarior, ne in perfidiam malitiam nequitiamque mutentur. Et quando ista contingunt (tanto utique plura, quanto illi sunt plures) et in nostram notitiam perferuntur, quibus cor nostrum flagris uratur, quis potest, nisi qui talia sentit, advertere? Mortuos quippe audire mallemus, quamvis et hoc sine dolore non possimus audire. Quorum enim nos vita propter amicitiae solacia delectabat, unde fieri potest, ut eorum mors nullam nobis ingerat maestitudinem? Quam qui prohibet, prohibeat, si potest, amica conloquia, interdicat amicalem vel intercidat affectum, humanarum omnium necessitudinum vincula mentis

all bonds of human relationship and make our minds a blank of cruel indifference; or else you must decree that we must adopt such an attitude to our friends as would rob friendship of its charm. If you cannot do all that, the death of those whose lives have given us pleasure is bound to be bitter. Hence grief is like a wound or an ulcer to the heart which is not devoid of feeling, and for the healing of it consolation is administered with loving care; for we must not argue that grief is not something which needs healing just because the healthier the mind, the more quickly and easily is grief healed in it. The deaths of close friends, particularly those whose services are of most value to human fellowship, affect the lives of mortal men with varying degrees of severity; none the less we should prefer to be told or to see that they were dead rather than that they had failed in loyalty or virtue, for then they would be dead in the soul itself. Of this huge mass of evils the earth is full; wherefore it is written: 'Is not human life on earth a time of testing?'[1] and the Lord Himself says: 'Woe unto the world because of occasions of stumbling'[2]; and again, 'Because wickedness has been multiplied, the love of many shall grow cold'.[3] This is why we congratulate our friends, if they are good men, when they die: though their death saddens us, their very death gives us all the surer comfort, for they have been freed of those evils by which even good men are worn down or are warped, or exposed to both of these dangers.

Chapter 9

But in the fellowship of the holy angels there is no need for us to fear that we shall be saddened by the death or the lapse of such friends as they. Such fellowship is indeed postulated by pagan philosophers who hold that the gods are friendly to us; they pass from this world to the universe with the purpose of thus embracing somehow or other the heavens as well, and so they define a fourth category of fellowship. But angels do not associate with us with the same degree of intimacy as do men (and this must be included among the sorrows of our human life); and, again, Satan, so we are told, changes himself into an angel of light[4] to tempt those who need to be taught by temptations or those who it is right should be deceived. For these reasons the plenteous mercy of God is needful to us, if we are to avoid mistaking the false friendship of evil spirits for the real friendship of good spirits, and thus exposing ourselves to enemies who are all the more able to do us harm as they excel in cleverness and power of deception. Indeed that plenteous mercy of God is needful to man and to his great

[1] Job vii. 1.   [2] Mt. xviii. 7.   [3] id. xxiv. 12.   [4] 2 Cor. xi. 14.

inmiti stupore disrumpat aut sic eis utendum censeat, ut nulla ex eis animum dulcedo perfundat. Quod si fieri nullo modo potest, etiam hoc quo pacto futurum est, ut eius nobis amara mors non sit, cuius dulcis est vita? Hinc enim est et luctus quoddam non inhumani cordis quasi vulnus aut ulcus, cui sanando adhibentur officiosae consolationes. Non enim propterea non est quod sanetur, quoniam quanto est animus melior, tanto in eo citius faciliusque sanatur. Cum igitur etiam de carissimorum mortibus, maxime quorum sunt humanae societati officia necessaria, nunc mitius, nunc asperius affligatur vita mortalium: mortuos tamen eos, quos diligimus, quam vel a fide vel a bonis moribus lapsos, hoc est in ipsa anima mortuos, audire seu videre mallemus. Qua ingenti materia malorum plena est terra, propter quod scriptum est: *Numquid non temptatio est vita humana super terram?* et propter quod ipse Dominus ait: *Vae mundo ab scandalis*, et iterum: *Quoniam abundavit*, inquit, *iniquitas, refrigescet caritas multorum.* Ex quo fit, ut bonis amicis mortuis gratulemur et, cum mors eorum nos contristet, ipsa nos certius consoletur, quoniam caruerunt malis, quibus in hac vita etiam boni homines vel conteruntur vel depravantur vel in utroque periclitantur.

CAPUT 9

In societate vero sanctorum angelorum, quam philosophi illi, qui nobis deos amicos esse voluerunt, quarto constituerunt loco, velut ad mundum venientes ab orbe terrarum, ut sic quodam modo complecterentur et caelum, nullo modo quidem metuimus, ne tales amici vel morte nos sua vel depravatione contristent. Sed quia nobis non ea, qua homines, familiaritate miscentur (quod etiam ipsum ad aerumnas huius pertinet vitae) et aliquando Satanas, sicut legimus, transfigurat se velut angelum lucis ad temptandos eos, quos ita vel erudiri opus est vel decipi iustum est: magna Dei misericordia necessaria est, ne quisquam, cum bonos angelos amicos se habere putat, habeat malos daemones fictos amicos, eosque tanto nocentiores, quanto astutiores ac fallaciores, patiatur inimicos. Et cui magna ista Dei misericordia necessaria est nisi magnae humanae

misery, for he is oppressed by so deep an ignorance that he is easily deluded by the pretences of the evil spirits. Those very philosophers of the city of wickedness of whom we have spoken believed that the gods were friendly to them, but they have most assuredly fallen into the hands of evilly-disposed spirits who hold in bondage the whole of that city, which with those spirits will one day endure everlasting punishment. The rites, or rather blasphemies, and the foul spectacles with which men honour the crimes of their deities and think to render homage and win atonement are sufficient evidence of the nature of these deities; they are actually the authors of these deeds of shame and demand that their worshippers also shall be guilty of them.

Chapter 10

These deities offer deceits and temptations of many kinds from which not even the saints are free, nor the faithful worshippers of the one true and supreme God. For in this world of man's frailty and in these evil days even anxiety on that score is not without value; it makes us seek with all the more ardent yearning that freedom from care in which is the fullest and the most assured peace. For in peace will be found those gifts of nature which are given to our nature by the Creator of all things in nature—the gifts which are not only good but also eternal, gifts consisting not only in the mind healed by wisdom but also in the body which will be renewed by its resurrection; in peace will be found virtues, which are not in conflict with vice and evil, but which have as the reward of victory an eternal peace which no adversary can disturb. That eternal peace is final happiness, a finality of perfection which excludes the notion of being finished. In this world we are indeed said to be happy when we have such little peace as a good life here can give us; but happiness of this kind, if compared with the happiness which we call final happiness, is found to be sheer misery. And so when, as mortal men in a mortal world, we have such peace as we can have in this life, if we live aright, virtue puts its blessings to a right use; but, even when we have not peace, virtue makes use even of the evils which man suffers. But virtue is true virtue only when it refers all the goods of which it makes good use, and all its actions in making good use of good and evil, and indeed its own self to that end in which we shall find a peace of such quality and such degree that it cannot be surpassed.

Chapter 11

It would therefore be possible to say that the end of our good is peace, just as we have also said it is eternal life; this would agree with the

miseriae, quae ignorantia tanta premitur, ut facile istorum simulatione fallatur? Et illos quidem philosophos in impia civitate, qui deos sibi amicos esse dixerunt, in daemones malignos incidisse certissimum est, quibus tota ipsa civitas subditur, aeternum cum eis habitura supplicium. Ex eorum quippe sacris vel potius sacrilegiis, quibus eos colendos, et ex ludis inmundissimis, ubi eorum crimina celebrantur, quibus eos placandos putarunt eisdem ipsis auctoribus et exactoribus talium tantorumque de-decorum, satis ab eis qui colantur apertum est.

Caput 10

Sed neque sancti et fideles unius veri Dei summique cultores ab eorum fallaciis et multiformi temptatione securi sunt. In hoc enim loco infirmi-tatis et diebus malignis etiam ista sollicitudo non est inutilis, ut illa securi-tas, ubi pax plenissima atque certissima est, desiderio ferventiore quaera-tur. Ibi enim erunt naturae munera, hoc est, quae naturae nostrae ab omnium naturarum creatore donantur, non solum bona, verum etiam sempiterna, non solum in animo, qui sanatur per sapientiam, verum etiam in corpore, quod resurrectione renovabitur; ibi virtutes, non contra ulla vitia vel mala quaecumque certantes, sed habentes victoriae praemium aeternam pacem, quam nullus adversarius inquietet. Ipsa est enim beatitudo finalis, ipse perfectionis finis, qui consumentem non habet finem. Hic autem dicimur quidem beati, quando pacem habemus, quantulacumque hic haberi potest in vita bona; sed haec beatitudo illi, quam finalem dici-mus, beatitudini comparata prorsus miseria reperitur. Hanc ergo pacem, qualis hic potest esse, mortales homines in rebus mortalibus quando habemus, si recte vivimus, bonis eius recte utitur virtus; quando vero eam non habemus, etiam malis, quae homo patitur, bene utitur virtus. Sed tunc est vera virtus, quando et omnia bona, quibus bene utitur, et quid-quid in bono usu bonorum et malorum facit, et se ipsam ad eum finem refert, ubi nobis talis et tanta pax erit, qua melior et maior esse non possit.

Caput 11

Quapropter possemus dicere fines bonorum nostrorum esse pacem, sicut aeternam diximus vitam, praesertim quia ipsi civitati Dei, de qua nobis est

sacred psalm which addressed the city of God, the theme of this laborious work, in the following words: 'Praise the Lord, O Jerusalem, Praise thy God, O Sion: for he strengthened the bars of thy gates: he has blessed thy sons within thee, even he who set peace to be thy boundaries'.[1] When the bars of its gates shall have been made strong, no one shall then go into it and no one shall go out of it. By boundaries or ends we ought here to understand the peace which we wish to exhibit as final: the mystical name of the city of God, Jerusalem, means 'the vision of peace' as we have already said. But in our finite world the word 'peace' is so often used in a context in which there can be no possibility of eternal life that I prefer to call the end in which the city will realise its supreme good eternal life rather than peace. The Apostle says about this end, 'Now freed from sin, but having become the slaves of God, you have a reward leading to sanctification, but you have as your end eternal life'.[2] But on the other hand there is objection to the phrase eternal life. People with no acquaintance with Holy Scripture can interpret eternal life to include the life of the wicked, either following philosophers who regard the soul as immortal or following a doctrine of our faith which regards the punishments of the wicked as endless; for the wicked cannot be tortured eternally unless they also live for ever. And so precisely for this reason the end in which the city of God will realise its supreme good ought to be called either peace in eternal life or eternal life in peace, and the definition then becomes intelligible to all. So great a good is peace that even in earthly and mortal conditions to hear of it is pleasant, and nothing more desirable can be desired, nothing better in fact can be found. I should like to speak a little longer about this, and I think I shall not burden the reader: I do it because peace is the end of the city which I am describing, and also because of its inherent attractiveness, since peace is dear to all of us.

Chapter 12

You will agree with me in recognising the truth of this, if you consider human life and consider also nature, of which human life is a part; for there is no one so constituted as to be unwilling to possess peace any more than he is unwilling to feel joy. The very men who will wars will only victory; they are anxious therefore to reach a glorious peace by means of war; for victory is simply the subjugation of resistance, and, when that is achieved, peace will reign. Peace therefore is the objective even in the waging of war, and this is true also of those who aim at giving full play to martial qualities in the exercise of military control and in fighting. Hence

[1] Ps. cxlvii. 12 sqq.   [2] Rom. vi. 22.

ista operosissima disputatio, in sancto dicitur psalmo: *Lauda Hierusalem Dominum, conlauda Deum tuum Sion; quoniam confirmavit seras portarum tuarum, benedixit filios tuos in te, qui posuit fines tuos pacem.* Quando enim confirmatae fuerint serae portarum eius, iam in illam nullus intrabit nec ab illa ullus exibit. Ac per hoc fines eius eam debemus hic intellegere pacem, quam volumus demonstrare finalem. Nam et ipsius civitatis mysticum nomen, id est Hierusalem, quod et ante iam diximus, visio pacis interpretatur. Sed quoniam pacis nomen etiam in his rebus mortalibus frequentatur, ubi utique non est vita aeterna, propterea finem civitatis huius, ubi erit summum bonum eius, aeternam vitam maluimus commemorare quam pacem. De quo fine apostolus ait: *Nunc vero liberati a peccato, servi autem facti Deo, habetis fructum vestrum in sanctificationem, finem vero vitam aeternam.* Sed rursus quia vita aeterna ab eis, qui familiaritatem non habent cum scripturis sanctis, potest accipi etiam malorum vita, vel secundum quosdam etiam philosophos propter animae inmortalitatem vel secundum etiam fidem nostram propter poenas interminabiles impiorum, qui utique in aeternum cruciari non poterunt, nisi etiam vixerint in aeternum: profecto finis civitatis huius, in quo summum habebit bonum, vel pax in vita aeterna vel vita aeterna in pace dicendus est, ut facilius ab omnibus possit intellegi. Tantum est enim pacis bonum, ut etiam in rebus terrenis atque mortalibus nihil gratius soleat audiri, nihil desiderabilius concupisci, nihil postremo possit melius inveniri. De quo si aliquanto diutius loqui voluerimus, non erimus, quantum arbitror, onerosi legentibus, et propter finem civitatis huius, de qua nobis sermo est, et propter ipsam dulcedinem pacis, quae omnibus cara est.

Caput 12

Quod mecum quisquis res humanas naturamque communem utcumque intuetur agnoscit; sicut enim nemo est qui gaudere nolit, ita nemo est qui pacem habere nolit. Quando quidem et ipsi, qui bella volunt, nihil aliud quam vincere volunt; ad gloriosam ergo pacem bellando cupiunt pervenire. Nam quid est aliud victoria nisi subiectio repugnantium? quod cum factum fuerit, pax erit. Pacis igitur intentione geruntur et bella, ab his etiam, qui virtutem bellicam student exercere imperando atque pugnando. Unde pacem constat belli esse optabilem finem. Omnis enim

it may be agreed that peace is the desired end of war; for everyone seeks peace even in the act of making war, but no one seeks war in the act of making peace. Those who are willing that the peace in which they live should be disturbed do not thereby show hatred of peace, but show their desire to alter it in accordance with their own wishes: they do not object to peace as such, but they want it to be such as they desire. They may have rebelled and separated themselves from the rest of the community, but, unless they maintain some semblance of peace with their fellow-conspirators or their supporters, they do not achieve their object; even brigands want peace among their confederates to enable them to threaten the peace of the rest with greater violence and in greater safety. Let us imagine an individual so overwhelmingly strong and so chary of confederates that he puts himself in the power of no ally, but all alone traps and overpowers his victim, falling upon all whom he can and murdering them and carrying off their goods. Even he maintains some shadow of peace with those whom he cannot kill or those from whom he wishes to conceal his deeds. In his house he is really anxious to be on peaceful terms with his wife and children and anyone else there; no doubt he gets pleasure from their obedience to his will. If he does not receive obedience, he fumes, he uses violence, he punishes, and, if necessary, even through his rage restores peace in the house since he realises that peace cannot exist unless some ruling principle —which in the home is himself—enforces the subjection of everything else in that same household-fellowship. Let us now imagine that he is offered the abject obedience of a larger number of men, a city or a nation, rendering him the same obedience that he exacted in his household; he would not now hide himself like a robber in his lair, but would exalt himself as a king for all to behold—though his greed and malignity would remain.

It can be seen therefore that everyone wishes to maintain peace with his own people, whom he wants to live according to his will. He wishes, if he can, to make his own all those against whom he wars, and to impose upon them when subjugated the laws of his own peace.

Let us now draw another picture, this time a picture of the kind of being sometimes met with in poetry or in fairy story, one whom the writers preferred to describe as a half-man, rather than as a man, just because of his untamed wildness which prevented him living in fellowship. This creature's kingdom was the loneliness of an eerie cave; so extraordinarily evil was his nature that his name—Cacus—was derived from it—in Greek κακός is the Latin *malus* [and in English 'evil']; he had no wife to offer him words of affection or to return his, no small children to play with and none growing up for him to control; no friends whose conversation he might enjoy. He did not even speak to his father Vulcan, over whom he

homo etiam belligerando pacem requirit; nemo autem bellum pacificando. Nam et illi qui pacem, in qua sunt, perturbari volunt, non pacem oderunt, sed eam pro arbitrio suo cupiunt commutari. Non ergo ut sit pax nolunt, sed ut ea sit quam volunt. Denique etsi per seditionem se ab aliis separaverint, cum eis ipsis conspiratis vel coniuratis suis nisi qualemcumque speciem pacis teneant, non efficiunt quod intendunt. Proinde latrones ipsi, ut vehementius et tutius infesti sint paci ceterorum, pacem volunt habere sociorum. Sed etsi unus sit tam praepollens viribus et conscios ita cavens, ut nulli socio se committat solusque insidians et praevalens quibus potuerit oppressis et extinctis praedas agat, cum eis certe, quos occidere non potest et quos vult latere quod facit, qualemcumque umbram pacis tenet. In domo autem sua cum uxore et cum filiis, et si quos alios illic habet, studet profecto esse pacatus; eis quippe ad nutum obtemperantibus sine dubio delectatur. Nam si non fiat, indignatur corripit vindicat et domus suae pacem, si ita necesse sit, etiam saeviendo componit, quam sentit esse non posse, nisi cuidam principio, quod ipse in domo sua est, cetera in eadem domestica societate subiecta sint. Ideoque si offerretur ei servitus plurium, vel civitatis vel gentis, ita ut sic ei servirent, quem ad modum sibi domi suae serviri volebat: non se iam latronem latebris conderet, sed regem conspicuum sublimaret, cum eadem in illo cupiditas et malitia permaneret. Pacem itaque cum suis omnes habere cupiunt, quos ad arbitrium suum volunt vivere. Nam et cum quibus bellum gerunt, suos facere, si possint, volunt eisque subiectis leges suae pacis inponere.

Sed faciamus aliquem, qualem canit poetica et fabulosa narratio, quem fortasse propter ipsam insociabilem feritatem semihominem quam hominem dicere maluerunt. Quamvis ergo huius regnum dirae speluncae fuerit solitudo tamque malitia singularis, ut ex hac ei nomen inventum sit (Graece namque malus κακòς dicitur, quod ille vocabatur), nulla coniux ei blandum ferret referretque sermonem, nullis filiis vel adluderet parvulis vel grandiusculis imperaret, nullo amici conloquio frueretur, nec Vulcani patris, quo vel hinc tantum non parum felicior fuit, quia tale monstrum

did have one advantage, namely, that he was more fortunate in not having produced such a monster as a son of his own. He gave nothing away to anyone, but carried off when he could everything and everyone whom he wished. Now even in that lonely cave of his, where, so the story goes, the ground was always warm with blood from some fresh slaughter, this monster desired nothing but peace, peace in which none would disturb him, in which no violence and no terror from outside would interrupt his rest.[1] In short, he was anxious to be at peace with his body, and all was well with him in proportion as he gained that. And so, since his limbs obeyed his orders implicitly, his aim was with all speed to impose peace upon his mortal frame whenever, through need of anything, it rebelled against itself or whenever it stirred up sedition within itself because threatened by the hunger, which, if unsatisfied, would part body from soul and keep them parted. Therefore he plundered and slew and devoured; yet, in spite of his cruelty and savagery, he was only striving in his own cruel and savage way after the peace and security of his own life. If he could have brought himself to possess in company with others the peace which he was concerned to establish in his own cave and in his own body, there would have been no need to call him evil or monster or half-man. Even if his physical appearance or the murky flames which he breathed out of his mouth terrified men from coming into fellowship with him, his savagery may not have been inspired by any desire to do harm but merely by the need to live. However, it is possible that such a creature never existed, or—which is easier to believe—at any rate was not quite as bad as the idle fancies of poets picture him: after all he had to be over-drawn or else the virtues of Hercules, his counterpart, would have lost in contrast. A creature of such a character—whether man or half-man—it is more reasonable to believe never existed, and the same is true of many poetical inventions. This view is supported by the evidence of the wildest of wild animals—and from them Cacus derived part of his wildness, for he is called half-beast[2] as well as half-man. It is by a kind of peace that they preserve their species; they mate, produce young, tend and feed their young, though many of them are solitary and keep to themselves—not sheep, deer, doves, starlings or bees, but lions, wolves, foxes, eagles, owls. The tiger becomes gentle and purrs over its cubs and licks them, its wildness now at peace. The kite flies solitarily over its prey, but it mates, builds a nest, sits on its eggs, feeds its young, and with all the peace it can, it preserves with the hen—a real materfamilias—a fellowship of the home.

How much more powerfully is man drawn by the laws of his nature to enter into fellowship and, so far as in him lies, to maintain peace with all men. Even evil men make war in defence of the peace of their own world

---

[1] Cf. Verg. *Aen.* viii. 195 sq.   [2] Cf. *Aen.* viii. 267.

ipse non genuit; nihil cuiquam daret, sed a quo posset quidquid vellet et quando posset quem vellet auferret: tamen in ipsa sua spelunca solitaria, cuius, ut describitur, semper recenti caede tepebat humus, nihil aliud quam pacem volebat, in qua nemo illi molestus esset, nec eius quietem vis ullius terrorve turbaret. Cum corpore denique suo pacem habere cupiebat, et quantum habebat, tantum bene illi erat. Quando quidem membris obtemperantibus imperabat, et ut suam mortalitatem adversum se ex indigentia rebellantem ac seditionem famis ad dissociandam atque excludendam de corpore animam concitantem quanta posset festinatione pacaret, rapiebat necabat vorabat et quamvis inmanis ac ferus paci tamen suae vitae ac salutis inmaniter ac ferociter consulebat; ac per hoc si pacem, quam in sua spelunca atque in se ipso habere satis agebat, etiam cum aliis habere vellet, nec malus nec monstrum nec semihomo vocaretur. Aut si eius corporis forma et atrorum ignium vomitus ab eo deterrebat hominum societatem, forte non nocendi cupiditate, sed vivendi necessitate saeviebat. Verum iste non fuerit vel, quod magis credendum est, non talis fuerit, qualis poetica vanitate describitur; nisi enim nimis accusaretur Cacus, parum Hercules laudaretur. Talis ergo homo sive semihomo melius, ut dixi, creditur non fuisse, sicut multa figmenta poetarum. Ipsae enim saevissimae ferae, unde ille partem habuit feritatis (nam et semiferus dictus est), genus proprium quadam pace custodiunt, coeundo gignendo pariendo, fetus fovendo atque nutriendo, cum sint pleraeque insociabiles et solivagae; non scilicet ut oves cervi columbae sturni apes, sed ut leones ⟨lupi⟩ vulpes aquilae noctuae. Quae enim tigris non filiis suis mitis inmurmurat et pacata feritate blanditur? Quis milvus, quantumlibet solitarius rapinis circumvolet, non coniugium copulat, nidum congerit, ova confovet, pullos alit et quasi cum sua matre familias societatem domesticam quanta potest pace conservat? Quanto magis homo fertur quodam modo naturae suae legibus ad ineundam societatem pacemque cum

and try to reduce all men and all things to abject obedience to one man; and that can come about only if they agree to promote his peace whether through love or fear. This illustrates how pride distortedly imitates God. For it hates equality of fellow beings under Him, but tries to impose upon them its own domination instead of His; thus it hates the just peace of God and loves an inequitable peace of its own. It cannot do without loving peace of some kind. Indeed no corruption of good is so contrary to nature as to destroy even the last traces of nature.

Compared with the peace of the righteous the peace of the wicked is not worthy to be called peace, as you will see if you know how to prefer the straight to the crooked, and arrangement to wilful disarrangement. Even what is wilfully disarranged is bound to have some kind of peace imposed upon it: the elements of its nature or the elements of which it is composed have some kind of peace within or proceeding from or in association with some part of nature: otherwise it would simply be nothing at all. For example, suspend someone head downwards; the position of the body and the order of his limbs are disarranged, since what nature demands should be uppermost is now below, and vice versa: that disarrangement has disturbed the peace of the body and causes it discomfort. All the same the soul still remains at peace with its body [that is, it has not thereby become hostile to the body], and fusses over its welfare: that is why the man feels pain. If discomfort drives the soul to take its departure from the body, what is left behind still possesses a kind of peace in its parts as long as the limbs continue to be knit together; and that is why the man remains suspended. The body, composed of earth, tends towards the earth, straining on the rope which suspends it, and so it strives towards its own ordered peace: its weight cries out, as it were, for a resting place; and, though the body is lifeless and without feeling, it cannot withdraw from its own natural ordered peace, either when it possesses that peace or when it travels towards it. Suppose that chemicals are applied and the body is embalmed to prevent its wasting or dissolution; still a kind of peace joins part to part and adjusts the mass of the body to the place in which it rests, a place which is then adapted to it and so offers it peace. Suppose now that the body is not embalmed, but is left to its natural course; it then undergoes a process of violent change as it splits up into gases unpleasant to the senses (for that is what meets our senses when flesh rots), until finally it is ready to find its appropriate place among the elements and it departs gradually, particle by particle, into their peace. Nothing in fact can be exempted from the laws of the great Creator who orders all things and administers the peace of the universe: and even if from the corpse of some larger living creature minute animals are born, by the same law of the Creator each of these little bodies serves

hominibus, quantum in ipso est, omnibus obtinendam, cum etiam mali pro suorum pace belligerent omnesque, si possint, suos facere velint, ut uni cuncti et cuncta deserviant; quo pacto, nisi in eius pacem vel amando vel timendo consentiant? Sic enim superbia perverse imitatur Deum. Odit namque cum sociis aequalitatem sub illo, sed inponere vult sociis dominationem suam pro illo. Odit ergo iustam pacem Dei et amat iniquam pacem suam. Non amare tamen qualemcumque pacem nullo modo potest. Nullius quippe vitium ita contra naturam est, ut naturae deleat etiam extrema vestigia.

Itaque pacem iniquorum in pacis comparatione iustorum ille videt nec pacem esse dicendam, qui novit praeponere recta pravis et ordinata perversis. Quod autem perversum est, etiam hoc necesse est ut in aliqua et ex aliqua et cum aliqua rerum parte pacatum sit, in quibus est vel ex quibus constat; alioquin nihil esset omnino. Velut si quisquam capite deorsum pendeat, perversus est utique situs corporis et ordo membrorum, quia id, quod desuper esse natura postulat, subter est, et quod illa subter vult esse, desuper factum est; conturbavit carnis pacem ista perversitas et ideo molesta est: verum tamen anima corpori suo pacata est et pro eius salute satagit, et ideo est qui doleat; quae si molestiis eius exclusa discesserit, quamdiu compago membrorum manet, non est sine quadam partium pace quod remanet, et ideo est adhuc qui pendeat. Et quod terrenum corpus in terram nititur et vinculo quo suspensum est renititur, in suae pacis ordinem tendit et locum quo requiescat quodam modo voce ponderis poscit, iamque exanime ac sine ullo sensu a pace tamen naturali sui ordinis non recedit, vel cum tenet eam, vel cum fertur ad eam. Si enim adhibeantur medicamenta atque curatio, quae formam cadaveris dissolvi dilabique non sinat, adhuc pax quaedam partes partibus iungit totamque molem adplicat terreno et convenienti ac per hoc pacato loco. Si autem nulla adhibeatur cura condendi, sed naturali cursui relinquatur, tamdiu quasi tumultuatur dissidentibus exhalationibus et nostro inconvenientibus sensui (id enim est quod in putore sentitur), donec mundi conveniat elementis et in eorum pacem paulatim particulatimque discedat. Nullo modo tamen inde aliquid legibus summi illius creatoris ordinatorisque subtrahitur, a quo pax universitatis administratur; quia, etsi de cadavere maioris animantis animalia minuta nascantur, eadem lege creatoris quae-

its small soul in the peace which is its health. Even if the flesh of dead men be devoured by animals, the same laws will be found to operate throughout creation and to make for the health of each species of mortal things, imposing peace through the adjustment of like to like, no matter in what direction movement may take place nor what combinations may occur, nor what changes and transformations.

Chapter 13

And so the peace of the body is ordered adjustment of its parts; the peace of the irrational part of the soul is ordered rest from the appetites; the peace of the rational part of the soul is ordered unity of thought and action.

The peace of the body and soul together is ordered life and health in the living creature; the peace of mortal man and God is ordered obedience in faith under eternal law; the peace of men is ordered agreement.

The peace of the household is ordered agreement of those who dwell together, whether they command or whether they obey; the peace of the city is ordered agreement of its citizens, whether they command or whether they obey; the peace of the heavenly city is the fellowship of enjoying God and enjoying one another in God, a fellowship held closely together by order and in harmony; the peace of all created things is the tranquillity bestowed by order; order is the arrangement of equal and unequal which assigns to each its proper place.

The miserable, therefore, in so far as they are miserable, are assuredly not at peace, for they are without the tranquillity bestowed by order, which admits of no unrest. All the same they cannot be outside and beyond order, for their misery is deserved and is their due; they cannot, it is true, be associated with the happy, but their very disassociation is brought about by the law of order. In so far as they are free from unrest, they adapt themselves with some degree of suitable adjustment to the state in which they find themselves, and for this reason they have some degree of tranquillity which proceeds from order; and therefore they have some degree of peace. But the real cause of their misery is this: even if they enjoy a measure of freedom from care and feel no actual pain, they are not in such state that they are necessarily secure and free from pain; and their misery is increased if they have not the peace which accompanies obedience to the law of order by which creation is governed. When they do feel pain, their peace is broken in whatever quarter they feel pain, though they can still have peace wherever the fires of pain do not burn and their bodily framework is not in process of being destroyed. Just as

que corpuscula in salutis pace suis animulis serviunt; etsi mortuorum carnes ab aliis animalibus devorentur, easdem leges per cuncta diffusas ad salutem generis cuiusque mortalium congrua congruis pacificantes, quaqua versum trahantur et rebus quibuscumque iungantur et in res quaslibet convertantur et commutentur, inveniunt.

Caput 13

Pax itaque corporis est ordinata temperatura partium, pax animae in-rationalis ordinata requies appetitionum, pax animae rationalis ordinata cognitionis actionisque consensio, pax corporis et animae ordinata vita et salus animantis, pax hominis mortalis et Dei ordinata in fide sub aeterna lege oboedientia, pax hominum ordinata concordia, pax domus ordinata imperandi atque oboediendi concordia cohabitantium, pax civitatis ordi-nata imperandi atque oboediendi concordia civium, pax caelestis civitatis ordinatissima et concordissima societas fruendi Deo et invicem in Deo, pax omnium rerum tranquillitas ordinis. Ordo est parium dispariumque rerum sua cuique loca tribuens dispositio. Proinde miseri, quia, in quan-tum miseri sunt, utique in pace non sunt, tranquillitate quidem ordinis carent, ubi perturbatio nulla est; verum tamen quia merito iusteque sunt miseri, in ea quoque ipsa miseria sua praeter ordinem esse non possunt; non quidem coniuncti beatis, sed ab eis tamen ordinis lege seiuncti. Qui cum sine perturbatione sunt, rebus, in quibus sunt, quantacumque con-gruentia coaptantur; ac per hoc inest eis ordinis nonnulla tranquillitas, inest ergo nonnulla pax. Verum ideo miseri sunt, quia, etsi in aliqua securitate non dolent, non tamen ibi sunt, ubi securi esse ac dolere non debeant; miseriores autem, si pax eis cum ipsa lege non est, qua naturalis ordo administratur. Cum autem dolent, ex qua parte dolent, pacis pertur-batio facta est; in illa vero adhuc pax est, in qua nec dolor urit nec compago ipsa dissolvitur. Sicut ergo est quaedam vita sine dolore, dolor autem sine

there can be life of a kind without pain, but no pain without life of some kind, so in the same way there can be a kind of peace without war, but there cannot be war without some kind of peace. The truth of this follows not from the character of war as such, but from the necessity of war being waged by or in beings who are to some degree or other created natures; and they could not be created natures without having peace of some kind as an essential part of themselves.

It follows then that there can be a created nature in which there is no evil and even in which there can be no evil; there can be no created natures of such kind as to be devoid of good; not even the nature of the devil himself, in so far as it is a created nature, is evil. It is self-will that makes it evil. He has not stood in the truth,[1] though he has not thereby avoided the judgment of the truth; he has not remained in the tranquillity of order but he has not therefore escaped from the power of Him who orders all things. That element of God's goodness which is in the devil as a created nature does not withdraw him from the justice of God by which order is maintained through punishment; in punishment God does not assail the good which He has created, but the evil of which the devil himself is guilty. God does not take away all that He gave to a created nature; He takes away some and some He leaves, that there may still be someone left to feel pain at the loss of what He has taken away. Pain is itself evidence of good taken away and of good left; for, unless some good were left, a man would not be able to feel pain at the loss of the good that had been lost. For the sinner is more a sinner if he rejoices in the loss of his state of virtue; he who suffers the anguish of the rack feels pain at the loss of his physical well-being (unless indeed he were to gain profit from his punishment). Now a virtuous state and physical well-being are both goods and the loss of a good ought to cause pain rather than joy—unless of course the loss of a good, for example, physical well-being, is offset by the enjoyment of a greater good, for example, a state of virtue; therefore it is more appropriate that the wicked should feel pain at his punishment than that he should derive pleasure from his sin. For, just as to feel joy at surrendering a good through sin is evidence of an evil will, so pain through the loss of a good in punishment is evidence of a good nature. For the man who feels pain at the loss of the peace which is inherent in his own nature feels that pain because there are some remnants of peace left in him which put his own nature on good terms with itself. It is a legitimate consequence that in the last punishment the wicked should bewail in their sufferings the loss of the goods which are inherent in their own nature, feeling that they are taken from them by a most just God—a God whom they despised when He was a most generous giver.

[1] John viii. 44.

aliqua vita esse non potest: sic est quaedam pax sine ullo bello, bellum vero esse sine aliqua pace non potest; non secundum id, quod bellum est, sed secundum id, quod ab eis vel in eis geritur, quae aliquae naturae sunt; quod nullo modo essent, si non qualicumque pace subsisterent.

Quapropter est natura, in qua nullum malum est vel etiam in qua nullum esse malum potest; esse autem natura, in qua nullum bonum sit, non potest. Proinde nec ipsius diaboli natura, in quantum natura est, malum est; sed perversitas eam malam facit. Itaque in veritate non stetit, sed veritatis iudicium non evasit; in ordinis tranquillitate non mansit, nec ideo tamen a potestate ordinatoris effugit. Bonum Dei, quod illi est in natura, non eum subtrahit iustitiae Dei, qua ordinatur in poena; nec ibi Deus bonum insequitur quod creavit, sed malum quod ille commisit. Neque enim totum aufert quod naturae dedit, sed aliquid adimit, aliquid relinquit, ut sit qui doleat quod ademit. Et ipse dolor testimonium est boni adempti et boni relicti. Nisi enim bonum relictum esset, bonum amissum dolere non posset. Nam qui peccat, peior est, si laetatur in damno aequitatis; qui vero cruciatur, si nihil inde adquirat boni, dolet damnum salutis. Et quoniam aequitas ac salus utrumque bonum est bonique amissione dolendum est potius quam laetandum (si tamen non sit compensatio melioris; melior est autem animi aequitas quam corporis sanitas): profecto convenientius iniustus dolet in supplicio, quam laetatus est in delicto. Sicut ergo laetitia deserti boni in peccato testis est voluntatis malae, ita dolor amissi boni in supplicio testis est naturae bonae. Qui enim dolet amissam naturae suae pacem, ex aliquibus reliquiis pacis id dolet, quibus fit, ut sibi amica natura sit. Hoc autem in extremo supplicio recte fit, ut iniqui et impii naturalium bonorum damna in cruciatibus defleant, sentientes eorum ablatorem iustissimum Deum, quem contempserunt benignissimum largitorem. Deus ergo naturarum omnium sapientissimus conditor et iustissimus ordinator, qui terrenorum ornamentorum maximum instituit mortale genus humanum, dedit hominibus quaedam bona huic vitae congrua, id est pacem temporalem pro modulo mortalis vitae in ipsa salute et incolumitate ac societate sui generis, et quaeque huic paci vel tuendae vel recuperandae necessaria sunt (sicut ea, quae apte ac convenienter adiacent sensibus, lux vox, aurae spirabiles aquae potabiles, et quidquid ad alendum tegendum curandum ornandumque corpus congruit), eo pacto aequissimo, ut, qui mortalis talibus bonis paci mortalium adcommodatis recte usus fuerit, accipiat ampliora atque meliora, ipsam scilicet inmortalitatis pacem eique convenientem gloriam et honorem in vita aeterna ad fruendum Deo et proximo in Deo; qui autem perperam, nec illa accipiat et haec amittat.

So, then, God is the all-wise creator of all natures, ordering all according to His justice, who established the race of mortal men as the greatest of the glories of this earth. To men He gave certain goods appropriate to life here, namely, temporal peace sufficient for the span of human life, to be enjoyed in physical well-being and in security and in fellowship with human kind. He gave too all that is necessary for the preservation or the recovery of peace, as, for example, all those things which are most suitably adapted to the senses, light, sound, air to breathe, water to drink, and all that conduces to the nourishment, protection, care and adornment of the body. But God gave all these gifts on the one most just condition, that whoever as mortal man rightly uses these goods which are designed specially for the peace of mortals shall receive other more generous and nobler goods—namely the peace of immortality, and the glory and honour which accompany it, in everlasting life, that he may enjoy God and his neighbour in God; but that whosoever uses these goods badly shall never receive the later gifts and shall lose those which originally he was given.

Chapter 14

Every use which we make of temporal things is referred to the enjoyment of earthly peace in the earthly city; in the heavenly city the standard of reference is the enjoyment of eternal peace.

Now, if we were alive as irrational creatures, we should crave nothing except the ordered adjustment of the parts of the body and rest from the appetites; and therefore we should want nothing but rest for the flesh and an abundance of pleasures so that the peace of the body might contribute to the peace of the soul; for, in the absence of the peace of the body, the peace of the irrational soul is thwarted, since it cannot achieve rest from the appetites. On the other hand peace of the body and peace of the soul, when they exist together, contribute to that peace which the soul and the body have in relation to one another, that is, the peace of an ordered life and of well-being in the living creature. Just as living creatures show that they love the peace of the body when they seek to escape pain, and that they love the peace of the soul when they follow pleasure for the satisfaction of the needs of the appetites, so in avoiding death they give sufficient evidence of their love of that peace which unites soul and body. But man is possessed of a rational soul, and therefore he subordinates to the peace of the rational soul all that he has in common with the beasts, to the end that he may set his mind upon some object and in pursuance of that object embark upon a particular course of action; the result is that he gains an ordered unity of thought and action, which we defined earlier as the peace

Caput 14

Omnis igitur usus rerum temporalium refertur ad fructum pacis terrenae in terrena civitate; in caelesti autem civitate refertur ad fructum pacis aeternae. Quapropter si inrationalia essemus animantia, nihil appeteremus praeter ordinatam temperaturam partium corporis et requiem appetitionum; nihil ergo praeter quietem carnis et copiam voluptatum, ut pax corporis prodesset paci animae. Si enim desit pax corporis, impeditur etiam inrationalis animae pax, quia requiem appetitionum consequi non potest. Utrumque autem simul ei paci prodest, quam inter se habent anima et corpus, id est ordinatae vitae ac salutis. Sicut enim pacem corporis amare se ostendunt animantia, cum fugiunt dolorem, et pacem animae, cum propter explendas indigentias appetitionum voluptatem sequuntur: ita mortem fugiendo satis indicant, quantum diligant pacem, qua sibi conciliantur anima et corpus. Sed quia homini rationalis anima inest, totum hoc, quod habet commune cum bestiis, subdit paci animae rationalis, ut mente aliquid contempletur et secundum hoc aliquid agat, ut sit ei ordinata cognitionis actionisque consensio, quam pacem rationalis animae dixeramus. Ad hoc enim velle debet nec dolore molestari nec

of the rational soul. To gain this he must wish neither to be plagued by pain nor to be thrown into confusion by regret nor to be extinguished by death, so that his knowledge may be knowledge of something of value and his life and character may be fashioned in accordance with that knowledge.

But such is the frailty of the human mind, that his very thirst for knowledge may lead him into some pestilential error. He needs therefore divine direction which he can obey with a feeling of being guided; and he needs divine help which he may obey without feeling he has lost his liberty. As long as he is in a mortal body, he is in a strange country away from his Lord; therefore he walks by faith and not by sight.[1] That is why he refers all peace, whether of the body or the spirit or of the body and the spirit jointly, to that peace which man has in partnership with the immortal God, that there may be to him ordered obedience in faith under eternal law.

Now God our Teacher lays down for man two main precepts, 'love God and love your neighbour', in which he finds three things to love, namely, God, himself, and his neighbour, and he who loves God does not go wrong in loving himself. It follows from this that it is for the love of God that a man takes thought also for his neighbour whom he is bidden to love as himself—his wife, his son, his household, and all men for whom he can take thought—and he wishes thought to be taken for himself by his neighbour, if he should happen to need it. The result will be that he will find himself rendered at peace, as far as it depends upon himself, with every man in the peace of men, which is ordered agreement; and in this phrase 'order' means, first, harming no one and, secondly, actually helping whomsoever one can. Naturally such a man's first instinct is to care for his own people; he finds more occasions and readier means of doing so, whether because of the order imposed by natural ties or that imposed by the broader fellowship of men. Hence the Apostle says, 'But if any provideth not for his own and specially his own household, he hath denied the faith and is worse than an unbeliever'.[2] From this source is derived the peace of the household, that is the ordered agreement of those who dwell together, whether they command or whether they obey. For command over others is then accompanied by thought for them, as a husband takes thought for and so commands his wife or parents their sons or masters their slaves. Those for whom thought is taken obey, as women obey their husbands, sons their parents, slaves their masters. But in the house of the just man who lives by faith and still dwells in a strange land far from the heavenly city—in his house even those who command are the slaves of those whom they apparently command. For they exercise com-

[1] 2 Cor. v. 7.   [2] Tim. v. 8.

desiderio perturbari nec morte dissolvi, ut aliquid utile cognoscat et secundum eam cognitionem vitam moresque componat. Sed ne ipso studio cognitionis propter humanae mentis infirmitatem in pestem alicuius erroris incurrat, opus habet magisterio divino, cui certus obtemperet, et adiutorio, ut liber obtemperet. Et quoniam, quamdiu est in isto mortali corpore, peregrinatur a Domino: ambulat per fidem, non per speciem; ac per hoc omnem pacem vel corporis vel animae vel simul corporis et animae refert ad illam pacem, quae homini mortali est cum inmortali Deo, ut ei sit ordinata in fide sub aeterna lege oboedientia. Iam vero quia duo praecipua praecepta, hoc est dilectionem Dei et dilectionem proximi, docet magister Deus, in quibus tria invenit homo quae diligat, Deum, se ipsum et proximum, atque ille in se diligendo non errat, qui Deum diligit: consequens est, ut etiam proximo ad diligendum Deum consulat, quem iubetur sicut se ipsum diligere (sic uxori, sic filiis, sic domesticis, sic ceteris quibus potuerit hominibus), et ad hoc sibi a proximo, si forte indiget, consuli velit; ac per hoc erit pacatus, quantum in ipso est, omni homini pace hominum, id est ordinata concordia, cuius hic ordo est, primum ut nulli noceat, deinde ut etiam prosit cui potuerit. Primitus ergo inest ei suorum cura; ad eos quippe habet opportuniorem facilioremque aditum consulendi, vel naturae ordine vel ipsius societatis humanae. Unde apostolus dicit: *Quisquis autem suis et maxime domesticis non providet, fidem denegat et est infideli deterior.* Hinc itaque etiam pax domestica oritur, id est ordinata imperandi oboediendique concordia cohabitantium. Imperant enim, qui consulunt; sicut vir uxori, parentes filiis, domini servis. Oboediunt autem quibus consulitur; sicut mulieres maritis, filii parentibus, servi dominis. Sed in domo iusti viventis ex fide et adhuc ab illa caelesti civitate peregrinantis etiam qui imperant serviunt eis, quibus videntur imperare.

mand not through any lust of domination but because theirs is the responsibility to take thought for others, not through any arrogant desire to lord it over others, but because theirs is the mercy which provides for others.

Chapter 15

This is the conception of 'command' which the order inherent in nature prescribes, and these are the conditions under which God has created man. For He says, 'Let him have dominion over the fishes of the sea and the birds of the sky and all creeping things which creep upon the earth'.[1] It was not His will that man, a creature possessed of reason and created in His image, should have dominion, unless over irrational creatures; it was His will that man should have dominion over beasts and not over men. Hence the first righteous men [the patriarchs] were appointed to be shepherds of flocks rather than kings of men; so that even in this way God gave an indication of what is demanded by the order which governs created beings and what is exacted by the deserts of sinners. For the condition of slavery is rightly understood to be a condition imposed upon the sinner. That explains why we never read of a slave in any passage of Scripture until Noah, a just man, used the term in condemning the sin of his son,[2] who earned the title of slave by his own misdeed and not by nature. The derivation of the word for 'servile' in Latin is held to be as follows; prisoners who by the rights of war could have been put to death were reduced to a 'servile' state because they were 'preserved' alive by their conquerors, *servus* thus being derived from *servare*. This process of turning a 'preserved' captive into a slave takes place only as a penalty incurred by sin. For, even when a just war is being fought, the opposite side is battling in defence of sin, and even when victory goes in favour of the wicked it is a divine judgment humiliating the defeated by correcting or punishing their sins. To this, Daniel, a man of God, bears witness; when he was in captivity, he confessed to God his sins and those of his people,[3] and his righteous grief testified that sin was the reason of the captivity which he endured.

So the primal cause of slavery is sin and its result is that one man is subordinated to another, fettered by his servile status; this always occurs through the judgment of God, with whom there is no injustice and who knows how to apportion differing punishments appropriate to the deserts of those who do wrong. But 'every man who commits sin is the slave of sin',[4] says the most high Lord, and that is why many religious men, who

[1] Gen. i. 26.   [2] Gen. ix. 25.   [3] Dan. ix. 5.   [4] John viii. 34.

Neque enim dominandi cupiditate imperant, sed officio consulendi, nec principandi superbia, sed providendi misericordia.

CAPUT 15

Hoc naturalis ordo praescribit, ita Deus hominem condidit. Nam: *Dominetur*, inquit, *piscium maris et volatilium caeli et omnium repentium, quae repunt super terram.* Rationalem factum ad imaginem suam noluit nisi inrationabilibus dominari; non hominem homini, sed hominem pecori. Inde primi iusti pastores pecorum magis quam reges hominum constituti sunt, ut etiam sic insinuaret Deus, quid postulet ordo creaturarum, quid exigat meritum peccatorum. Condicio quippe servitutis iure intellegitur inposita peccatori. Proinde nusquam scripturarum legimus servum, antequam hoc vocabulo Noe iustus peccatum filii vindicaret. Nomen itaque istud culpa meruit, non natura. Origo autem vocabuli servorum in Latina lingua inde creditur ducta, quod hi, qui iure belli possent occidi, a victoribus cum servabantur servi fiebant, a servando appellati; quod etiam ipsum sine peccati merito non est. Nam et cum iustum geritur bellum, pro peccato e contrario dimicatur; et omnis victoria, cum etiam malis provenit, divino iudicio victos humiliat vel emendans peccata vel puniens. Testis est homo Dei Daniel, cum in captivitate positus peccata sua et peccata populi sui confitetur Deo et hanc esse causam illius captivitatis pio dolore testatur. Prima ergo servitutis causa peccatum est, ut homo homini condicionis vinculo subderetur; quod non fit nisi Deo iudicante, apud quem non est iniquitas et novit diversas poenas meritis distribuere delinquentium. Sicut autem supernus Dominus dicit: *Omnis, qui facit peccatum, servus est peccati,* ac per hoc multi quidem religiosi dominis iniquis, non tamen liberis

are the slaves of wicked masters, are the slaves of masters who are not free; for 'a man is made over as a slave to that which has conquered him'.[1] A man is much more fortunate in being a slave to another man than to a lustful passion, since—to quote only one example—a lust for power devastates the hearts of men by the savagery of the power which it exerts over them. In that ordered peace in which one set of men are made subordinate to another set, humility greatly profits those who are slaves, while arrogance greatly harms those who are masters. But no man is the slave either of another man or of sin because of the nature in which God originally created man. No! even slavery enforced as a punishment is ordered by that law which bids the order inherent in created things to be preserved and forbids its disarrangement; for, if there had been no misdeed transgressing that law, there would have been nothing which called for the constraint exerted by penal slavery. For these reasons the Apostle warns slaves to be subject to their masters and to be their slaves wholeheartedly and with good will[2]; he means that, if they cannot win their freedom from their masters, they should of themselves bring a certain freedom into their slavery by being slaves not in craftiness and fear but in faithfulness and love, until inequality passes away and all overlordship and all power of man over man is made empty of meaning, and God is all in all.[3]

Chapter 16

Even if our righteous forefathers did have slaves, at any rate they managed the peace of the household in such a way that, though as regards temporal goods they made a distinction between the lot of the sons of the household and the status of slaves, yet, when it was a question of the worship of God, which holds out hope of eternal goods, they took thought for every member of their household and showed each the same affection. This attitude is insisted upon by the order which is inherent in nature; from it the title of 'father of a family', that is, of a household, is sprung; and indeed it is so widely adopted now that even harsh masters like to be called by this name. But those who are truly fathers of their household take thought for each member of it just as if they were all sons, with a view to promoting the worship and service of God; for they ardently yearn to reach that heavenly home in which the obligation to rule mortal men will not be laid upon them, for the reason that there will no longer be obligation to take thought for those who have already attained felicity in the immortality of that heavenly home. Until they arrive there, fathers of households must

[1] 2 Pet. ii. 19.   [2] Eph. vi. 5.   [3] 1 Cor. xv. 28.

serviunt: *A quo enim quis devictus est, huic et servus addictus est.* Et utique felicius servitur homini, quam libidini, cum saevissimo dominatu vastet corda mortalium, ut alias omittam, libido ipsa dominandi. Hominibus autem illo pacis ordine, quo aliis alii subiecti sunt, sicut prodest humilitas servientibus, ita nocet superbia dominantibus. Nullus autem natura, in qua prius Deus hominem condidit, servus est hominis aut peccati. Verum et poenalis servitus ea lege ordinatur, quae naturalem ordinem conservari iubet, perturbari vetat; quia si contra eam legem non esset factum, nihil esset poenali servitute cohercendum. Ideoque apostolus etiam servos monet subditos esse dominis suis et ex animo eis cum bona voluntate servire; ut scilicet, si non possunt a dominis liberi fieri, suam servitutem ipsi quodam modo liberam faciant, non timore subdolo, sed fideli dilectione serviendo, donec transeat iniquitas et evacuetur omnis principatus et potestas humana et sit Deus omnia in omnibus.

Caput 16

Quocirca etiamsi habuerunt servos iusti patres nostri, sic administrabant domesticam pacem, ut secundum haec temporalia bona filiorum sortem a servorum condicione distinguerent; ad Deum autem colendum, in quo aeterna bona speranda sunt, omnibus domus suae membris pari dilectione consulerent. Quod naturalis ordo ita praescribit, ut nomen patrum familias hinc exortum sit et tam late vulgatum, ut etiam inique dominantes hoc se gaudeant appellari. Qui autem veri patres familias sunt, omnibus in familia sua tamquam filiis ad colendum et promerendum Deum consulunt, desiderantes atque optantes venire ad caelestem domum, ubi necessarium non sit officium imperandi mortalibus, quia necessarium non erit officium consulendi iam in illa inmortalitate felicibus; quo donec veniatur, magis debent patres quod dominantur, quam servi tolerare quod serviunt. Si

be patient under their need to be masters, even more patient than slaves must be of their slavery. But, if anyone in a house is disobedient and so thwarts the peace of the household, he is corrected to the degree which human fellowship allows, either by the lash of the tongue or of the whip, or by any other form of punishment which is just and lawful; and correction is intended to be for the profit of him who is corrected, to make him fit himself again into the peace from which he has sprung apart. Just as no one can claim to be a benefactor who by his active aid causes someone to lose a greater good, so no one can with a clear conscience spare a wrongdoer and so allow him to fall into still greater evil. To have a clear conscience in such a matter you must not only do no evil to others, but you must hold them back from sin or punish their sin, in order that the experience of punishment may bring about the reformation of the sinner, or else that the example made of him may deter others from like sin.

A man's home ought to be the beginning of the state or a small fragment of it; every beginning looks towards some end proper to its own genus, and every part looks towards that whole, regarded as a whole, of which it is a part. From this it clearly follows that the peace of the household looks towards the peace of the city; that is to say, the ordered agreement of those who dwell together in a household, whether they command or whether they obey, looks towards the ordered agreement of citizens, whether they command or whether they obey. The result is that the head of a household ought to take his principles from the law of the city in order that by those principles he may so rule his own household as to bring it into harmony with the peace of the city.

Chapter 17

The household of men who do not live by faith pursues an earthly peace derived from the material things and the blessings of this temporal life. The household of men who live by faith awaits those eternal things which are promised for the future, and uses all earthly and temporal things as a stranger in a strange land; it is careful that these things shall not captivate and lead astray that faculty by which man travels towards God, but rather shall sustain it and so enable it to bear more easily the burdens of the body which is doomed to corruption and weighs down the spirit,[1] and to do as little as possible to increase those burdens. Thus it comes about that both types of men and both types of household have something in common in the use which they make of the things necessary to this mortal life, but each type sets before itself its own specific end in the use which it makes

[1] Wisd. ix. 15.

quis autem in domo per inoboedientiam domesticae paci adversatur, corripitur seu verbo seu verbere seu quolibet alio genere poenae iusto atque licito, quantum societas humana concedit, pro eius qui corripitur utilitate, ut paci unde dissiluerat coaptetur. Sicut enim non est beneficentiae adiuvando efficere, ut bonum quod maius est amittatur: ita non est innocentiae parcendo sinere, ut in malum gravius incidatur. Pertinet ergo ad innocentis officium, non solum nemini malum inferre, verum etiam cohibere a peccato vel punire peccatum, ut aut ipse qui plectitur corrigatur experimento, aut alii terreantur exemplo. Quia igitur hominis domus initium sive particula debet esse civitatis, omne autem initium ad aliquem sui generis finem et omnis pars ad universi, cuius pars est, integritatem refertur, satis apparet esse consequens, ut ad pacem civicam pax domestica referatur, id est, ut ordinata imperandi oboediendique concordia cohabitantium referatur ad ordinatam imperandi oboediendique concordiam civium. Ita fit, ut ex lege civitatis praecepta sumere patrem familias oporteat, quibus domum suam sic regat, ut sit paci adcommoda civitatis.

Caput 17

Sed domus hominum, qui non vivunt ex fide, pacem terrenam ex huius temporalis vitae rebus commodisque sectatur; domus autem hominum ex fide viventium expectat ea, quae in futurum aeterna promissa sunt, terrenisque rebus ac temporalibus tamquam peregrina utitur, non quibus capiatur et avertatur quo tendit in Deum, sed quibus sustentetur ad facilius toleranda minimeque augenda onera corporis corruptibilis, quod adgravat animam. Idcirco rerum vitae huic mortali necessariarum utrisque hominibus et utrique domui communis est usus; sed finis utendi cuique

of those things; and the end of one is very different from the end of the other.

Similarly, the earthly city, which does not live by faith, seeks an earthly peace and pins down to a particular purpose the agreement of its citizens, whether they command or obey, the purpose being that the wills of men may achieve a measure of concordance as regards the things which pertain to this mortal life. But the heavenly city, or rather that part of it which sojourns in mortality here on earth and lives by faith, must necessarily make use of the earthly peace of which we have just spoken, until mortality itself, to which such peace is a necessity, shall pass away. Hence, the heavenly city lives, as it were, the life of a prisoner in a strange land in the midst of the earthly city. But it has already been promised its redemption and has received the gift of the Spirit as a pledge of its future, and so it does not hesitate to obey the laws of the earthly city which control all that conduces to the maintenance of this mortal life; for thus it will preserve the harmony of the two cities in things relating to that mortality which both share alike.

The earthly city possessed saints or sages of its own, but of a kind of which divine philosophy strongly disapproves. Led astray by their own fancies or deluded by evil spirits they believed that a multiplicity of gods had to be appeased by man-made ritual and that various spheres were subordinated to these gods and belonged to them according to their variously assigned functions; to one god belonged the body, to another the mind; similarly with parts of the body—the head, the neck; so, too, with parts of the mind—intellect, learning, anger, desire; concrete things which go to make up life also had their gods—herds, corn, wine, oil, woods, money, sailing, wars and victories, marriage, birth, fecundity, and so on. But the heavenly city knew that only one God should be worshipped and in loyalty it held that service should be rendered to Him in that service which the Greeks called λατρεία and which is due to Him alone. Hence this city could not share the laws of religion with the earthly city, and in defence of its own laws it was bound to part company, and so to antagonise those who held different views. It had to endure anger and hatred and the full onset of their persecution—save when at moments it dismayed the hearts of its adversaries by the terror of its numbers, and always by divine help.

While, then, the heavenly city sojourns upon earth, it summons its citizens from all nations and in spite of differing languages it gathers together a fellowship of sojourners. It takes no account of differences of customs, laws and institutions which are necessary for securing or maintaining earthly peace. It repeals or cancels none of them; rather it preserves and adopts what is permissible to it amid the diversity of the various nations; but it keeps its eye fixed upon the one and the same end of earthly

suus proprius multumque diversus. Ita etiam terrena civitas, quae non vivit ex fide, terrenam pacem appetit in eoque defigit imperandi oboediendique concordiam civium, ut sit eis de rebus ad mortalem vitam pertinentibus humanarum quaedam compositio voluntatum. Civitas autem caelestis vel potius pars eius, quae in hac mortalitate peregrinatur et vivit ex fide, etiam ista pace necesse est utatur, donec ipsa, cui talis pax necessaria est, mortalitas transeat; ac per hoc, dum apud terrenam civitatem velut captivam vitam suae peregrinationis agit, iam promissione redemptionis et dono spiritali tamquam pignore accepto legibus terrenae civitatis, quibus haec administrantur, quae sustentandae mortali vitae adcommodata sunt, obtemperare non dubitat, ut, quoniam communis est ipsa mortalitas, servetur in rebus ad eam pertinentibus inter civitatem utramque concordia. Verum quia terrena civitas habuit quosdam suos sapientes, quos divina improbat disciplina, qui vel suspicati vel decepti a daemonibus crederent multos deos conciliandos esse rebus humanis atque ad eorum diversa quodam modo officia diversa subdita pertinere, ad alium corpus, ad alium animum, inque ipso corpore ad alium caput, ad alium cervicem et cetera singula ad singulos; similiter in animo ad alium ingenium, ad alium doctrinam, ad alium iram, ad alium concupiscentiam; inque ipsis rebus vitae adiacentibus ad alium pecus, ad alium triticum, ad alium vinum, ad alium oleum, ad alium silvas, ad alium nummos, ad alium navigationem, ad alium bella atque victorias, ad alium coniugia, ad alium partum ac fecunditatem et ad alios alia cetera; caelestis autem civitas ⟨cum⟩ unum Deum solum colendum nosset eique tantum modo serviendum servitute illa, quae Graece λατρεία dicitur et non nisi Deo debetur, fideli pietate censeret: factum est, ut religionis leges cum terrena civitate non posset habere communes proque his ab ea dissentire haberet necesse atque oneri esse diversa sentientibus eorumque iras et odia et persecutionum impetus sustinere, nisi cum animos adversantium aliquando terrore suae multitudinis et semper divino adiutorio propulsaret. Haec ergo caelestis civitas dum peregrinatur in terra, ex omnibus gentibus cives evocat atque in omnibus linguis peregrinam colligit societatem, non curans quidquid in moribus legibus institutisque diversum est, quibus pax terrena vel conquiritur vel tenetur, nihil eorum rescindens vel destruens, immo etiam servans ac sequens, quod licet diversum in diversis nationibus, ad unum tamen eundemque finem terrenae pacis intenditur, si religionem,

peace as does the earthly city, provided always that the religion which teaches the duty of worshipping the one all-highest and true God is not thereby hampered.

Hence, in its sojourn here, the heavenly city makes use of the peace provided by the earthly city; in all that relates to the mortal nature of man it preserves and indeed seeks the concordance of human wills, in so far as it can do this without prejudice to its piety and religion. It refers that earthly peace to the heavenly peace, which is truly such peace that it alone can be regarded and described as peace—at any rate the peace of a rational creature; for it is the highest degree of ordered and harmonious fellowship in the enjoyment of God and of one another in God. When this stage is reached, then there will be life,—not life subject to death, but life that is clearly and assuredly life-giving. There will be a body,—not a body which is animal, weighing down the soul as it decays, but a spiritual body experiencing no need and subordinated in every part to the will. This is the peace which the heavenly city has while it sojourns here in faith, and in this faith it lives a life of righteousness. To the establishing of that peace it refers all its good actions, whether they be towards God or towards one's neighbour; for the life of this city is utterly and entirely a life of fellowship.

Chapter 18

Let us pass now to that 'differentia' which Varro adopted from the New Academics who believe that all knowledge is uncertain—the city of God utterly detests all doubt on this matter, taking such doubt to be madness. As regards knowledge which the mind comprehends by reason, the city of God holds that the body, which is corruptible and therefore burdens the soul, allows us only fragmentary knowledge (the Apostle, too, says that we know in part)[1]; but, small as it is, that knowledge is most certain knowledge. The city of God trusts the senses as giving evidence about all concrete things; the mind uses the senses through the mechanism of the body, and not to think their evidence ever credible is a more piteous delusion than to think it credible. The city also trusts the Holy Scriptures, both the Old and New Testament, which we call canonical; from them is derived the faith by which the righteous man lives. By that faith we walk without any doubt as long as we sojourn here away from the Lord. Provided we keep that faith sure and certain, we may feel doubt on things which we neither apprehend by the senses nor comprehend by reason and on things which have not been made manifest to us by the canon of Scrip-

[1] 1 Cor. xiii. 9.

qua unus summus et verus Deus colendus docetur, non impedit. Utitur ergo etiam caelestis civitas in hac sua peregrinatione pace terrena et de rebus ad mortalem hominum naturam pertinentibus humanarum voluntatum compositionem, quantum salva pietate ac religione conceditur, tuetur atque appetit eamque terrenam pacem refert ad caelestem pacem, quae vere ita pax est, ut rationalis dumtaxat creaturae sola pax habenda atque dicenda sit, ordinatissima scilicet et concordissima societas fruendi Deo et invicem in Deo; quo cum ventum erit, non erit vita mortalis, sed plane certeque vitalis, nec corpus animale, quod, dum corrumpitur, adgravat animam, sed spiritale sine ulla indigentia ex omni parte subditum voluntati. Hanc pacem, dum peregrinatur in fide, habet atque ex hac fide iuste vivit, cum ad illam pacem adipiscendam refert quidquid bonarum actionum gerit erga Deum et proximum, quoniam vita civitatis utique socialis est.

CAPUT 18

Quod autem adtinet ad illam differentiam, quam de Academicis novis Varro adhibuit, quibus incerta sunt omnia, omnino civitas Dei talem dubitationem tamquam dementiam detestatur, habens de rebus, quas mente atque ratione comprehendit, etiamsi parvam propter corpus corruptibile, quod adgravat animam (quoniam, sicut dicit apostolus, *ex parte scimus*), tamen certissimam scientiam, creditque sensibus in rei cuiusque evidentia, quibus per corpus animus utitur, quoniam miserabilius fallitur, qui numquam putat eis esse credendum; credit etiam scripturis sanctis et veteribus et novis, quas canonicas appellamus, unde fides ipsa concepta est, ex qua iustus vivit; per quam sine dubitatione ambulamus, quamdiu peregrinamur a Domino; qua salva atque certa de quibusdam rebus, quas neque sensu neque ratione percepimus neque nobis per scripturam canoni-

ture or have not become known to us on the evidence of witnesses whom it would be ridiculous to disbelieve; in feeling doubt on such things we do not expose ourselves to any valid criticism.

Chapter 19 is omitted

Chapter 20

Since the supreme good of the city of God is everlasting and perfect peace —not the kind of peace which mortals pass through in the journey between birth and death, but the peace in which immortals remain without suffering anything at all which can mar it—it is undeniable that life under those conditions affords the greatest possible happiness and that in comparison with it life here affords the greatest misery, no matter how full it may be of goods of the mind and of the body and outward riches. Yet, if a man so orders his present life as to refer the use he makes of it to the final goal of that eternal life which he loves passionately and hopes with all steadfastness to attain, he can be said without absurdity to be happy even now, but happy in that hope of his rather than in things as they are now.[1] Without that hope things as they are now offer a sham happiness, indeed profound misery. The world does not enjoy true goods of the mind—for wisdom is not true wisdom if it displays prudence and vision, courage in action, temperance and self-restraint, justice in the distribution of goods, but does not at the same time direct its gaze upon that final goal, where God shall be all in all[2] in assured eternity and in perfect peace.

Chapter 21

For this reason[3] it is relevant to redeem a promise made in the second book of this work and to demonstrate as shortly and clearly as I can that the Roman Commonwealth was never a commonwealth which satisfied the definition employed by Scipio in Cicero's books 'On the Commonwealth.'[4] . .

Book II, Chapter 21 (inserted here in full)

Now, if to say that the Roman commonwealth was scandalously corrupt is to invite ridicule and if the pagans are indifferent to the shame and dis-

[1] *Spe illa potius quam re ista.* For the meaning see p. 247; briefly *res ista* is 'that pagan world of yours'.
[2] 1 Cor. xv. 28.   [3] For the connection of thought, see p. 247.
[4] Cf. Cic. *de Rep.* ii. 42 sqq.; iii. 5.

cam claruerunt nec per testes, quibus non credere absurdum est, in nostram notitiam pervenerunt, sine iusta reprehensione dubitamus.

Caput 20

Quam ob rem summum bonum civitatis Dei cum sit pax aeterna atque
perfecta, non per quam mortales transeant nascendo atque moriendo, sed
in qua inmortales maneant nihil adversi omnino patiendo: quis est qui
illam vitam vel beatissimam neget vel in eius comparatione istam, quae
hic agitur, quantislibet animi et corporis externarumque rerum bonis
plena sit, non miserrimam iudicet? Quam tamen quicumque sic habet, ut
eius usum referat ad illius finem, quam diligit ardentissime ac fidelissime
sperat, non absurde dici etiam nunc beatus potest, spe illa potius quam re
ista. Res ista vero sine spe illa beatitudo falsa et magna miseria est; non
enim veris animi bonis utitur, quoniam non est vera sapientia, quae
intentionem suam in his, quae prudenter discernit, gerit fortiter, cohibet
temperanter iusteque distribuit, non ad illum dirigit finem, ubi erit Deus
omnia in omnibus, aeternitate certa et pace perfecta.

Caput 21

Quapropter nunc est locus, ut quam potero breviter ac dilucide expediam,
quod in secundo huius operis libro me demonstraturum esse promisi,
secundum definitiones, quibus apud Ciceronem utitur Scipio in libris de
re publica, numquam rem publicam fuisse Romanam...

[LIBER II

Caput 21

Sed si contemnitur qui Romanam rem publicam pessimam ac flagitiosis-

honour with which the scandalous corruption of morals has disfigured the commonwealth and care only that it shall stand firm and be permanent, they had better listen to Cicero who goes further than Sallust's 'scandalous corruption' and maintains that in his time the commonwealth had utterly perished and that it did not remain a commonwealth at all. He introduces into an imaginary conversation the character of Scipio—the same Scipio who had annihilated Carthage—and makes him discourse upon the commonwealth at the very period of Roman History when there were forebodings that it was on the point of perishing through that very corruption which Sallust describes. For the conversation was supposed to take place at the time of the murder of one of the Gracchi, which was the beginning, according to Sallust, of the civil wars. (In the same books there is a reference to the death of Gracchus.) At the end of the second book Scipio uses the analogy of music; 'stringed instruments or wind instruments and human voices or a choir of voices require a harmony of separate notes to be maintained; any change or discord is intolerable to trained ears; the harmony is composed of notes of different pitch carefully controlled and adjusted and the result is a concordant and co-ordinated composition. In the same way a city composed of high, low and intermediate grades of society (which correspond to the notes in the analogy) sings together if reason takes control and dissimilar elements come into agreement; what musicians call harmony in a choir is in a city concord, the best and most compelling bond of security in any and every commonwealth, and concord cannot by any manner of means exist if unaccompanied by righteousness'.[1] After this the discussion ranged more widely and went into greater detail, the theme being the value of righteousness to a city and the loss which its absence inflicts. At this point Philus, one of those who took part in the discussion, took up the thread and asked for a more thorough treatment of this problem of righteousness with special reference to the common belief that a commonwealth cannot be governed without injustice. Scipio agreed that this knotty question ought to be thrashed out, but he added that nothing had so far been said which would advance their discussion, unless proof were given not only of the proposition, 'a commonwealth cannot be governed without injustice', but also of the truth of its antithesis, 'a commonwealth cannot be governed without the highest degree of justice'. The elaboration of this theme was postponed till the next day when the debate was carried on with considerable conflict of opinion. Philus undertook to state the case for the first view, though he was careful to repudiate it as his own opinion, and he conscientiously pleaded the case of injustice versus justice, attempting to demonstrate by plausible arguments and illustrations that the one was profitable to a

---

[1] *de Rep.* ii. 42 sq.

simam dixit, nec curant isti quanta morum pessimorum ac flagitiosissimorum labe ac dedecore impleatur, sed tantummodo ut consistat et maneat: audiant eam non, ut Sallustius narrat, pessimam ac flagitiosissimam factam, sed, sicut Cicero disputat, iam tunc prorsus perisse et nullam omnino remansisse rem publicam. Inducit enim Scipionem, eum ipsum qui Carthaginem extinxerat, de re publica disputantem, quando praesentiebatur ea corruptione, quam describit Sallustius, iam iamque peritura. Eo quippe tempore disputatur, quo iam unus Gracchorum occisus fuit, a quo scribit seditiones graves coepisse Sallustius. Nam mortis eius fit in eisdem libris commemoratio. Cum autem Scipio in secundi libri fine dixisset, 'ut in fidibus aut tibiis atque cantu ipso ac vocibus concentus est quidam tenendus ex distinctis sonis, quem inmutatum aut discrepantem aures eruditae ferre non possunt, isque concentus ex dissimillimarum vocum moderatione concors tamen efficitur et congruens: sic ex summis et infimis et mediis interiectis ordinibus, ut sonis, moderata ratione civitatem consensu dissimillimorum concinere, et quae harmonia a musicis dicitur in cantu, eam esse in civitate concordiam, artissimum atque optimum omni in re publica vinculum incolumitatis, eamque sine iustitia nullo pacto esse posse,' ac deinde cum aliquanto latius et uberius disseruisset, quantum prodesset iustitia civitati quantumque obesset, si afuisset, suscepit deinde Philus, unus eorum qui disputationi aderant, et poposcit, ut haec ipsa quaestio diligentius tractaretur ac de iustitia plura dicerentur, propter illud, quod iam vulgo ferebatur rem publicam regi sine iniuria non posse. Hanc proinde quaestionem discutiendam et enodandam esse adsensus est Scipio responditque nihil esse, quod adhuc de re publica dictum putaret, quo possent longius progredi, nisi esset confirmatum non modo falsum esse illud, sine iniuria non posse, sed hoc verissimum esse, sine summa iustitia rem publicam regi non posse. Cuius quaestionis explicatio cum in diem consequentem dilata esset, in tertio libro magna conflictione res acta est. Suscepit enim Philus ipse disputationem eorum, qui sentirent sine iniustitia geri non posse rem publicam, purgans praecipue, ne hoc ipse sentire crederetur, egitque sedulo pro iniustitia contra iustitiam, ut hanc esse utilem rei publicae, illam vero

commonwealth and the other was not. At the request of the whole company Laelius then attacked the task of defending justice, maintaining with all his power that there was nothing so hostile to the interests of the commonwealth as injustice and that a commonwealth could not carry on, or indeed stand at all, without a high degree of justice.

After this view had received due consideration Scipio returned to points which had been let drop, bringing up again his own previous definition and putting forward for favourable consideration his brief definition of the commonwealth as the weal of the people. But he stipulated that by 'people' he did not mean *any* gathering of a crowd of men, but a gathering united in fellowship by agreement as to what was right and by a common pursuit of interest. He reminded his hearers of the value of a clear definition in the conduct of an argument, and from the definitions which he had advanced already he inferred that a commonwealth, that is the weal of the people, came into being when it was well and justly governed, by a king alone or by an aristocracy or by the people as a whole. Suppose now, Scipio continued, that the king is unjust (and he called him 'a tyrant', as did the Greeks) or the aristocracy is unjust (and their combination he termed 'a faction'), or the people itself is unjust (he could find no current description for such a people except to call it also 'a tyrant')—then the commonwealth is not only unsound through being corrupt, which was the theme of the previous day's discussion, but simply does not exist; the chain of logic in the definition proves this, for there is no weal of the people if it is in the hands of a tyrant or a faction, and the people is no longer a people if it is unjust, since it fails to satisfy the definition of a people, namely, a multitude of men united in fellowship by a common agreement as to what is right and by a common pursuit of interest.

Therefore, at the time when the Roman commonwealth was of the character described by Sallust, it had ceased to be, in his words, 'scandalously corrupt', but had really ceased to exist, at any rate according to the line of argument adopted in the discussion of the commonwealth by the outstanding leaders of that day. For example, Cicero, speaking in the fifth book in his own person and not in the character of Scipio or anyone else, first quotes the verse of Ennius: 'It is by the moral excellence of ancient days that the commonwealth of Rome is now upheld, and by her men,' and he goes on to say[1]: 'Its truth no less than its brevity makes it sound to me as though it had been uttered by an oracle. For neither the men without a commonwealth to match them in moral excellence nor the moral excellence without the leadership of men of similar qualities could have founded or sustained for so long so great a commonwealth

[1] *de Rep.* v. i.

inutilem, veri similibus rationibus et exemplis velut conaretur ostendere. Tum Laelius rogantibus omnibus iustitiam defendere adgressus est asseruitque, quantum potuit, nihil tam inimicum quam iniustitiam civitati nec omnino nisi magna iustitia geri aut stare posse rem publicam.

Qua quaestione, quantum satis visum est, pertractata Scipio ad intermissa revertitur recolitque suam atque commendat brevem rei publicae definitionem, qua dixerat eam esse rem populi. Populum autem non omnem coetum multitudinis, sed coetum iuris consensu et utilitatis communione sociatum esse determinat. Docet deinde quanta sit in disputando definitionis utilitas, atque ex illis suis definitionibus colligit tunc esse rem publicam, id est rem populi, cum bene ac iuste geritur sive ab uno rege sive a paucis optimatibus sive ab universo populo. Cum vero iniustus est rex, quem tyrannum more Graeco appellavit, aut iniusti optimates, quorum consensum dixit esse factionem, aut iniustus ipse populus, cui nomen usitatum non repperit, nisi ut etiam ipsum tyrannum vocaret: non iam vitiosam, sicut pridie fuerat disputatum, sed, sicut ratio ex illis definitionibus conexa docuisset, omnino nullam esse rem publicam, quoniam non esset res populi, cum tyrannus eam factiove capesseret, nec ipse populus iam populus esset, si esset iniustus, quoniam non esset multitudo iuris consensu et utilitatis communione sociata, sicut populus fuerat definitus.

Quando ergo res publica Romana talis erat, qualem illam describit Sallustius, non iam pessima ac flagitiosissima, sicut ipse ait, sed omnino nulla erat secundum istam rationem, quam disputatio de re publica inter magnos eius tum principes habita patefecit. Sicut etiam ipse Tullius non Scipionis nec cuiusquam alterius, sed suo sermone loquens in principio quinti libri commemorato prius Enni poetae versu, quo dixerat:

Moribus antiquis res stat Romana virisque,

'quem quidem ille versum, inquit, vel brevitate vel veritate tamquam ex oraculo quodam mihi esse effatus videtur. Nam neque viri, nisi ita morata civitas fuisset, neque mores, nisi hi viri praefuissent, aut fundare aut tam diu tenere potuissent tantam et tam fuse lateque imperantem rem public-

which flung its rule so far and so widely. In times which none of us can remember the moral tradition handed down by our forefathers used to attach to itself men of outstanding character, while men of such calibre maintained the traditional tone and the institutions of their ancestors. Our own age, on the other hand, has taken over the commonwealth as though it were a picture of high merit but fading through age; not only have we omitted to restore its former colours, but we have taken no care to preserve even the outlines of the shapes it contained. What remains of the old standards which Ennius said were the support of the commonwealth? They are forgotten and regarded as out of date; so far are we from observing them that we have reached the stage of not even knowing what they were. As for the men—the old standards have perished through sheer dearth of men to maintain them; and for this calamity it is not enough that we should be asked to give an explanation, rather we ought to be put in the dock on a capital charge. For it is due to our vices and not to any blow of fortune that the commonwealth of which we keep the name has long since been lost to us in substance.'

That was Cicero's admission, made long after the death of Africanus whom he introduced into the discussion on the commonwealth in his books, but still before the coming of Christ. Now, if these views had been held and expressed after the diffusion and predominance of Christianity, what pagan would not believe that the facts described by Cicero were to be attributed to the Christians? But why did not the Roman gods see to it that the commonwealth should not then perish and be lost—the commonwealth which, long before Christ came in the flesh, Cicero had so mournfully lamented as being already lost?

Let the panegyrists of Rome examine her character by considering those ancient morals and those men of old, and see whether true justice really flourished therein or whether perchance it was then not a really living principle inherent in those morals but only a painted picture—a view which Cicero himself unconsciously suggested when he used the metaphor of painting. But we will examine this another time, God willing. For in its own appropriate place I shall endeavour to show that, if you adopt Cicero's own definitions of commonwealth and people (which in concise form he put into Scipio's mouth and which were supported by many other expressions of opinion voiced by himself or those whom he introduced into the discussion), Rome never was a commonwealth, since true justice never resided there. If you adopt other definitions more easily accepted, in her own manner and within a limited measure Rome was a commonwealth and was administered better by the ancient Romans than by their successors. But justice which is true justice resides only in that commonwealth whose founder and governor is Christ—if indeed you are

cam. Itaque ante nostram memoriam et mos ipse patrius praestantes viros adhibebat, et veterem morem ac maiorum instituta retinebant excellentes viri. Nostra vero aetas cum rem publicam sicut picturam accepisset egregiam, sed evanescentem vetustate, non modo eam coloribus isdem quibus fuerat renovare neglexit, sed ne id quidem curavit, ut formam saltem eius et extrema tamquam liniamenta servaret. Quid enim manet ex antiquis moribus, quibus ille dixit rem stare Romanam, quos ita oblivione obsoletos videmus, ut non modo non colantur, sed iam ignorentur? Nam de viris quid dicam? Mores enim ipsi interierunt virorum penuria, cuius tanti mali non modo reddenda ratio nobis, sed etiam tamquam reis capitis quodam modo dicenda causa est. Nostris enim vitiis, non casu aliquo, rem publicam verbo retinemus, re ipsa vero iam pridem amisimus.'

Haec Cicero fatebatur, longe quidem post mortem Africani, quem in suis libris fecit de re publica disputare, adhuc tamen ante adventum Christi; quae si diffamata et praevalescente religione Christiana sentirentur atque dicerentur, quis non istorum ea Christianis inputanda esse censeret? Quam ob rem cur non curarunt dii eorum, ne tunc periret atque amitteretur illa res publica, quam Cicero longe, antequam Christus in carne venisset, tam lugubriter deplorat amissam? Viderint laudatores eius etiam illis antiquis viris et moribus qualis fuerit, utrum in ea viguerit vera iustitia an forte nec tunc fuerit viva moribus, sed picta coloribus; quod et ipse Cicero nesciens, cum eam praeferret, expressit. Sed alias, si Deus voluerit, hoc videbimus. Enitar enim suo loco, ut ostendam secundum definitiones ipsius Ciceronis, quibus quid sit res publica et quid sit populus loquente Scipione breviter posuit (adtestantibus etiam multis sive ipsius sive eorum quos loqui fecit in eadem disputatione sententiis), numquam illam fuisse rem publicam, quia numquam in ea fuit vera iustitia. Secundum probabiliores autem definitiones pro suo modo quodam res publica fuit, et melius ab antiquioribus Romanis quam a posterioribus administrata est; vera autem iustitia non est nisi in ea re publica, cuius conditor rectorque

prepared to call it a commonwealth, as you might be, since undeniably it is the weal of the people. If, however, the word commonwealth, which is in common use in other contexts and in other senses, is too far removed from the ordinary practice of *our* speech, we can certainly say that true justice resides in that city of which Holy Scripture says, 'Glorious things are spoken of thee, city of God.'[1]

Book XIX, Chapter 21 (resumed)

He briefly defines a commonwealth as the weal of the people. If this definition is true, the Roman commonwealth never was a commonwealth because it was never the weal of the people, which he laid down as a definition of a commonwealth. He defined a people as the gathering together of a multitude of men united in fellowship by a common agreement as to what is right[2] and by common pursuit of interest. The sense which he attaches to common agreement as to what is right he explains in the course of his argument, proving thereby that a commonwealth cannot be carried on without righteousness; therefore where there is not true righteousness, there can be no right. For what is done with right is certianly done righteously, but what is done unrighteously cannot be done with right. Inequitable institutions set up by men are not to be described or even deemed as embodying right, for even men assert that the right is that which has flowed from the fountain of righteousness and that it is untrue to say, as is commonly held by mistaken schools of thought, that the right is what is to the interest of the stronger. Hence, where there is no true righteousness, there cannot be a gathering of men united in fellowship by common agreement as to what is right, and therefore there can be no people, at any rate on the lines of Scipio's or Cicero's definition. And, if there is no people, there can be no weal of the people, but only the weal of some kind of multitude which could not be dignified by the name of people. Therefore, if the commonwealth is the weal of the people, if a people not united in fellowship by agreement as to what is right is not a people, and if there is no right where there is no righteousness, the certain conclusion is to be drawn that where there is no righteousness there is no commonwealth.

[The argument may now be taken a stage further.] Righteousness is that virtue which assigns to each its due. What kind of righteousness

---

[1] Ps. lxxxvii. 3.

[2] It must be understood that the words translated 'right' and 'righteousness' are *ius* and *iustitia*: in some contexts 'justice' would come nearer the meaning, but it is then impossible to keep the play of 'ius' and 'iustitia': in other contexts 'justice' is further away from the meaning than 'righteousness'.

Christus est, si et ipsam rem publicam placet dicere, quoniam eam rem populi esse negare non possumus. Si autem hoc nomen, quod alibi aliterque vulgatum est, ab usu nostrae locutionis est forte remotius, in ea certe civitate est vera iustitia, de qua scriptura sancta dicit: *Gloriosa dicta sunt de te, civitas Dei.*]

LIBER XIX

Caput 21

. . Breviter enim rem publicam definit esse rem populi. Quae definitio si vera est, numquam fuit Romana res publica, quia numquam fuit res populi, quam definitionem voluit esse rei publicae. Populum enim esse definivit coetum multitudinis iuris consensu et utilitatis communione sociatum. Quid autem dicat iuris consensum, disputando explicat, per hoc ostendens geri sine iustitia non posse rem publicam; ubi ergo iustitia vera non est, nec ius potest esse. Quod enim iure fit, profecto iuste fit; quod autem fit iniuste, nec iure fieri potest. Non enim iura dicenda sunt vel putanda iniqua hominum constituta, cum illud etiam ipsi ius esse dicant, quod de iustitiae fonte manaverit, falsumque esse, quod a quibusdam non recte sentientibus dici solet, id esse ius, quod ei, qui plus potest, utile est. Quocirca ubi non est vera iustitia, iuris consensu sociatus coetus hominum non potest esse et ideo nec populus iuxta illam Scipionis vel Ciceronis definitionem; et si non populus, nec res populi, sed qualiscumque multitudinis, quae populi nomine digna non est. Ac per hoc, si res publica res est populi et populus non est, qui consensu non sociatus est iuris, non est autem ius, ubi nulla iustitia est: procul dubio colligitur, ubi iustitia non est, non esse rem publicam. Iustitia porro ea virtus est, quae sua cuique distribuit. Quae igitur iustitia est hominis, quae ipsum homi-

then can the righteousness of man be which steals man himself away from the true God and makes him subject to foul deities? Is this to assign to each his due? If you rob a man of his estate when he has bought it and hand it over to someone who has no right to it, you are unrighteous; if you rob God of yourself when he is your sovereign lord and your maker, and become the slave of evil spirits, are you then righteous?

In these same books 'On the Commonwealth', a keen and valiant defence of righteousness against unrighteousness is maintained. A case had just been put up in defence of unrighteousness in which the plea was made that a commonwealth could not exist and be carried on except through unrighteousness, and it was taken to be firmly established that the enslavement of one man to another was unrighteous, but that unless the imperial city to which the great commonwealth of empire belonged practised such unrighteousness it could not rule its provinces. To this argument the reply was made in defence of righteousness that the righteousness of such a rule lay in the advantage which slavery offered to the provincials; such rule is to their advantage if it is justifiably exercised, and it is so exercised if the wicked are deprived of power to inflict wrong; the conquered will thus find their lot improved, because before they were conquered they were in worse plight. To support this argument a noteworthy illustration was taken as though from the heart of nature itself; if the rule of a superior power is unrighteous, why does God rule man, the mind rule the body, and the reason rule lust and other evil desires of the mind? This illustration satisfactorily established beyond doubt that slavery is advantageous to some, and that enslavement to God is advantageous to all men. The mind enslaved to God exercises justifiable rule over the body, and inside the mind itself the reason, if subordinate to the Lord God, exercises similar control over lust and other evil desires.

Wherefore, when a man does not serve God, what degree of righteousness can you suppose to be in him? For, if the mind does not serve God, its control over the body cannot be righteous, neither can the control of human reason over evil desires. If there is no righteousness in such a man, it is certain that there can be none in a gathering composed of such men. Hence it is not here that we must look for that common agreement as to what is right which turns a multitude into a people—that people whose weal constitutes a 'commonwealth'. [That is really the chief argument:] for there is little to be said about 'interest'; in the words of the definition, you remember, a gathering of men is called a people if it is united by a common pursuit of interest. If you watch carefully, you will see that those who live a life of impiety do not serve their own interest; all who live a life of impiety serve, not God, but evil spirits, who are all the more impious as they demand sacrifice to be offered to themselves,

nem Deo vero tollit et inmundis daemonibus subdit? Hocine est sua cuique distribuere? An qui fundum aufert eius, a quo emptus est, et tradit ei, qui nihil habet in eo iuris, iniustus est; et qui se ipsum aufert dominanti Deo, a quo factus est, et malignis servit spiritibus, iustus est?

Disputatur certe acerrime atque fortissime in eisdem ipsis de re publica libris adversus iniustitiam pro iustitia. Et quoniam, cum prius ageretur pro iniustitiae partibus contra iustitiam et diceretur nisi per iniustitiam rem publicam stare gerique non posse, hoc veluti validissimum positum erat, iniustum esse, ut homines hominibus dominantibus serviant; quam tamen iniustitiam nisi sequatur imperiosa civitas, cuius est magna res publica, non eam posse provinciis imperare: responsum est a parte iustitiae ideo iustum esse, quod talibus hominibus sit utilis servitus, et pro utilitate eorum fieri, cum recte fit, id est cum improbis aufertur iniuriarum licentia, et domiti melius se habebunt, quia indomiti deterius se habuerunt; sub-ditumque est, ut ista ratio firmaretur, veluti a natura sumptum nobile exemplum atque dictum est: 'Cur igitur Deus homini, animus imperat corpori, ratio libidini ceterisque vitiosis animi partibus?' Plane hoc exemplo satis edoctum est quibusdam esse utilem servitutem, et Deo quidem ut serviatur utile esse omnibus. Serviens autem Deo animus recte imperat corpori, inque ipso animo ratio Deo Domino subdita recte im-perat libidini vitiisque ceteris. Quapropter ubi homo Deo non servit, quid in eo putandum est esse iustitiae? quando quidem Deo non serviens nullo modo potest iuste animus corpori aut humana ratio vitiis imperare. Et si in homine tali non est ulla iustitia, procul dubio nec in hominum coetu, qui ex hominibus talibus constat. Non est hic ergo iuris ille consensus, qui hominum multitudinem populum facit, cuius res dicitur esse res publica. Nam de utilitate quid dicam, cuius etiam communione sociatus coetus hominum, sicut sese habet ista definitio, populus nuncupatur? Quamvis enim, si diligenter adtendas, nec utilitas sit ulla viventium, qui vivunt impie, sicut vivit omnis, qui non servit Deo servitque daemonibus, tanto magis impiis, quanto magis sibi, cum sint inmundissimi spiritus, tamquam

though they are the foulest of spirits, as though they were gods. [But there is no need to elaborate this argument about 'interest':] I think my treatment of 'common agreement as to what is right' is thorough enough to make it sufficiently clear that a people in which righteousness does not dwell is not a people whose weal can be said to be common.

It may be said in reply that the Romans in their commonwealth served not foul spirits but good and holy gods: but surely I need not go over and over the arguments which I have stated fully enough already, and more than enough. Anyone who has read the foregoing books and reached this point can surely have no remaining doubt that the Romans served evil and impure spirits—unless he is extremely dense or shamelessly contentious.

No more about the character of the gods to whom they sacrificed: enough to say that in the law of the true God it is written: 'He that sacrificeth unto any gods but the Lord only shall be rooted out'.[1] The God who gave this ordinance and joined such a threat to it did not will that sacrifice should be offered to other gods, whether good or bad.

Chapter 22

To this the retort may be made, 'Who is that God of yours, and how do you justify this claim to such obedience from the Romans as would forbid them to offer sacrifice to any god but Himself?' Really, it argues great blindness to keep on asking this question. He is the God whose prophets foretold the state of the world as we now see it. He is the God who gave Abraham the answer, 'In your seed shall all nations be blessed'.[2] This blessing of all nations came about in Christ (who according to the flesh was sprung from the seed of Abraham); even those who have remained enemies of this name recognise it, whether willingly or unwillingly. He is that God whose divine Spirit spake by those who foretold what we have since seen accomplished through the Church, now spread, as we see, through the whole world: all this I have set out in my earlier books. He is the God whom Varro, the most learned of the Romans, recognised as Jupiter, though he did not quite know what he was saying; all the same I think his view worth quoting precisely because a man of such learning was not able to account Him no god at all nor to reckon Him the meanest: he believed that he was the god whom he thought to be the greatest god of all. Finally, He is that God whom Porphyry, the most learned of philosophers and the most bitter enemy of Christians, admitted to be a great god—even though he was led to do so by the oracles of those whom he imagined to be gods.

[1] Exod. xxii. 20.   [2] Gen. xxii. 18.

diis sacrificari volunt: tamen quod de iuris consensu diximus satis esse
arbitror, unde appareat per hanc definitionem non esse populum, cuius res
publica esse dicatur, in quo iustitia non est. Si enim dicunt non spiritibus
inmundis, sed diis bonis atque sanctis in sua re publica servisse Romanos:
numquid eadem totiens repetenda sunt, quae iam satis, immo ultra quam
satis est diximus? Quis enim ad hunc locum per superiores huius operis
libros pervenit, qui dubitare adhuc possit malis et inpuris daemonibus
servisse Romanos, nisi vel nimium stolidus vel inpudentissime con-
tentiosus? Sed ut taceam quales sint, quos sacrificiis colebant: in lege veri
Dei scriptum est: *Sacrificans diis eradicabitur nisi Domino tantum.* Nec
bonis igitur nec malis diis sacrificari voluit, qui hoc cum tanta com-
minatione praecepit.

CAPUT 22

Sed responderi potest: 'Quis iste Deus est aut unde dignus probatur, cui
deberent obtemperare Romani, ut nullum deorum praeter ipsum colerent
sacrificiis?' Magnae caecitatis est, adhuc quaerere, quis iste sit Deus. Ipse
est Deus, cuius prophetae praedixerunt ista quae cernimus. Ipse est Deus,
a quo responsum accepit Abraham: *In semine tuo benedicentur omnes gentes.*
Quod in Christo fieri, qui secundum carnem de illo semine exortus est,
idem ipsi qui remanserunt huius nominis inimici, velint nolintve, cog-
noscunt. Ipse est Deus, cuius divinus Spiritus per eos locutus est, quorum
praedicta atque completa per ecclesiam, quam videmus toto orbe diffusam,
in libris superioribus posui. Ipse est Deus, quem Varro doctissimus
Romanorum Iovem putat, quamvis nesciens quid loquatur; quod tamen
ideo commemorandum putavi, quoniam vir tantae scientiae nec nullum
istum Deum potuit existimare nec vilem. Hunc enim eum esse credidit,
quem summum putavit deum. Postremo ipse est Deus, quem doctissimus
philosophorum, quamvis Christianorum acerrimus inimicus, etiam per
eorum oracula, quos deos putat, deum magnum Porphyrius confitetur.

Chapter 23

(The greater part of this long chapter, here omitted, is devoted to exposing the inconsistency of Porphyry. It concludes:)

Our conclusion, therefore, is this: righteousness implies that the one highest God rules over a city which obeys Him through His grace and carries out his order not to sacrifice to any other god but Himself; that, as a result, in all men who belong to that city and obey God the mind faithfully rules over the body, and the reason over sinful desires, according to a properly ordered system of rule; that a gathering and a people of righteous men, no less than the individual righteous man, lives by faith, working through the love with which man loves God as He ought to be loved, and his neighbour as himself. Where there is not such righteousness as this, there is no gathering of men united in fellowship by common agreement as to what is right and by common pursuit of interest; hence most emphatically there is no people—if the definition of people just given is true; therefore there is no commonwealth, since there is no weal of the people where there is no people.

Chapter 24

Suppose, however, that a different definition of people is proposed, a definition, for example, like this: 'A people is a gathering of a multitude of rational beings united in fellowship by sharing a common love of the same things.' In that case, to see the character of each people you have to examine what it loves. No matter what it loves, it can in any case be called without absurdity a people, since it is not a gathering of a multitude of cattle, but of rational creatures, united in fellowship by sharing a common love of the same things; it is a better or a worse people according as it is united in loving higher or lower things.

Now, in the terms of that definition of ours, the Roman people is a people and its weal is beyond doubt a commonwealth. But history tells us (and in the foregoing books I have quoted freely from Roman history) what were the things which the Roman people loved in its earliest days and in its later days; history tells us of the change in its character which led it into bloody insurrections and thence to 'social' wars and civil wars: it tells us how the unity which is, as it were, the salvation of a people was shattered and ruined. Yet, even so, I would not deny the Romans the title of people or say that its weal was not a commonwealth, as long as it remains, in some sense, a gathering of a multitude of rational beings, united in fellowship by sharing a common love of the same things. What

CHAPTER 23

Caput 23

.. Quapropter ubi non est ista iustitia, ut secundum suam gratiam civitati oboedienti Deus imperet unus et summus, ne cuiquam sacrificet nisi tantum sibi, et per hoc in omnibus hominibus ad eandem civitatem pertinentibus atque oboedientibus Deo animus etiam corpori atque ratio vitiis ordine legitimo fideliter imperet; ut, quem ad modum iustus unus, ita coetus populusque iustorum vivat ex fide, quae operatur per dilectionem, qua homo diligit Deum, sicut diligendus est Deus, et proximum sicut semet ipsum—ubi ergo non est ista iustitia, profecto non est coetus hominum iuris consensu et utilitatis communione sociatus. Quod si non est, utique populus non est, si vera est haec populi definitio. Ergo nec res publica est, quia res populi non est, ubi ipse populus non est.

Caput 24

Si autem populus non isto, sed alio definiatur modo, velut si dicatur: 'Populus est coetus multitudinis rationalis rerum quas diligit concordi communione sociatus', profecto, ut videatur qualis quisque populus sit, illa sunt intuenda, quae diligit. Quaecumque tamen diligat, si coetus est multitudinis non pecorum, sed rationalium creaturarum et eorum quae diligit concordi communione sociatus est, non absurde populus nuncupatur; tanto utique melior, quanto in melioribus, tantoque deterior, quanto est in deterioribus concors. Secundum istam definitionem nostram Romanus populus populus est et res eius sine dubitatione res publica. Quid autem primis temporibus suis quidve sequentibus populus ille dilexerit et quibus moribus ad cruentissimas seditiones atque inde ad socialia atque civilia bella perveniens ipsam concordiam, quae salus est quodam modo populi, ruperit atque corruperit, testatur historia; de qua in praecedentibus libris multa posuimus. Nec ideo tamen vel ipsum non esse populum vel eius rem dixerim non esse rem publicam, quamdiu manet qualiscumque rationalis multitudinis coetus, rerum quas diligit concordi communione sociatus. Quod autem de isto populo et de ista re

I have said of the Roman people and its commonwealth, I must be understood to have said and to mean as applying also to Athens or any of the Greek states, to Egypt, to the Assyrian Babylon which preceded the Babylon of Rome, since in their commonwealth they exercised imperial rule whether on a large or a small scale, and indeed it can be applied to any other nation.

To put the matter in general form, a city of wicked men in which God's order to offer no sacrifice, except to Himself, is not obeyed, nor His order, which follows upon the other, that the mind should exercise proper and constant rule over the body, and the reason over evil desires—such a city is without the truth of righteousness.

Chapter 25

For though the mind may give the impression of exercising a praiseworthy rule over the body, and the reason over evil desires, yet if the mind and the reason are not enslaved to God, as God himself enjoined that they should be, they certainly cannot exercise a proper rule over the body and over evil desires. For what sort of a dominion over the body and evil desires can a mind exercise which is ignorant of the true God, which is not subject to His rule but is prostituted to the most evil spirits who corrupt it? On the contrary, these very virtues which such a mind thinks it has and which enable it to rule the body and evil desires are themselves vices rather than virtues if they have reference to the attainment or the continued possession of any objective other than God Himself. Admittedly, certain people may regard them as true and honourable virtues, on the ground that they are not referred back to any standard outside themselves and are desired purely for their own sakes; but even then they are swollen with arrogance and so are to be ranked as vices and not virtues. For, just as that which gives life to flesh is not derived from the flesh, but is above and beyond it, so that which gives happiness to the life of man comes not from man, but is above and beyond man: and the same is true not only of man but of every heavenly power and every heavenly virtue.

Chapter 26

Hence, as the life of the flesh is the spirit, so the happiness of a man's life is God: on this the sacred literature of the Hebrews says, 'Happy is the people which has the Lord as its own God'.[1] Miserable, therefore, is the

[1] Ps. cxliv. 15.

publica dixi, hoc de Atheniensium vel quorumcumque Graecorum, hoc de Aegyptiorum, hoc de illa priore Babylone Assyriorum, quando in rebus publicis suis imperia vel parva vel magna tenuerunt, et de alia quacumque aliarum gentium intellegar dixisse atque sensisse. Generaliter quippe civitas impiorum, cui non imperat Deus oboedienti sibi, ut sacrificium non offerat nisi tantummodo sibi, et per hoc in illa et animus corpori ratioque vitiis recte ac fideliter imperet, caret iustitiae veritate.

Caput 25

Quamlibet enim videatur animus corpori et ratio vitiis laudabiliter imperare, si Deo animus et ratio ipsa non servit, sicut sibi esse serviendum ipse Deus praecepit, nullo modo corpori vitiisque recte imperat. Nam qualis corporis atque vitiorum potest esse mens domina veri Dei nescia nec eius imperio subiugata, sed vitiosissimis daemonibus corrumpentibus prostituta? Proinde virtutes, quas habere sibi videtur, per quas imperat corpori et vitiis, ad quodlibet adipiscendum vel tenendum rettulerit nisi ad Deum, etiam ipsae vitia sunt potius quam virtutes. Nam licet a quibusdam tunc verae atque honestae putentur esse virtutes, cum referuntur ad se ipsas nec propter aliud expetuntur: etiam tunc inflatae ac superbae sunt, ideo non virtutes, sed vitia iudicanda sunt. Sicut enim non est a carne sed super carnem, quod carnem facit vivere: sic non est ab homine, sed super hominem, quod hominem facit beate vivere; nec solum hominem, sed etiam quamlibet potestatem virtutemque caelestem.

Caput 26

Quocirca ut vita carnis anima est, ita beata vita hominis Deus est, de quo dicunt sacrae litterae Hebraeorum: *Beatus populus, cuius est Dominus Deus ipsius.* Miser igitur populus ab ipso alienatus Deo. Diligit tamen etiam

people which is estranged from that God. Yet even this people loves peace of a kind (a peace, too, of which it is impossible to disapprove), though in the end it will not possess that peace since it does not make good use of its peace before its end comes. To us Christians, too, it is of vital concern that a people should for the time being possess this peace in this life; for, as long as the two cities are intermingled, we also make use of the peace of the modern Babylon: though the people of God is in the process of being set free from this peace by faith, nevertheless for the time being it sojourns here in the midst of it. This explains why the apostle exhorted the Church to pray for its kings and those in exalted positions and adds the words, 'That we may live a quiet and calm life in all piety and charity.'[1] So, too, the prophet Jeremiah, when he foretold[2] to the ancient people of God their captivity and gave them the divine command to go in all obedience to Babylon serving their God patiently even in that adversity, actually exhorted them to offer prayer for the peace of Babylon, saying, 'For in her peace is your peace'; he meant, of course, that temporal peace which for the time being is shared alike by the good and the evil.

Chapter 27

But the peace which is peculiar to us [Christians] is, in this world, a peace with God through faith, and, in eternity, a peace with God through sight. Nevertheless, whether we have in mind that temporal peace which is common to all or our own peace, in this world peace is of such quality as to offer rather comfort to our misery than the joy of happiness. So, too, with our righteousness; though it is true righteousness, because the final good, which it takes as its standard, is true, still in this life it is so limited that it comes into being rather through the remission of our sins than through any perfection of our virtues. Evidence of this is furnished by the prayer which is used by the whole of the heavenly city sojourning here in the lands of the earth; through every one of its members it cries to God, 'Forgive us our debts as we also forgive our debtors'.[3] This prayer is of no avail to benefit those whose faith is dead because it is not accompanied by works: it is of benefit to those whose faith works through love. For, though the reason may be subjected to God, still, in our state as mortals occupying bodies which will perish and which weigh down the soul, the rule which reason exercises over evil desires is not complete, and therefore the righteous feel the need of such a prayer as this. It may be quite true that reason does rule over evil desires, but it is a rule that is

---

[1] 1 Tim. ii. 2.   [2] Jer. xxix. 7.   [3] Mt. vi. 12.

ipse quandam pacem suam non inprobandam, quam quidem non habebit in fine, quia non ea bene utitur ante finem. Hanc autem ut interim habeat in hac vita, etiam nostri interest; quoniam, quamdiu permixtae sunt ambae civitates, utimur et nos pace Babylonis; ex qua ita per fidem populus Dei liberatur, ut apud hanc interim peregrinetur. Propter quod et apostolus admonuit ecclesiam, ut oraret pro regibus eius atque sublimibus, addens et dicens: *Ut quietam et tranquillam vitam agamus cum omni pietate et caritate*, et propheta Hieremias, cum populo Dei veteri praenuntiaret captivitatem et divinitus imperaret, ut oboedienter irent in Babyloniam Deo suo etiam ista patientia servientes, monuit et ipse ut oraretur pro illa dicens: *Quia in eius est pace pax vestra*, utique interim temporalis, quae bonis malisque communis est.

Caput 27

Pax autem nostra propria et hic est cum Deo per fidem et in aeternum erit cum illo per speciem. Sed hic sive illa communis sive nostra propria talis est pax, ut solacium miseriae sit potius quam beatitudinis gaudium. Ipsa quoque nostra iustitia, quamvis vera sit propter verum boni finem, ad quem refertur, tamen tanta est in hac vita, ut potius remissione peccatorum constet quam perfectione virtutum. Testis est oratio totius civitatis Dei, quae peregrinatur in terris. Per omnia quippe membra sua clamat ad Deum: *Dimitte nobis debita nostra, sicut et nos dimittimus debitoribus nostris*. Nec pro eis est efficax haec oratio, quorum fides sine operibus mortua est; sed pro eis, quorum fides per dilectionem operatur. Quia enim Deo quidem subdita, in hac tamen condicione mortali et corpore corruptibili, quod adgravat animam, non perfecte vitiis imperat ratio, ideo necessaria est iustis talis oratio. Nam profecto quamquam imperetur, nequaquam sine conflictu vitiis imperatur; et utique subrepit aliquid in

certainly not exercised without a conflict: in fact, given the condition of human frailty, even if you contend well in that conflict or succeed in conquering, subjecting and maintaining dominion over such enemies, something always creeps in unnoticed which causes sin to be committed, not perhaps the sin of ready act, but certainly the sin of unguarded phrase or fleeting thought. For this reason, as long as rule over evil desire has to be exercised, peace cannot be complete: for against the evil elements which offer resistance a hazardous campaign has to be carried on to crush them, while the triumph over those which have been defeated brings a respite which is not yet assured; the rule which keeps them under is not yet free of anxiety. We are subject, then, to temptations, of which it is tersely said in the divine utterances, 'Is not the life of man upon earth a time of testing?'[1] In the face of this, who would presume to say that his life is such that he can dispense with saying to God, 'Forgive us our debts'? Only the proud man; he cannot claim to be a great man, for he is puffed up and swollen with pride, and him God in His righteousness resists, God who bestows His grace upon the humble. Wherefore it is written, 'God resists the proud, but to the humble he gives grace'.[2]

And so in this life each individual's righteousness consists in this, that God should rule man who should render Him obedience, that the mind should rule the body, and the reason the evil desires even when they fight against it, either by subduing them or resisting them, that God Himself should be asked to grant grace for merit and pardon for sin and that He should be thanked for all benefits received from Him.

But in that final peace things will be otherwise; to that peace righteousness looks for its standards and it is in order to obtain that peace that righteousness exists; man's nature, healed by its immortality and set free from corruption, will experience no evil desires, and each one of us will be rid of all that can thwart us whether it comes from outside or inside himself. Hence, there will be no need for reason to rule evil desires, for there will be none; God will rule man, the mind will rule the body, and obedience will be as acceptable and easy as life and kingship then will be happy. Such things shall be eternal there for all and for each, and it will be certain that they are eternal. Therefore the peace of this happiness or the happiness of this peace will be the supreme good.

Chapter 28

But for those who do not belong to that city of God there shall be on the contrary everlasting misery, which is also called the second death, for the

---

[1] Job. vii. 1.   [2] James iv. 6; 1 Pet. v. 5.

hoc loco infirmitatis etiam bene confligenti sive hostibus talibus victis subditisque dominanti, unde si non facili operatione, certe labili locutione aut volatili cogitatione peccetur. Et ideo, quamdiu vitiis imperatur, plena pax non est, quia et illa, quae resistunt, periculoso debellantur proelio, et illa, quae victa sunt, nondum securo triumphantur otio, sed adhuc sollicito premuntur imperio. In his ergo temptationibus, de quibus omnibus in divinis eloquiis breviter dictum est: *Numquid non temptatio est vita humana super terram?* quis ita vivere se praesumat, ut dicere Deo: *Dimitte nobis debita nostra* necesse non habeat nisi homo elatus? nec vero magnus, sed inflatus ac tumidus, cui per iustitiam resistit, qui gratiam largitur humilibus. Propter quod scriptum est: *Deus superbis resistit, humilibus autem dat gratiam.* Hic itaque in unoquoque iustitia est, ut oboedienti Deus homini, animus corpori, ratio autem vitiis etiam repugnantibus imperet, vel subigendo vel resistendo, atque ut ab ipso Deo petatur et meritorum gratia et venia delictorum ac de acceptis bonis gratiarum actio persolvatur. In illa vero pace finali, quo referenda et cuius adipiscendae causa habenda est ista iustitia, quoniam sanata inmortalitate atque incorruptione natura vitia non habebit nec unicuique nostrum vel ab alio vel a se ipso quippiam repugnabit, non opus erit ut ratio vitiis, quae nulla erunt, imperet; sed imperabit Deus homini, animus corpori, tantaque ibi erit oboediendi suavitas et facilitas, quanta vivendi regnandique felicitas. Et hoc illic in omnibus atque in singulis aeternum erit aeternumque esse certum erit, et ideo pax beatitudinis huius vel beatitudo pacis huius summum bonum erit.

Caput 28

Eorum autem, qui non pertinent ad istam civitatem Dei, erit e contrario miseria sempiterna, quae mors etiam secunda dicitur, quia nec anima ibi

soul cannot be said to be alive there, if it is estranged from the life of God, nor the body either, if it is subject to eternal pains: hence, the second death will be more ruthless than death here, since it will not be possible for it to be terminated by death. Now, war is held to be the opposite of peace (as misery is the opposite of happiness and death of life); if, then, peace is proclaimed and extolled as one of the ends of good men, it is reasonable to ask, conversely, what kind of war we must understand to be among the ends of the wicked. If you ask this question, you should note what element it is in war that makes it harmful and destructive: you will find this element to be nothing but the enmity and the conflict of things among themselves. No more oppressive or bitter war can be imagined than a war in which there is conflict between the will and the passions—a war in which neither gains the victory which will put an end to their enmities, and in which violent pain wars with our bodily nature without either yielding to the other. On earth, when such a conflict occurs, either pain wins and death takes away all feeling, or nature wins and restored health removes pain. But hereafter pain remains to scourge, and nature lives on to experience feeling; both continue that punishment may continue. These are the ends assigned to good men, and then the ends assigned to the wicked; the first are to be desired, the second to be avoided: but to one set of ends or to the other the good and the evil will travel, passing through judgment; on this judgment I will discourse in the following book, so far as God grants me the power.

vivere dicenda est, quae a vita Dei alienata erit, nec corpus, quod aeternis doloribus subiacebit; ac per hoc ideo durior ista secunda mors erit, quia finiri morte non poterit. Sed quoniam sicut miseria beatitudini et mors vitae, ita bellum paci videtur esse contrarium: merito quaeritur, sicut pax in bonorum finibus praedicata est atque laudata, quod vel quale bellum e contrario in finibus malorum possit intellegi. Verum qui hoc quaerit, adtendat quid in bello noxium perniciosumque sit, et videbit nihil aliud quam rerum esse inter se adversitatem atque conflictum. Quod igitur bellum gravius et amarius cogitari potest, quam ubi voluntas sic adversa est passioni et passio voluntati, ut nullius earum victoria tales inimicitiae finiantur, et ubi sic confligit cum ipsa natura corporis vis doloris, ut neutrum alteri cedat? Hic enim quando contingit iste conflictus, aut dolor vincit et sensum mors adimit, aut natura vincit et dolorem sanitas tollit. Ibi autem et dolor permanet ut affligat, et natura perdurat ut sentiat; quia utrumque ideo non deficit, ne poena deficiat. Ad hos autem fines bonorum et malorum, illos expetendos, istos cavendos, quoniam per iudicium transibunt ad illos boni, ad istos mali: de hoc iudicio, quantum Deus donaverit, in consequenti volumine disputabo.

COMMENTARY

Attention is drawn to *Notes to Extracts and Chapters*
in Notes II on page 277.

Extract 1, Book i, preface

The first lines of this chapter are so important that the phrases are considered one by one.

The first two words—the most glorious city, *gloriosissimam civitatem*—point back to the eighty-seventh Psalm. St Augustine quotes the Psalms perhaps more than any other book of the Bible; he wrote a Commentary on the Psalms and in his later life was specially devoted to them.[1] St Augustine does not elaborate the thought of this Psalm; but the general meaning of it must have been present to his mind in his references to it, particularly to the verse 'Glorious things are spoken of thee, O city of God'. The Psalm expresses a point of view not common in the O.T. and its language is not often paralleled. It may be paraphrased thus[2]:

'Jehovah loves his foundations upon the holy mountains—*Jerusalem and its Temple*—he loves the Gates of Zion more than all the dwellings of Jacob. Glorious things are spoken of thee, O city of God—*the rest of the Psalm explains what are the glorious things; the glory is described by Jehovah Himself who speaks thus:* 'Rahab (*Egypt*) and Babylon I shall include among those that know Me—*that is, as my worshippers.* It shall be said that Philistia, Tyre and Ethiopia, each one of them, are born in Zion—*that is, are re-born in Zion as adopted citizens and worshippers of Jehovah.* Of Zion herself it is said "One man after another is re-born in her and the Most High Himself shall stablish her". When Jehovah—*Jehovah still speaks*—makes a list of the nations who worship Him, He shall record that such and such a nation was reborn in Zion. In thee—*that is, Jerusalem*—are all who sing and dance for joy; all the springs of my happiness—*that is, the Psalmist's*—are in thee.'

The glory of Zion, therefore, is that she shall incorporate as citizens and worshippers of Jehovah the nations of the earth, giving them equal partnership as members of a family enrolled in the register of Jehovah.

From one point of view the Jewish spirit fostered an exclusiveness which was unrivalled in the ancient world. The Jews were the chosen people of God, unlike all others; their land, their law, their religion were His gifts. Thus separating themselves from other nations, they could not but regard the rest of the world as inferior and as enemies. But one day that inferiority would be asserted in real fact, and God would break His

[1] See e.g. R. E. Prothero, *The Psalms in Human Life*, Chapter I.
[2] According to one interpretation; for others see Note, p. 278.

136

enemies, that is, the enemies of the Jews, and a King of the line of David would lead in triumph the captive kings of the world.

From another point of view the Jews' conception of their mission was inclusive rather than narrow. The prophets sometimes drew a picture of the nations coming in willing submission to Jehovah in His holy city; the Redeemer of Israel shall be the God of the whole earth, and Jerusalem the centre of worship for all nations; 'the Gentiles shall come to thy light and kings to the brightness of thy rising.' In some passages the nations come as suppliants and remain as tributaries; in others the idea of Israel's pre-eminence almost disappears.

But this Psalm expresses, perhaps more clearly than any other passage, the idea of the enrolment of the nations on equal terms with the Jews; they are to be reborn as members of the Jewish family; even her hereditary enemies, Egypt and Babylon, are to be received as kinsmen, not as captives or suppliants, but as enrolled citizens. Here, then, we have a conception of the unity of mankind—a fellowship of men in the recognition of Jehovah.

Something of this, it might be presumed, must have been present to the mind of St Augustine, for the general meaning must have been clear to him in the 'old Latin' or *Itala* version of the Scriptures which he used, or from the Septuagint to which he attached the greatest importance, regarding it as inspiredly written.

At the same time there are elements in the city of God as described in the Psalm (so interpreted) which St Augustine could not have adopted. The idea of nations coming to the city is foreign to him. To him the nations, as such, represent or generally typify 'the earthly city', *terrena civitas*; but within every nation there are individual men who have belonged or belong to the city of God. He never contemplates the conversion of whole nations. The earthly and the heavenly city grow side by side and are 'inseparably interwoven' to the end. There is to be no general theocracy. Secondly, though Jewish worship and law and prophecy were in themselves superior to those of the Gentiles and though they still enshrine examples and prototypes of value for Christians, yet Zion is no longer the centre to which the citizen of God will turn. The focus-point is now the worship of God through Christ. Herein is the city of God glorious—not in the gathering of nations to Zion, but in the drawing of individuals, wherever they may be, to allegiance to God, here and hereafter. Such is the point of view of the *dcD*.

But as a matter of fact we do know from a source other than the *dcD* what interpretation St Augustine put upon this Psalm; for he deals with it in his *Enarrationes in Psalmos*, which is a collection of sermons and rhetorical treatises, some perhaps not actually delivered. The opening

may be quoted in full. 'The Psalm which has just been sung is brief if you count up the words, but it is tremendous in the burden of its thought. The whole Psalm has been read aloud, and you notice how short a time it took from beginning to end. . . . In this Psalm the praises of a certain city are sung; of it we are citizens in so far as we are Christians; we are resident aliens in it as long as we are mortal men; to it we press on, but the way to it is barred by thorns and brambles and could not be found till the king of the city made Himself the Way, that we might reach the city.' The exposition is long, full of interesting digressions and over-subtle interpretations of kindred texts, and the Latin text differs from the Hebrew basis of the R.V. The main thesis[1] is as follows: 'Its foundations are upon the holy mountains'—the mountains are the right place for a city, and the foundations are the Apostles and Prophets with Christ as the cornerstone of the foundations; the citizens are the stones. 'The Lord loves the gates of Zion above all the dwellings of Jacob'—and the Apostles and Prophets are the gates and we enter by Christ who is the door. The dwelling-places of Jacob stand for all states or cities, actual and imaginary. 'Glorious things are spoken of thee, city of God'—and the glorious things are that 'I (Jehovah) shall bear in mind Raab and Babylon, for the benefit of those (therein) who know me; Gentiles and Tyre and the people of the Ethiopians, these have been in thee'—that is, Gentiles even from the remotest countries shall belong to the city. But how would Gentiles come to Zion? 'A man shall say "Zion is my mother";'—they will come to Zion through a man—'And that man was born in her, and that man himself founded the City, even the All-Highest.' In other words Christ recognised Zion as His mother; He founded her that He might be born in her and the founder was Himself God. And how is this known? 'The Lord will tell it in the writings of the peoples and the leaders.' The leaders are those who are made leaders in the city itself, and they may be men of humble status—fishermen and publicans—for God chooses the weak things of the world. In this there is ground for rejoicing. 'The dwelling-place of all men who are made joyful, so far as men know real joy,[2] is in thee.'

The development of the 'earthly Zion' into the 'Holy City', the 'new Jerusalem', of the New Testament is familiar enough. The 'city of God' becomes the 'Jerusalem that is above',[3] an ideal city, no longer a city with an earthly citadel whether in Jerusalem or elsewhere. Nevertheless, the name Zion and the city of the living God still attract the early writers of the New Testament and have attracted Christians ever since. The writer of the Epistle to the Hebrews, for example, speaks of the city in

[1] For the Latin text see Notes, p. 278.
[2] St A's explanation of *tanquam*.   [3] Gal. iv. 26.

Heaven which God has made ready[1]; 'here we have no abiding city, but we seek that city which is to come.'[2] In one passage of the Epistle there seems almost to be an echo of the ideas of the eighty-seventh Psalm, 'Ye have already approached Mount Zion and the city of the living God, Jerusalem in Heaven, and ye have approached thousands of angels, a vast gathering and assembly of the first born, whose names are now entered in the roll of citizens in Heaven.'[3]

In this last passage the points which are of interest are (1) Jerusalem is now the ideal city, not the city of Palestine, as it was to the Psalmist; (2) the Greek word for 'gathering' is the classical word ($\pi\alpha\nu\acute{\eta}\gamma\upsilon\rho\iota\varsigma$) for a gathering for religious festivals, while the word for 'assembly' ($\acute{\epsilon}\kappa\kappa\lambda\eta\sigma\acute{\iota}\alpha$) is the word used (a) for the people assembled for legislative purposes; (b) for the Church; (3) the Epistle, as well as the Psalmist, imagines a citizen-roll ($\acute{\alpha}\pi\sigma\gamma\rho\acute{\alpha}\phi\eta$) in which the names of the citizens are already entered; (4) the city is composed of angels and men, and it will be seen later that the sharing of the city by angels and men is an idea on which St Augustine lays emphasis. But to him the city is, at the same time, in Heaven and on earth and is therefore not wholly ideal but partly actual. Whether St Augustine equated the city with the Church is a question which we must ask later.[4]

This 'Holy City' the seer of Apocalypse saw coming down new out of Heaven from God.[5] If this means the sudden dawn of a millennium on earth, the idea would be unacceptable to St Augustine who nowhere suggests that he looks forward to any golden age; in his view the earthly city, the counterpart of the city of God, will go on to the end of the world. If the vision points to the progressive realisation of a spiritual fact, now partly actual, but eventually to be fully actual, it would be in harmony with St Augustine's thought, though foreign to his manner of expression.

'City of God' or 'Citizenship in the City of God', *civitatem Dei* (see p. 20).

It would be inappropriate here to describe the power which the idea of citizenship exercised in the Graeco-Roman world. The Greek city-state developed a high conception of citizenship. Yet, until the philosophers took it in hand, it was an exclusive and narrow conception; privilege was closely guarded and was extended, if at all, with grudging caution. Rome, on the other hand, was generous; for she granted, though not readily at first, the rights and duties of citizenship to conquered enemies, and so turned them into devoted allies; later, as her imperial rule developed, she learned the secret, till then undiscovered, of reconciling an intensely eager

---

[1] Heb. xi. 16. [2] Heb. xiii. 14; cf. xi. 14. [3] Heb. xii. 22, 23.
[4] See p. 157. [5] Rev. iii. 12; xxi. 2.

local citizenship with loyalty to the Roman civilising mission. Though by the time of St Augustine the townships of the Empire had lost the proud independence of the second century A.D., partly through the extension of the franchise to the Roman world by Caracalla in A.D. 212, partly through the tight control resulting from the administration of Diocletian and later Emperors, yet the conception of citizenship still exerted its fascination upon educated minds as a political ideal, even though seen only in retrospect; for there were many who cast their eyes back over Roman history with sad regret.

But, as St Augustine read the Epistles of St Paul, written 350 years before, he would find nothing but pride in the Roman citizenship of which St Paul boasted as his inheritance; he was proud, too, of his citizenship of Tarsus, 'no mean city.'[1] For the present purpose, however, the passages are of most interest which reflect in metaphor St Paul's consciousness of citizenship. 'In all good conscience have I been a good citizen in the sight of God?'[2] which in the context can only mean that he had been a good citizen in that ideal Jewish state of which Jehovah was sovereign. Writing to the Philippians St Paul uses the same word with a different meaning, 'Only behave as good citizens in a way worthy of the Gospel of Christ,'[3] and here the state of which his readers are to be citizens can be nothing but the kingdom of Christ. Similarly, 'our commonwealth ($\pi o\lambda i\tau\epsilon\nu\mu a$) is already existing for us in heaven'[4] implies that the status of citizen may be seized now, and in the phrase 'ye are fellow citizens with the saints'[5] the present tense implies actual and not potential citizenship to be realised hereafter. The last word is significant; for, if it does not go so far as St Augustine in claiming that men share with angels membership of the city of God, at any rate they share it now with the saints who have already gone to their rest. To St Paul then the city already exists, and men on earth are to become its citizens. The city exists, in so far as it exists, here and now, and in heaven and hereafter: for between the two times and the two places no line can be drawn.

'As it exists in its present temporal pilgrimage among the pagans,' *sive in hoc temporum cursu inter impios peregrinatur.* For St Augustine, as for St Paul, the city in part exists here and now. It therefore has no affinity with any city or Utopia or millennium which is imagined as starting at some date not yet reached, or as lying outside time. Here and now it sojourns as a stranger in a strange land, and the strangeness of its environment is partly due to the *impii*, the pagans, among whom the earthly section of the city must live its life.

---

[1] Acts xxii. 28; xxi. 39. [2] Acts xxiii 1. [3] Phil. i 27.
[4] Phil. iii 20. [5] Eph. ii 19.

The picture of the Jews as dwellers in strange lands cherishing the hope of the promised land is familiar enough. The idea was caught up by the writers of the Epistles and from that day to this the life of the Christian as a pilgrimage has been a familiar image in every form of Christian writing and teaching. Here we need only point out that in the passages in the Epistles which use the idea of 'sojourning', the Greek word frequently used is the word denoting the status of 'resident aliens' (πάροικοι) officially recognised in the Greek city state; it is also combined with 'strangers' (ξένοι) that is, utter 'foreigners'. Yet another word 'pilgrim' (παρεπίδημος) is combined with 'foreigner', or with 'sojourner'; it simply denoted a foreigner residing in a place but possessing no rights at all.[1] The Vulgate translation (*peregrini, peregrinor*) maintains the technical idea of foreigner, for the *peregrini* were aliens resident in Rome but not possessing civic rights.

Christians then are sojourners in a strange land. Yet St Paul seems in one passage to contradict himself. Christians are no longer 'strangers or sojourners', for they are fellow citizens with the saints.[2] There is, of course, no real contradiction; seen by the side of the 'world' they are 'sojourners', seen by the side of the saints they are 'fellow-citizens'. But it is in contrast with the 'world' that Christians usually see themselves.

There is one passage, however, which bears more closely upon the text of St Augustine. In the famous chapter on faith in the Epistle to the Hebrews (xi) it is said that:

'By faith Abraham, on hearing his call, at once obeyed, to go forth into a place which he was to receive as his inheritance, and he went forth, while he knew not whither he was going. By faith he went to a land of his promise, as into a land belonging to another, and dwelt there as a sojourner, living in tents with Isaac and Jacob, the heirs with him of the same promise: for he expected to be given the city which has the foundations, whose architect and builder is God.'

The points worth notice here are (i) that Abraham did not know his route except that it led to the one city that was permanent, in contrast with the shifting camping places of his nomad life; his journey meant sojourning in strange lands; (ii) it was through his faith that he heard and on hearing obeyed the call, that he bore the trials of his enforced sojourn in the lands of others, that he cherished the vision of the permanent city of God. And in verse 13 the matter is summed up again: 'It was according to their faith that all these died—that is, the patriarchs—in faith, for they had not yet seen the fulfilment of the promises: they saw the vision of fulfilment from afar off and they rejoiced in it; they admitted that they were strangers and sojourners in the land; and men who make such

---

[1] Eph. ii. 19; 1 Pet. ii. 2; Heb. xi. 13.   [2] Eph. ii. 19.

admission as that make it evident for all to see that they are searching for a fatherland' (πατρίδα).

Faith is, not unexpectedly, the next term in St Augustine's definition of the city.

'Drawing its life from faith,' *ex fide vivens*. The phrase may originally come from Habakkuk,[1] where the full wording is 'the righteous man lives by faith'.[2] But between the prophet and the saint come the Epistles, in which the phrase and the thought are too familiar to need illustration; briefly 'faith' is used in the sense of 'confidence in things not seen'.[3] Though the city may not be visible, it is none the less real. At the same time the reminiscence of the 'righteous man' living by faith helps to prepare the reader for the tremendous emphasis which throughout will be laid by St Augustine—beginning with the next phrase—on the part which righteousness plays in the city. It is the main qualification for citizenship.

So far the city is on earth: but a section of it is now in heaven, as the next words go on to say.

'In the permanence of the eternal abiding-place which it now awaits in patience,' *in illa stabilitate aedis aeternae, quam nunc expectat per patientiam*. The passage seems to echo the phrase from the Epistle to the Hebrews, 'the city which has the foundations'; for 'permanence, *stabilitas*', refers to the nature of the structure—built to be permanent—rather than to the mere idea of continuousness.

'Till righteousness be turned into judgment,' *quoadusque iustitia convertatur in iudicium*. The end of the period of waiting will be marked by the triumph of righteousness, which will demand judgment being passed upon the unrighteous; during the period of waiting the unrighteous have flourished, and righteousness seems to be betrayed; but then righteousness will be seen to be justified. The word *iustitia*—as was explained on p. 14—carries the double notion of 'justice' and 'righteousness', as this its first occurrence exemplifies; justice demands that righteousness should now at last judge the unrighteous.

'Which it will fully obtain one day in final victory and perfected peace,' *deinceps adeptura per excellentiam victoria ultima et pace perfecta*. Victory is given at last and the reward of victory is peace. As will be seen, St Augustine has much to say upon peace as a universal aim.[4]

Such is the brief definition of the city with which St Augustine opens his work. His next sentence explains why the work was written. It was written, first in fulfilment of a promise, secondly, to counter the pagans who preferred their own gods to the God who was founder of the city.

'To defend that city. . . . . Marcellinus,' *hoc opere . . . suscepi*.

---

[1] Hab. ii. 4.   [2] cf. *dcD* xix. 14.   [3] cf. Heb. xi. 1.
[4] See especially the latter part of Book xix.

(i) The promise had been made to a certain Marcellinus, who is described in this passage as 'my very dear son' and elsewhere as 'my very dear friend and earnest student of the sacred writings' and as 'most acceptable to us in the love of Christ'.[1] In A.D. 411—that is, not long after the conquest of Rome by Alaric—the Emperor Honorius sent Marcellinus to Carthage to preside over a conference of the Catholics and the Donatists and to settle the dispute between them. Being a tribune and a lawyer he conducted the enquiry with impartiality[2] and decided in favour of the Catholics. The minutes of the meeting which are extant are recapitulated in St Augustine's *Breviculus collationis*.[3] But he was accused by the Donatists of taking bribes, and three letters of St Augustine urge him not to be harsh in his treatment of the misguided sectarians. Later he was put to death during the revolt of Heraclian, A.D. 413.

During his visit to Africa Marcellinus, who was a Christian, had been brought into close touch with Volusianus, the proconsul of Africa, who though a pagan had shown considerable interest in the Christian religion. Marcellinus was anxious for his conversion.

Accordingly we find in the correspondence of St Augustine letters to and from St Augustine and Volusianus, and also Marcellinus. In one letter (cxxxv) Volusianus asks St Augustine to clear up certain problems which were puzzling him, especially concerning the Incarnation. The next letter is from Marcellinus to St Augustine asking him not only to reply to Volusianus' questions, but also to explain to him the extent and the manner in which the ethics of the Sermon on the Mount apply to ordinary social and political life. In letter cxxxvii (17)[4] St Augustine deals with the problems. But the letter is of special interest because it seems to anticipate the theme of the *dcD*. '"Thou shalt love the Lord thy God with thy whole heart and thy whole soul and thy whole mind" and "thou shalt love thy neighbour as thyself". Herein is contained all physics, for all the causes of all natural things reside in God their Creator. Herein is all ethics, since a good and upright life cannot be moulded unless the objects of its love are the right objects and they are loved as they should be loved—namely God and one's neighbour. Herein is all logic, since the truth and the light of the reasonable soul can be only God. Herein is the welfare of every state worthy of praise, for a state cannot be founded nor preserved to the best advantage unless it rests upon and is held together by faith and lasting concord—unless the object of its love is the good of all which at its highest and truest is God—unless men love one another in Him with all sincerity, basing their love for one another on their love for Him from Whom they cannot conceal the motive of their love.'

[1] *Ep.* cxc. 20; clxvi. 7.   [2] *C. Th.* xvi. 5. 52 quotes an imperial decree recording this.
[3] *Patrol. Lat.* xliii. 613–650.   [4] Written A.D. 412.

In another letter (cxxxviii) to Marcellinus St Augustine refutes the view that Christianity had brought ruin upon the Roman Empire, and he goes on to condemn the morality of stage plays and to state some of the arguments in favour of Christianity. These are matters which are dealt with at length in the *dcD*.

This correspondence therefore may well have furnished the impulse for the writing of the work itself or may indicate that the purpose was already in the mind of St Augustine. But there is no direct reference to any express promise to Marcellinus to undertake the work; the promise may have been made verbally or in some letter not preserved.

But, if in some way St Augustine had made a promise to Marcellinus, he had already promised himself the task of writing upon the two cities. In a treatise begun in A.D. 401, though not finished till A.D. 415, St Augustine says[1] that two cities, with their foundations in the race of man, have been marked out by the two loves of which man is capable, love of others and love of self; one is the city of the righteous, the other of the unrighteous: 'These cities are intermixed in this temporal life, and in this way the world goes on, until they shall be separated in the final judgment, and the one of them, together with the good angels, attain everlasting life in their king, while the other, together with the bad angels, will be sent with their own king into everlasting fire. Perhaps, if God so will it, I will discourse upon these two cities at greater length in another work.'

The theme is touched upon in the same way in the treatise, *de rudibus catechizandis*, written about A.D. 400: 'Two cities, one of the wicked, the other of the saints, persist from the beginning of the human race until the end of this age; now they are intermingled physically, though distinct as concerns their wills; in the day of judgment they will be separated physically as well. For all men who love pride and all temporal domination, together with the empty pomp and outward show of arrogance, and all spirits who love such things and seek their own glory by the subjugation of men—all these are bound together in one fellowship of men: even if they fight with one another for their objectives, they are plunged into the same abysses by the weight of their own greed, and so are united again in the likeness of their characters and their deserts. On the other hand all men and all spirits who seek in humility the glory of God rather than their own and pursue Him in piety—all these belong to one fellowship. None the less the most merciful God is patient towards wicked men and offers to them opportunity of penitence and correction.'[2]

Thus, though the correspondence with Marcellinus is the occasion of the writing of the *dcD*, and the occasion is reinforced by the capture of the 'eternal city' by Alaric, the thought of the two cities had clearly been in

[1] *de gen. ad litt.* xi. 20. [2] *c.* 31.

St Augustine's mind years earlier,[1] and the resolution to write about them at some time had been recorded in a published treatise.

Marcellinus is addressed at the beginning of the first book of the *dcD* and also of the second book; no reference is made to him later. We know that he died on the Ides of September A.D. 413. Hence the *dcD* was begun early in A.D. 413 or perhaps in 412.

(ii) In the second place the *dcD* was written to counter the pagans, as the sub-title (*contra paganos*) also shows. If the work had been begun when the idea of writing it first occurred to its author, it would doubtless have been written 'to counter the pagans', and many of its arguments against pagan standards in religion and ethics would have been the same. But the sack of Rome gave a new urgency to its writing and cannot but have affected its form and content. For the fall of Rome shook the foundation of men's belief in the past and hope for the future. The need therefore was apparent for a philosophy of life and an interpretation of history which would steady the bewildered minds of men; the greater the need, the greater the opportunity, and the *dcD* rose to the occasion.

'A great and difficult task,' *magnum opus et arduum*. My proposed work is ambitious, says St Augustine, for it is no easy task to convince the proud of the virtue of humility. Humility is not the mark of a nation which regards as its highest boast the power to 'spare the conquered and to break the proud in war'. To claim this right is a mark of pride, for 'God alone resists the proud'.

This is a noteworthy passage, which the rest of the book develops. How is the downfall of the Roman Empire to be explained? It is due to pride, the sin which no man can claim to punish; to claim that right is an arrogant usurpation of divine right. The collapse of Rome is not to be judged upon the human plane: neither Alaric nor his Goths are the judges of Rome: rather they are the instruments through which judgment was passed at the level of divine justice, and the right of God to punish those who usurp His place was vindicated in history.

This point of view is only hinted at in the paragraph of the text under consideration; there is no utter condemnation of Rome, whose name is not even mentioned. St Augustine's readers are not invited to condemn Rome; in the first place, it would scarcely have been a tactful beginning, and, secondly, St Augustine himself would not so invite them, for he admires much of the Roman achievement. But his readers are told at once what is the root cause of the weakness and collapse of the Empire, and they are told by having the very lines which glorify the secret of Roman power quoted against them as containing the secret of her ruin. They are

[1] For reff. to the two cities in other of A's writings see note on p. 278.

then shown that this cause operates according to a divine law (*divinae legis*) well known to Christians. On the first page, therefore, his readers are prepared for the doctrine that historical events cannot be assessed except in the light of the divine governance of the world operating according to law. The collapse of Rome therefore is not inexplicable; the consternation which it causes naturally follows if Romans have been led to find their secret and their mission in the very behaviour which justifies their downfall.

'Pride' and 'humility' are ideas which permeate the *dcD* and indeed all St Augustine's writings. The fall of the angels was due to pride (cf. p. 150); the fall of man was due to pride (cf. p. 148): and both called out divine justice and mercy.

To St Augustine pride is the root of all sin, as will be apparent in later chapters. To the Graeco-Roman world 'pride' had been a notion familiar enough; the pride of the individual, of the family, of the nation, and the resulting 'envy' of heaven and sure nemesis—these were commonplaces to tragedians and moralists and historians. But by the time of St Augustine the sequence, pride-envy-punishment, had lost its cogency; for centuries the Empire of Rome had left no room for the spectacle of nations waxing or waning. The rise of the individual to power and wealth and his fall to destruction was common enough, but the change in his fortune was attributable to infidelity to the Empire or to the civil power. Or else the notion of a far-reaching divine justice was superseded by a belief in the influence of a goddess of chance, and chance excludes reason. Or, the success or disaster was due to the power of daemons into whose motives men could not pry: in short, the caprice of fortune or of daemons leaves no room for explanation.

Though the ancient world had once taken seriously the conception of pride and nemesis, it had not gone beyond prescribing that men should avoid pride; it had not progressed from the negative notion to the positive ideal of humility, which is the peculiarly Christian virtue. If pride runs through the *dcD* as the cause of evil, humility may equally be said to be preached throughout as the prerequisite to the righteousness of the city of God.

It may be observed that the sentence of Vergil from which St Augustine takes his quotation runs in full as follows: 'These are the skills which you shall acquire to form your culture—to impose habits of peace, to spare the conquered, and to break the proud in war.' The first of Rome's missions is to impose peace; St Augustine has already spoken of peace, not as the first, but as the ultimate stage in the struggle for righteousness, and in the nineteenth book he has much to say of the peace which proceeds from 'order'. But to him peace is the peace proceeding from within,

from a willing submission to a law of order, and not from an order imposed from outside by a victorious power.

'The earthly city', *civitas terrena*. It is a natural temptation to interpret 'the earthly city' as the collective term for historical states and communities which had existed before St Augustine's time or were contemporary with him, and in particular to equate it with the Roman Empire. Though no doubt in this passage St Augustine has Rome in mind, such an interpretation would be wrong, as will be seen in the course of the book. The *civitas terrena* as such, no less than the *civitas Dei*, is a conception, not a fact, though it is partly composed of fact; both are 'ideal' in the sense of being 'ideas' not wholly realised. The 'earthly city' is the antithesis of the city of God; if, as has been seen, the city of God necessarily excludes, the 'earthly city' is all that is excluded. But, as the city of God has never wholly existed as a *civitas*, for it takes its citizens from the past and from the present and the future and from a multitude of places—so the earthly city has not existed as a *civitas*. It, too, covers the past, the present and the future, and it cannot be identified with any state which has been, or is, since within a given state there are elements of good which are more related to the city of God than opposed to it. The city of God is a fellowship excerpted, as it were, from all time and all places, identified with none, but built up conceptually from fragments which had and have and will have historical existence. The same is true of its negation; it, too, can be identified wholly with no community at any given time or place. It, too, is a conception framed out of historical fragments. It is important to St Augustine's thought to realise that the 'earthly city' as such is, in the colloquial sense, 'no earthly city.'

Before leaving St Augustine's preface we may note that Dante, who used the *dcD* extensively in his *de Monarchia*, ends his first chapter with a sentence reminiscent of St Augustine. 'I lay my hand', he says, 'to a task which is difficult (*arduum*) and indeed beyond my powers, but I put my trust not so much in my own virtues as in that light of the lavish Giver "who gives to all liberally and upbraideth not".' Again, like countless other panegyrists of Rome, Dante quotes (ii. 7) Vergil's lines, *Tu regere imperio* . . . as summing up Rome's divine mission, and he holds (ii. 5) that Rome's Empire sprang from the fountain of 'piety'—the very word which St Augustine will not use of her and which he reserves for Christians. To him the Roman claim to a divine mission, so confidently reasserted by Dante in support of the Holy Roman Empire, is an act of arrogance, which is also impiety, since it usurps the rights of God. None the less he holds that Roman history was, in a sense which we shall see later, under the Providence of God.

THE ORIGIN OF THE TWO CITIES

Extracts 2-6

We pass now to the origin of the two cities. Why should there be two cities, one good, one bad? This question raises for St Augustine the problem of evil—why there is evil and whence it comes.

At this point a word is necessary as to the purpose of the reflections that follow. The teaching of St Augustine about evil and its nature, the original corruption of man's nature and the question of free-will occupy a large proportion of his writings, especially those directed against the Pelagian heresy. Again, the *dcD* includes much discussion of these questions both in the twelfth and fourteenth books, from which the extracts are taken, and elsewhere. Of all this no account is taken in the notes that follow. The purpose of the extracts is limited (*a*) to showing whence in St Augustine's view comes the cleavage between the two cities and (*b*) to raising the problems which are inherent in his theory of that cleavage and in any treatment of the problem of evil. The purpose of the notes is to make explicit these problems, to put them in relation to one another, and to make a starting point for further studies.

The original difference, says St Augustine, is to be found in a difference of will, with the result that the will which becomes different becomes evil. What is the cause of this difference?

The Christian is committed by his faith to reject two possible explanations. The first is that evil is to be traced to a power that is the rival of God and of equal power with Him; on this theory the universe is to be explained as a Dualism, an explanation which the Christian will not accept. But the alternative to Dualism, namely Monism, which assumes one supreme source of all being, seems to present a tremendous difficulty; for, if all creation is the work of one creator, evil, no less than good, must be his work, and such a conclusion is contrary to the Christian doctrine that God is good and therefore cannot be the author of evil. The first sentence of the first extract strikes this note clearly; the created natures of the good and the bad angels alike are identical essentially, and God their creator is good. But the problem remains, why or how did any difference arise?

The passages chosen for the selection may be summed up as follows: the will, from its very nature as will, has the power of turning inwards towards itself, or outwards towards God and His will. If it turns inwards, it does so because it feels that its own resources are sufficient for itself, and such a feeling is pride and its object is self. The pride of self-sufficiency, then, is the beginning of evil. Though pride may seem to be something

148

fine and even triumphant, nevertheless it is mean and inferior. For it prefers something less, the finite self, to something greater, the infinite God. If we ask why the will turns inwards towards itself, we can give no ultimate reason; all we can say is that there is a falling away from the real nature, a failure of strength, a failure to realise what it might have realised, a default from the higher to the lower, and the accompaniment to such failure and defection is unhappiness. Hence there is no 'efficient' cause for the evil will, for the cause is inside it: the cause is deficient rather than efficient. But, as St Augustine sees, this is not explanation, but is rather description; and he says frankly that he cannot pretend to knowledge of this mystery of evil. But he goes on to assert again that evil cannot be due to God who created man's nature; therefore the will was created good. Its default can be due only to an act of its own rather than to any positive act outside itself; the evilness of evil lies in the fact that it is man's way rather than God's way. Evil is man's nature spoilt, and its treatment consists not in the addition of anything as an antidote or a specific, nor in the removal of anything, but only in the healing of what was spoilt. Hence the will is free, but it is free to wrest itself out of the straight. The will was made free by God, and the God who made it free is the God who, if it has spoilt itself, has power to make it whole again, or to make it safe, or to 'save' it. If, then, the root of sin is pride of will, the only means of preventing the will from corrupting itself is to pursue humility, a humility which, therefore, is seen to be, paradoxically, the greatest thing in the world.

This attempted analysis or tentative description of the origin and nature of the evil will rests primarily upon an ethical and spiritual basis. Though St Augustine, as a result of his early moral experiences and his sudden and violent conversion, is exceptionally conscious of the evilness of evil and the tendency of man to choose the worse however much he strives for the better, nevertheless this consciousness is in some degree a characteristic common to most men who attach any importance to moral life and reflect upon the nature of the moral will. All speculation upon the origin and nature of the evil in man springs logically from this consciousness, and all stories, supposedly historical or frankly allegorical, assume and spring from this experience. Speculation upon it is bound, from the nature of the theme, to force certain problems to the forefront, and to suggest various but similar answers to them.

The theory that the origin of evil is to be found in the defect of will, in a failure or default due to choice, seems to presuppose that the will was originally free from that defect—unless the will was originally created with the defect in it, a supposition which compromises the goodness of its Creator. Hence the tendency arises to assume an original state of perfection before the will corrupted itself. This assumption is made in the passage

of St Augustine before us, and much more clearly and emphatically elsewhere in the *dcD* and in his other writings. Indeed the theory of 'original
righteousness' passed into the Christian thought of the West largely
through the authority of St Augustine; in St Paul, though there are a few
rhetorical turns of phrase which may suggest it, the theory is conspicuously
absent.

The next step in speculation is to ask when this defect or weakness first
occurred; for this question is natural unless we are to assume an infinite
regress, or in other words we are to be satisfied with a psychological
description and are to give up any attempt to say when or where the defect
first (originally) occurred. The question has given rise to several answers,
not all of which can be mentioned here. In the passages selected St
Augustine assigns the first default to the angels before the creation of
man, and the angels, being made by God, were good but by preferring
themselves to God fell from original righteousness and sinned.

To this solution put forward by St Augustine modern thought is apt to
reply as follows: 'Why go back to angels? Why not start with man? for
we know nothing about angels; to introduce a hypothetical unknown is
not to help explanation. Further, they do not solve the problem, for the
problem of evil remains.' To the theory of 'original righteousness' in the
angels objection is not usually taken, since nothing is known about the
origin of angels, while something is known about the early development
of man on this planet.

But speculation finds it impossible to begin with man, for not all the evil
with which we are familiar springs from man. 'All creation groaneth and
travaileth;' sub-human nature appears to be infected with evil; blind and
ruthless cruelty—nature red in tooth and claw—seems to operate throughout creation and appears to give the lie to the provident and merciful love
which Christians assume to lie at the heart of the universe. Further, evil
seems sometimes to be supra-human; there have been times when evil and
corruption have seemed to descend, as though from outside, upon portions
of the human race, and to carry them down to depths of depravity of which
it would have been difficult to imagine man capable. The individual, too,
at times feels as though there were some agency working from without to
compel him to do that which he would not. All this may be summed up in
St Paul's conviction that he fought not against men but against 'principalities and powers'.

If, then, evil is to be found at sub-human, human and supra-human
levels, its origin must be pushed back to a time prior to the appearance of
man on the planet. This is the necessity which the hypothesis of a self-
corruption of the angels is intended to meet. Stories about some such pre-
terrestrial corruption take many forms in pagan and Christian tradition.

In the Old Testament the crude story of the angels who lusted after the women of men[1] was quickly superseded by other stories, and in particular by the Adam story, which, however, is concerned to account for the entry of evil into man and ignores the origin of evil in the sub-human and supra-human spheres. But the story of Michael and the dragon which occurs in Enoch and in Revelation is an attempt on lines familiar to pagan mythology to push back the origin of all evil to a pre-human stage, and to find the origin of evil in a self-corruption of angels. Modern restatements of the problem are compelled to do much the same; though they discard the term 'angels', they assume a corruption proceeding from within which vitiates the life-stream of the universe or contaminates the world-soul, and in such a conception they account for the origin of evil in all forms of life, whether on the human plane or above or below it. Whether the conception of a life-stream or a world-soul is easier than the older notion of angels may be doubted by some. But St Augustine at any rate found much the same problem as his modern successors, and his hypothesis is not on very different lines from theirs. For him and for them the problem rests primarily upon psychological and ethical experience; and for him and for them it is necessary to find some one point at which the corruption occurred and to place that point in the period before the appearance of man; for him and for them original righteousness is assumed in some plane of being, for, if it is not, the conception of corruption is illogical.

In the passage selected St Augustine describes the origin of evil in man in the same way as he has already described its origin in angels. He begins by emphasising that the human will was made upright and good; he goes on to describe how it corrupted itself by preferring what was less for what was greater, by turning in upon itself and satisfying its own selfish pride. Here lies the psychological origin of human sin. Elsewhere in his voluminous works St Augustine erects an elaborate doctrine of the fall of man, adopting the story of the fall of the first man Adam as the historical cause and occasion of the entry of sin into the world upon the human plane. All this speculation and all criticism of it is here ignored as irrelevant to the present purpose.

St Augustine assumes the original righteousness of man—the human will was created good. It will be remembered that, when we considered original righteousness earlier, we found that, if the goodness of the Creator was to be safeguarded, and the infinite regress was to be avoided, created beings, at some point or some plane of existence, had to be assumed to be originally righteous in order that they might be corrupted. And the hypothesis of the self-corruption of angels before the creation was put forward by St Augustine, and the hypothesis of the corruption of the life-stream

[1] Gen. vi.

or world-soul by modern speculation. But when we come to man, we need not assume original righteousness, for evil has already originated before the appearance of man, and we cannot assume it if we adopt the findings of modern thought. Neither history nor science finds any trace of a time when man was in a state of original righteousness. On the contrary they postulate an amoral state from which man emerged into moral consciousness. Christian thought holds that the process of such emergence was under divine intention and guidance, and that the difference between 'amoral' and 'moral' ultimately presupposes something which cannot be explained otherwise; but such a point of view does not necessitate 'original righteousness' which is historically untrue. Some of the metaphors, therefore, which St Augustine uses, 'fall' or 'flaw', cannot be admitted, if they are pressed to involve an original righteousness. On the other hand one of his phrases—though it occurs in the description of the self-corruption of the angels, and not of men—would be more consonant with modern views: 'the angels were unwilling to safeguard their strength for His service, and, instead of having a fuller being which they could have had if they had clung to Him who is the absolute being, preferred themselves to Him and so preferred that which was less. This was the first default'—a metaphor which is open to objection—'this was the first failure of strength.' In the phrase 'failure of strength' is to be found a better description of human evil in retrospect than the common term 'fall'—a word which has no biblical authority and seems to presuppose an original state of righteousness from which to fall. This 'weakness of will' in a creature intended to rise to higher level may have been brought about because that creature was influenced by powers of evil originating in a pre-human era and on a suprahuman plane; but, however that may be, the conception of failure to rise through weakness of will, failure to subordinate lower impulses to higher aims, is a notion more satisfactory to the modern view of the early history of man than the idea of 'flaw' or 'fall' or declension from some imagined state of perfection. If this weakness is inherited, as it appears to be, both biologically and socially, it may in a sense be called 'original sin'. But this is a term which must be used with great care: for it has long been associated with 'original righteousness', and with 'original guilt', a theory which rivets the first man's guilt upon his successors, and which is as objectionable morally as 'original righteousness' is objectionable historically.

The problem of the freedom of the will is not discussed here; for the selection of passages does not contain even such treatment of the problem as St Augustine undertakes in the *dcD*. But *Extract 5a* contains just enough to point the way to further consideration of the problem by the reader. The will is free when it is not in bondage to evil; when it turns to

good, it does so through a self-determination of itself. In other words, will, if it is will, is free: if it is in bondage to something outside itself, it is not will; if it determines itself in the direction of good, it can do so only by self-determination from within, and then it is will. But the weakness of will which is inherent in man of itself prevents the will determining itself in the direction of good, unless the will is healed and made whole by God; thus, in making the will whole, God frees it and makes it really will, that is, self-determined from within.

This brief passage is enough just to indicate the nature of the controversy of St Augustine with the Pelagians. To St Augustine the aid of God is a pre-requisite to that strength of the will which will bring about good. To the Pelagians each act of choice is an unaided choice of the will, and each act is the result of fresh choice; unless the act were due to an unaided choice, it could have no merit in the sight of God. To the Pelagians each man at each moment is the captain of his soul; to St Augustine he is determined by the inherent weakness of his will (which causes him to sin against his real nature and against God) unless God's grace strengthens his will and frees his whole personality. As man's weakness is due to causes—heredity, original sin, the inherent weakness of human nature—which are external to him, so external aid alone will give him the power to free himself from them.

To many people Pelagianism, which has affinities with Stoicism,[1] is attractive, for it seems to proclaim man's release from much that was once thought to bind him. It is based, however, on an incomplete analysis of human experience; in isolating one element, choice, it forgets other elements, namely weakness of will and the compelling power of habit. It virtually destroys religion, for it releases man, by virtue of unaided free-will, as much from God as from the devil. In fact, it reasserts the old contention of classical thought that 'virtue and vice alike are in our power'.[2] It affirms human perfectibility through knowledge and through a free choice between the alternatives presented by knowledge. While it emphasises personal responsibility, it destroys personality, for it neglects interest and love and affection, and fails to recognise that man cannot build his destiny in knowledge alone; for knowledge must be reinforced by will, and will by love if personality is to become whole and alive. Without love will is powerless, indeed almost meaningless.

Extract 6 is of great importance, as will be seen when the nineteenth book is reached. Love and will are the supreme ideas in St Augustine's view of human personality; and since he stresses that the city or state is a

[1] The contrast between Augustinianism at its best (i.e. without some of the extreme teachings as to original guilt and predestination) and Pelagianism at its most rigorous is virtually the contrast between Christianity and the classical outlook. See further, p. 263.
[2] Ar. *Eth.* 1113b. 6.

conglomerate of individuals, each with his loves and hates, the city itself assumes a character which is but the reflection of the loves and wills of its citizens. The state acquires no mysterious entity or personality, nor is it endowed with special virtues, because it is a state; its character is that of its citizens, whose characters depend upon the objects of their love and of their will. The city of God and the earthly city are divided by what they love and will, and human states are to be judged by the same criterion. The whole substance of the *dcD* will have been missed unless throughout its study it is recollected that not mind and knowledge but love and will form the basis of human character, that love is the source of power to influence the will, when knowledge by itself is helpless.

THE GROWTH OF THE CITIES

Extracts 7-12

The origin of the two cities being thus found in the different 'loves' reinforcing the will which is inherently weak, St Augustine goes on to consider their growth. They were launched on their careers on earth by Cain and Abel and have gone on ever since. The six extracts which follow show (*a*) the founders of the two cities, and the first symptoms of the internal dissension which has always been a characteristic of the 'earthly city' (No. 7), (*b*) the city of God before the advent of Christ (No. 8), (*c*) the growth of the Church (Nos. 9-12).

Having explained the origin of the two cities St Augustine launches them on their course. He takes Cain and Abel as their founders; Cain's title as the earthly founder is 'the diabolical jealousy which the evil feel towards the good, for no other reason than that they are evil and the good are good'. But the two brothers remind St Augustine of the other two brothers, Romulus and Remus, the founders of Rome; and he finds in them the prototype of the internal dissension which is characteristic of 'the earthly city'. And so from this point (xv. 5 to xviii. 46) there follows a long and rambling synopsis of Jewish history and reflections on the nature of the history of the Mediterranean, Rome naturally claiming the major part. Having reached the Christian era and the dispersion of the Jews as foretold by the prophets, St Augustine pauses to note that prophecies about Christ were made by men from other nations than the Jewish nation, as the Jews themselves are bound to admit. Job is an example: he surpassed his contemporaries in righteousness and loyalty to God[1]: and from this example it may be gathered that there were many others in

[1] Cf. Job i. 8.

other nations who belong to the heavenly Jerusalem, since to them also Christ Jesus was revealed.

From these selected passages it can be gathered that:

(*a*) the heavenly city is not synonymous with the Church, for it includes men who lived in pre-Christian times and many who came from divers nations[1]: and to this it may be added from numerous passages in the work that within the Church there are many who are *impii* and so do not belong to the heavenly city.

(*b*) the earthly city is not the Roman Empire, for it goes back to earlier times than Rome; nor, as will be seen later, is the Roman Empire as such condemned by St Augustine.

These are points which will be elaborated later. At the moment we may ask what is the title of non-Christians to membership of the heavenly city. Job's title appears to be righteousness and loyalty to God (*iustitia pietasque*): from him it can be inferred that others also had a similar title, for others 'have lived according to God and have pleased Him'.

St Augustine does not make clear in this passage what he means by the revelation of Christ to Job, nor how far he is prepared to go in opening the city to non-Christian Saints. The passage is set in a context discussing prophecy concerning the coming of Christ. But he goes on to say that none can satisfy this title unless he has a revelation of the one Mediator of God and man. The passage as it stands might be interpreted in two ways, either that to live as Job lived is in itself a revelation of Christ or that the only way in which Job's life can in any way be accounted for is to suppose that he had a direct revelation of Christ. There is no doubt that the second interpretation is what St Augustine intended. There is of course no Messianic prophecy in the Book of Job. But there is the famous chapter on Wisdom[2]; and, as we shall see, the Christian identified the Wisdom of God, spoken of in the Old Testament and the Wisdom literature, with the Logos of the Fourth Gospel and so with Christ. And there is also the famous passage, 'I know that my Vindicator liveth'—which has since been taken up into the Burial Service and into Handel's Messiah.[3]

The idea that the 'Word' inspired the Hebrew writers is very common in earlier writers. For example, Irenaeus (d. A.D. 202) says that 'all who foretold the coming of Christ received their inspiration from the Son'.[4] Tertullian (d. c. A.D. 240) says that Christ spake by Moses, 'for He was the spirit of the Creator,'[5] Origen (d. c. A.D. 254) that 'Christ the Word of God was in Moses and the prophets . . . and by His spirit they spake and did all things.'[6] And in St Augustine himself the patriarchs and prophets are described as 'citizens of that holy city' 'to whom by prophecy was

---

[1] Cf. xix. 17.   [2] Job xxviii.   [3] xix. 25.   [4] *adv. haer.* iv. 7. 2.
[5] *adv. Marc.* iii. 16.   [6] *de princ.* i. 1; iv. 15.

revealed the future humbleness of God our King and Lord Jesus Christ, so that by faith in it they might be healed from all pride and conceit', 'those holy men were members of the church although in this life they lived before the time when Christ the Lord was born according to the flesh.'[1] But perhaps this point of view, which is familiar to students of early Christian writers, may here be most conveniently illustrated by a passage from the 'Ecclesiastical History' of Eusebius, who died about A.D. 340. 'Even from the day of man's creation' the Divine Logos 'was recognised by all who were reputed to be conspicuous for righteousness and for pre-eminence in religion—recognised by the pure eyes of mental apprehension and reverenced as it is right to reverence the child of God. Thus did Moses the great servant and his friends recognise the Logos, and before him Abraham, foremost of all, and his children, and the righteous men and the prophets who have since appeared. And the Logos Himself never relaxing in piety to the Father has taught all men the knowledge of the Father'. Then follows a list of such revelations—for example, to Abraham by the oak of Mamre, to Jacob, to Joshua ('chief captain of the host of the Lord'). Finally the Wisdom books, argues Eusebius, add their testimony,[2] and he concludes with the words, 'Let this be our brief demonstration that the divine Logos pre-existed and appeared to some, if not to all men.' Eusebius then explains why the full revelation of the Divine Word was not given earlier; men were incapable of receiving it. Through the Hebrews, who 'clung to true religion', was spread an 'intro-duction to spiritual principles' till 'that same divine and heavenly Logos appeared at the beginning of the Roman Empire through man'. 'The very name of Jesus and particularly of Christ was honoured by the god-fearing prophets of old' continues Eusebius; but his proof rests upon verbal argu-ments which are inadmissible; for example, the word Christos which is the Greek of the Septuagint for the Anointed of the Lord is taken as evidence that the prophets foretold Christ.[3]

It is impossible to consider here the methods by which the early Chris-tian writers interpreted Scripture and the reasons for those methods. They saw in the O.T. types and symbols of Christianity, both the historical events and the doctrine. Whereas we should seek to trace and describe development and growth, they were concerned to argue that nothing had changed, that the Christian church and its doctrine were contained in the religion of the Jews. Indeed their point of view might almost be put in the words of Westcott written in 1851—'The Gospel was no sudden or soli-tary message. The legend of Pallas is the very converse of the Nativity. Christianity is in one sense as ancient as the Creation, resting on a founda-

[1] de cat. rud. 33.   [2] Gen. xviii. 1; xxxii. 30; Josh. v; Prov. viii. 12, 15, 16, 22-30.
[3] Eusebius, H. E. 1.2; cf. Justin, Tryph., 43-73.

tion wide as the world and old as time. Step by step the groundwork of the Church was laid in the silent depths, and at last when all was ready it rose above the earth that all men might consciously combine to rear the spiritual temple of the living God.'[1]

The early writers wished to emphasise with all their power that the God who is behind the N.T. is also the God who was behind the O.T.; that Christianity is not 'new-sprung'. That is one thing. It is a different thing to say that the patriarchs were conscious of having, as it were, a preview of the Second Person of the Christian revelation. In their anxiety to emphasise the unity of the two dispensations that is precisely what those writers do assert, and the passage of St Augustine under consideration is in the same line of thought.

But in fact there is no need to go outside the N.T. itself for a comparable passage. 'These things said Isaiah because he saw his glory and he spake of him'.[2] On this verse Dr. Temple wrote, 'The prophet had apprehended this[3] through a vision of the glory of Christ—who is thus identified with Jehovah; and this is correct, for Jehovah is God revealed; and God revealed is the Logos, Word, self-utterance of God; and the Logos is Jesus Christ.'[4]

Extract 9 makes it clear that the city of God is not co-extensive with the Church, for the good and the bad are gathered into the Church's net till the final separation. Many similar passages could be quoted. Yet very many passages could be quoted in which the city of God and the Church appear to be identical: the concluding words of *Extract 11* announce that the Church, not the city of God as might be expected, has travelled onwards since the time of Abel.

It is clear from a wider study than can be undertaken here that sometimes St Augustine seems to identify the Church and the city of God, in others to differentiate them. The truth is that in some contexts, as is appropriate to them, he treats the Church in its best aspects and in its best moments, not as identical with, but as representative of, the city of God; under other aspects, e.g. as containing unrighteous members, he treats it as sharply divided from the city of God. The same is true, as was seen earlier, of the earthly city; existing states, in their worst aspects, represent more nearly the 'city of unrighteousness'; in their better moments they are better than that city. Or it might be put in another way: the Church is the society which above all others devotes its efforts to the establishment of the city of God, and so may loosely be spoken of as the city, though strictly it contains many unworthy of the city. Individuals or societies

[1] *Introduction to the Study of the Gospels* (5th edition), p. 48.   [2] John xii. 41.
[3] That God causes the appropriate consequence of sin to result by the law of the order of creation.
[4] *Readings in St. John's Gospel*, p. 202 (complete edition, 1945).

157

who have no interest in the city of God belong to the earthly city; they conduct themselves and organise themselves apart from God. But occasionally St Augustine loosely speaks of political societies or 'states' as the earthly city. But this is only because, speaking generally, they have shown no concern for the city of God, not because such societies are from their nature the earthly city.

THE PROVIDENCE OF GOD AND THE ROMAN EMPIRE

Extracts 13-21

The nine extracts which follow (13-21) are taken from the fifth book, that is to say, from the concluding chapters of that part of the work in which St Augustine set out to show that the evils of the age cannot be attributed to the ban which Christianity lays upon the pagan cults.

They are given in this place (that is, after extracts from books fifteen and eighteen), because the summary of Jewish and Christian history and of 'secular' history which St Augustine gives in books fifteen to eighteen does not admit of summary and is not of great value. They are important because it is reasonable to ask (1) whether in St Augustine's view earthly states are of any value and whether the Roman Empire, in spite of its worship of false gods and false ideals, serves any good purpose at all in the scheme of things; (2) whether God's Providence extends to earthly states at all. In the nineteenth book, as we shall see, much will be said about secular government, and it is essential to an understanding of this book to see, if only in outline, what view St Augustine takes of history and in particular of the great organisation within which civilisation had moved for centuries.

Extract 13

The first few words are extremely important, not only for St Augustine's view of history, but as his criticism on ancient philosophy and as the key to the *dcD* and particularly book nineteen.

He assumes the existence of God. In another passage[1] he had argued that to look into nature and to find there measure, number and order compels the observer to look for the craftsman; or in other words, values are to be detected in nature, and not imported into it by man. Here the assumption is made that behind nature and history there is a God who is the source of values.

[1] *de Gen. contra Manich.* i. 25, 26.

But he immediately asserts that that God is a Trinity of Persons and is the Creator and Maker of all spirit and body. The implications of this as a criticism of classical thought are tremendous; only some of the headings can be indicated.

(i) In supposing the existence of one God Christianity found itself in harmony with Greek philosophic thought and with Hebrew prophecy, both of which, like Christianity, were in opposition to the polytheism of contemporary practice.

(ii) In assuming that this one God had created the world, Christianity was in harmony with the religion of the Hebrews, but differed profoundly from the speculations of Plato and Aristotle. To Plato God was the 'manufacturer' of the world, but He manufactured it according to an existing pattern, namely, the eternal forms or ideas which He did not create. To Aristotle God was the model or pattern on which the world was trying to create itself; God did not create it.

Even slight acquaintance with the culture and philosophy of the classical world makes sufficiently familiar the problems and difficulties with which earnest speculation and reflection upon experience were presented —the problem of the one and the many and how they could be reconciled, of the relation of form and matter, of the possibility of permanence and change, of the transcendence and immanence of God, of law and freedom, of eternity and time, of thought and sense.

In making God the Creator of the world Christianity asserted the unity of the natural world and the unity of all knowledge of that world. But it asserted even more; by assuming God and supposing that He created the world Christianity asserted its view that the existence of that natural world was not, and was not capable of being, derived by man through the medium of his senses, but was an assumption made by natural science, since only on that assumption could a science of the natural world exist.

Now classical thought, like much modern thought, believed either that the existence of a natural order was given by experience (which is not so), and therefore the assumption of a Creator was unnecessary, *or* that the natural order was illusion (which makes nonsense of man's life and makes natural science impossible). Christianity corrected the mistake of classical thought by pointing out that natural science must rest upon a supposition not given by experience, namely, that the world of nature exists, and that natural science, therefore, does make the assumption which the Christians make, namely, that the natural order was created by God. For what we presuppose (and we presuppose because we cannot prove, yet cannot not presuppose), we presuppose by an act which Christianity calls faith, and faith is religious in its nature. Therefore, in presupposing we are stating something which we hold about God.

In making the initial act of faith which cannot be avoided if we analyse the presuppositions of science correctly, that God created the world, Christianity includes the faith that He created man.

(iii) When St Augustine insists at this point that the God who created the world and man is a Trinity, he is again criticising ancient philosophy. Ancient philosophy and in particular Platonism was familiar with the idea of a self-differentiating unity which it called 'logos'—a principle which could subdivide itself while maintaining its essential unity. This the Christians asserted is true of God, and on this assumption are to be explained the manifold realms of nature. 'By Him all things were made and without Him was not anything made' is what is said of the Logos in the Fourth Gospel. But Christian belief differed from classical belief in maintaining that the Logos was made flesh.

The difficulty of ancient thought had always been to bring together the two worlds of thought and experience, the Creator and his creation, the one and the many. In the self-differentiating creativity of the Logos, revealed in time in Jesus Christ, Christians found the answer to their riddles.

(iv) But creation cannot be conceived as a single act, however much that act may differentiate itself into order and laws. As Greek philosophers had realised, motion is a characteristic of the natural world; and modern physics is replacing the idea of body by the idea of motion. But, once again, the idea that natural things move is not given to us by experience; the idea of motion is a presupposition necessary to enable us to put together the data of experience to make a science. Motion, therefore, is as much a presupposition as the natural world itself, since it is a motion within the natural world. To the idea, therefore, of God the Creator as a unity, and a self-differentiating unity causing the manifold realms of nature, we must add that of God the Creator as the source of motion, and the world of nature moves because it is moved by Him.

It is not, however, only in the realm of natural science that St Augustine invokes the idea of the Trinity to solve the difficulties of ancient thought; God is not only the 'creator of all body' but also of all spirit. This means that all the presuppositions which the sciences, other than natural science, make and which are presuppositions because they are not given by experience of sense-data and yet are necessary to scientists, imply the creative activity of a self-differentiating God who created and sustains with His activity the realm of spirit. The values, as, for example, truth and beauty and goodness, which are treated by their appropriate sciences are presupposed by these sciences, for they are not derivable from experience as such. And, since they are presupposed, they are thus stated to be due to the creative activity of God. For example, the conception of right and

wrong cannot be derived from experience; it is a presupposition of all moral philosophy, and to say this is to say that it is due to the creative activity of God.

(v) To sum up. To St Augustine the view which must be taken of history depends upon our view of man, and our view of man depends upon our view of creation, and the nature of the Creator. Hence the opening words of the chapter remind us of the nature of the Creator as the Christian believes it to be and by contrast they deny the theories of classical thought. It must be remembered that the doctrine of the Trinity was a weapon of philosophical discussion much more used in St Augustine's day than now, partly because philosophy occupied men's minds more than now, partly because the special problems of pagan philosophy were very live issues at the time, though the general problems are still as relevant now as then. From this starting point the chapter goes on to elaborate aspects of the creative activity of God which works itself out, following its own laws and imposing its own order, through all realms of being—through man, who seeks happiness and finds happiness and the peace of order in the sharing of the life of the Creator, down to the leaf of the tree and the feather in the wing of the bird which displays the order permeating the universe. Granted such a conception of God and such a view of His creative activity, how, asks St Augustine, can the kingdoms of man, i.e. history, be outside His care?

In the course of his long review of pagan history including its institutions, morality and religion, St Augustine insists that the life of the nations was vitiated because they worshipped false gods. It is easy to miss what St Augustine means by this constant assertion, and to assume that in his zeal for the god of Christianity he is simply affirming the jealousy of a jealous God. When he says that pagan thought and ambitions and the institutions which were their outcome went wrong because the pagans worshipped false gods, he means that they analysed their experience incorrectly; because their analysis was incorrect, they failed to see what were the absolute presuppositions upon which their sciences rested. For example, classical humanism, through faulty analysis of man's experience, believed that the values of morality were derived solely from that experience; hence there was no need to regard them as a presupposition necessary to any theory of good, and to any moral conduct. The result of this was that goodness was not regarded as an essential attribute of God, from whom human values are derived. Classical humanism, therefore, claimed to dispense with a god who was the author of good as known to men, and thus cut away from beneath it all valid philosophical basis for itself. When, then, St Augustine says that the classical world followed false gods, he means that it incorrectly analysed its experience, and so its science, that is, its inter-

pretation of life, was false; he is entitled, therefore, to say that its failure was the result of worshipping false gods. To him the Christian idea of God—involving as it does the Word becoming flesh—is the only solution of the philosophic tangles of the ancient world, because that idea is consistent with correct analysis of experience and indeed enables correct analysis to be made. History, then, can bear a meaning only in the light of the conscious creative activity of a God who is the author of creation, the principle of order and the source of motion in His creation, and this is what is meant by Providence.

Extracts 14-20

The selected extracts give three reasons why, in St Augustine's view, the Providence of God willed the Roman Empire.

(i) The first reason is to subdue the evils of the world. By 'evils', presumably, are meant anarchy, oppression and political strife and barbarism; in other words the *pax Romana* was willed by Providence. But it was only because the Romans showed such character as they did that their empire was willed; and this character is summed up in the sacrifice of personal ambition for the benefit of the Roman ideal. For the natural characteristic of the Roman was love of the glory of Rome: to be a subject people was inglorious, and to the triumphant ascendancy of Rome all effort was directed. Public spirit called forth sacrifice of personal ambition, even though it was public spirit in the cause of the earthly city.

To the qualities shown by the Romans St Augustine gives full recognition, not only admitting them as historical facts, but assigning them their worth in the divine plan of Providence. For they were recognised by God as meritorious and they obtained their reward; they won the Roman his place in the esteem of the world, in law, in literature, in history. Thus is the validity of the ideals pursued by the Romans established by Providence, whose purpose it was that whatever good men wrought should be recognised as good.

(ii) Secondly, Providence willed the Roman Empire in order to give to self-sacrifice its just reward; or in other words to vindicate the justice of God who assigns to moral values their due reward. But the reward—and there is a note of grim irony in the passage—the reward is on the same plane as the motives which inspire the self-sacrifice; the motive of the Romans' self-sacrifice was the winning of the admiration of men; and indeed they have won it—but no more, and no less. In mediating to the world Graeco-Roman civilisation they have given gifts to men, and for doing this Providence has given them their reward, since it is His will that men should have such gifts; but the reward is such as the givers asked.

None the less their moral efforts, though put forth not from the highest motives, can be lifted to a higher value, for they can become the example and the inspiration of those who are aware of higher motives, of the citizens of the heavenly city to whom the motive of goodness is love for God rather than the admiration of men. For of what value are the rankings which men give to one another? Yet Christians can learn from the secular state and its history; if Rome could inspire such devotion in her citizens, how much more should Christians be inspired by the city of God! Hence the greatest secular society in history was willed by Providence.[1]

(iii) It was willed by Providence in order to give examples to the heavenly city; that is to say, in history values are being realised, and from the process of their realisation on the plane of human history those who believe that these values testify to the operation of God in history can learn something of the nature of the will of God in operation and can direct their own conduct accordingly. For though, in St Augustine's view, moral values ultimately derive from God and therefore the highest morality springs from the consciousness of the will of God, nevertheless the moral aspiration and efforts of men ignorant of 'true religion' are, so far as they go, of significance. The secular society which is governed by good men, even if they are not Christian, is better than a society in which they are absent; indeed such a society may bear resemblances to the city of God itself. How much better than this is the society which is guided by a Christian ruler! Political organisations which pursue the good make for a better society and better citizens, but the climax is reached in a Christian society in the care of a Christian Emperor who is also a saint.

This view of history depends entirely upon the initial act of faith of the observer, upon some special insight (*sapientia*) brought to the interpretation of events by their interpreter. If he accepts the Providence of God, that is, the God of the Christian revelation, as the principle to which all events are to be referred, history becomes the process of the unfolding of values. And, when he approaches history from this point of view, he finds corroboration of what was initially a venture of faith. Such corroboration is precisely the task which St Augustine undertook in writing his long rambling review of secular history in books fifteen to eighteen of the *dcD*; the clue offered by faith shows the way to the interpretation of history.

It may easily be surmised from this account of St Augustine's view of history that any theory which left no room for the progressive unfolding

---

[1] Cf. 'It is obvious beyond all doubt to anyone of knowledge, faith and insight that our Lord Jesus Christ of his own favour increased and defended this city of Rome and raised it to its present pinnacle of success. It was his will to belong to this state above all others when he came to earth—in fact he must be declared to be a Roman citizen since he was enrolled in the Roman census.' Orosius, *adv. pag.* vi. 22, 8. For the last idea cf. Dante, *de mon.* ii. 12, *sub edicto Romanae auctoritatis nasci voluit* (and an amazing extension of it in the following chapter).

of purpose in history would receive little sympathy from him. We shall see at the beginning of the nineteenth book how St Augustine drives through the elaborate classical theories of the basis of human behaviour by his own straightforward enunciation of the one end which is truly man's. A view of history depends upon a view of human personality; and, as St Augustine finds classical teaching on personality deficient, he is not likely to agree with ancient views on history.

He has nothing to say specifically upon the philosophy of history held by Herodotus or Thucydides or Polybius or Livy, but by implication all classical theories are condemned. The pessimism of Herodotus proceeding from an outlook which sees nothing but a process of compensation, of equilibrium, of extremes cancelling out and therefore sees no progress in history—the fatalism of Thucydides inspired by a hopeless recognition of the irrationality of the 'accidental' against which the human spirit must battle—the fortune of Polybius and its identification with the success of Rome and the longings of Livy for the old Roman qualities embodied in a superman whom fortune and virtue, the powers behind the universe, would bless as the guarantee of human happiness—to these views St Augustine does not refer by name. But he has a scathing chapter[1] on the cyclical view of history—the view which suggests that there are cycles of civilisation which revolve bringing back the same typical positions, the same individuals and the same combinations of circumstances. In this condemnation are included all theories of history which seek to establish a future order by restoring a golden age of the past, as Livy wishes, and all theories of nature which suppose an unending grouping and regrouping of atoms to make the same patterns. To St Augustine such theories are absurd because they seek to explain the world by something which is solely intrinsic to it. Instead of admitting that the notion of the infinite is incomprehensible and yet of value, these theories try to solve the infinite by making it meet at both ends and so make a circle. Instead of admitting the unique value of each individual personality and each event, they reduce them all to a type and lose the individual in the typical. Instead of regarding history as a process reaching forward to a new but continuous creation, they regard it as having already done all that the limitations of itself allow it to do. St Augustine sums it all up in a striking phrase, 'Once and for all did Christ die for our sins,' which asserts the significance of each individual event and offers salvation as the end and culmination of the process of human history.

A very high value, therefore, is given to the Roman Empire in the Providence of God; indeed there is some resemblance in intention between the traditional role of Rome and the city of God itself. To St

[1] xii. 14.

Augustine Rome's great achievement may be summarised as the extension of the fellowship of citizenship to her whole Empire, which put Roman and provincial upon a plane of equality, and so made fellowship possible. It is true, he says, that the acquisition of the Empire was accompanied by the havoc of war, and that is the main reproach which can be brought against Rome. It is true also that universal citizenship might have been granted earlier than A.D. 212 and that the means of supporting the landless populace of Rome might have been acquired originally by agreement rather than by conquest. But these are small matters compared with the mighty ideals and achievements of a ruling people which in the fulfilment of its purpose cultivated virtues of self-denial and shared eventually its laws and its character with multitudes of men whom it took into the fellowship of citizenship.

Such chapters as these must be taken into account in estimating St Augustine's view of the Roman Empire. It may suit his purpose in some contexts, particularly when morals are under discussion, to malign Rome as the 'modern Babylon'; but it is a mistake to attribute to St Augustine the view that the Roman Empire was being justly extinguished, since the secular state was 'of the devil'. On the contrary, as we shall see later, the secular state is in his view based upon the ordinances of God and, therefore, is of Divine institution.[1] But in the meantime *Extract 19* serves as a useful anticipation. St Augustine maintains that the *civitas Dei* is the ideal which must inform political society at its best; its best implies a ruler combining the ability to govern with the true virtue which springs from 'true religion'; such a condition of affairs is, by the mercy of God, the best that men can possibly enjoy. But there is a second best. Though there is not 'true virtue' without 'true religion',[2] there is virtue without religion, and a state based upon such virtue is more 'useful' to its members than one which is not; such a state is 'justified' in the view of Providence, which knows more than we do about the manifold merits and deserts of men. Further, it offers fellowship, and, though such fellowship may not be comparable with that of the saints, it is none the less worthy of all praise and credit. Below this comes the empire of the unrighteous ruler who knows neither virtue nor true religion. But all these three categories of Empire are willed by the Providence of God for His own reasons, and if they are willed by God the secular state as such cannot be against His will. Of the nature of this state St Augustine has more to say in later chapters.[3]

Shortly before St Augustine claimed that the distinctive feature of Roman imperialism, namely its power to incorporate subject peoples within its all-embracing citizenship, formed the strongest title of the

---

[1] Cf. e.g. *prorsus divina providentia regna constituuntur humana.* v. 1.
[2] See further, p. 257.   [3] See below, pp. 236 sqq., 249 sqq.

Roman Empire to a place within the providential will of God, Claudian, the poet, wrote some lines which praised in extravagant terms the same characteristic of Roman rule; the points in which they resemble and differ from St Augustine's chapters invite brief study. The passage, which occurs in a poem written in praise of Stilicho[1] in A.D. 400, is as follows: 'It was Rome alone who took to her bosom the peoples she had conquered; she embraced the whole of mankind in a common name and cherished them as their mother and not as their queen; she gave the title of citizen to those whom she had subdued and she bound to herself far distant lands in the allegiance of child to parent. To Rome's institutions and to the peace they bring we owe it that the stranger is welcome in all lands, as though they were the place of his birth; . . . we owe it, too, that we are all members of one single family. And to the sway of Rome there shall be no bound. Other kingdoms were destroyed by luxury and its vices and by pride and the hatreds which it created.' Then follow historical examples of the waxing and waning of empires which all in turn yielded to Rome, whose power 'rested upon the sure prophecies of the Sibyl' and 'was given life by the sacred rites of Numa' and was protected by the numerous gods whom she drew to herself.

It is interesting to note that, while the pagan poet and the Christian bishop agree about the extension of Roman citizenship as Rome's supreme achievement, the very sins to which Claudian attributes the decay of earlier kingdoms are in St Augustine's view the cause of Rome's disaster— luxury and its vices, pride and its hatreds. In the very first paragraph of the *dcD* pride is singled out as the sin of paganism, and the very people whose highest boast is to 'war down the proud' is itself guilty of the pride which is its downfall. That Claudian attributes Rome's success to pagan gods is of course to be expected. It may be taken for granted that St Augustine was familiar with these lines, since he quotes from an earlier passage of the same book.

In *Extract 18* St Augustine says that the extension of the Roman citizenship was Rome's greatest achievement, but he adds that the extension to the whole of the Roman world should have taken place earlier than it did; it was a most welcome act and in the best interests of mankind (*gratissime, humanissime*). It is clear that, while he has in mind the whole process of the granting of the privileges of partial and complete citizenship, he refers specially to the *Constitutio Antoniniana*, the enactment of Caracalla in A.D. 212 by which Roman citizenship was given to all *peregrini* within the Empire (with certain exceptions).[2] It is not certain what

[1] iii. 150-61.
[2] The exceptions were the 'dediticii', but it is not agreed who these were: they may perhaps be taken to be barbarians settled within the Empire by Marcus Aurelius and the lowest class of freedmen as defined by the Lex Aelia Sentia of A.D. 4.

was the motive inspiring this enactment, for the two main sources of our information differ. On the one hand the historian Cassius Dio seems to suggest that, though ostensibly the aim was to 'confer honour', really it was to increase the revenue; for multitudes of new citizens would then become liable to the tax on inheritances. On the other hand a papyrus explains the motive differently. Caracalla had been saved from a plot against his life by his brother Geta; in gratitude to the immortal gods he considered that he was best able to render what was due to their majesty if he gave the title of Romans to the many thousands of subjects whom he took with him into the temples of the gods (presumably to render thanks). . . . 'For the multitude ought not only to suffer trials with me but also at last to be included in the victory; and this my decree will give unity to the greatness of the Roman people.' It will be easily seen that neither of these motives were likely to be of appeal to St Augustine—certainly not the second; and he was probably ignorant of both.

But apart from the motive the effect of the measure is variously interpreted. Some modern writers acclaim it as the logical end of a process of extension of privilege which had gone on for centuries; others,[1] though not necessarily denying this, point out that to widen privilege over the whole field is to destroy its value, and such was the intention. St Augustine describes it, as we have seen, as a 'humane' and 'welcome' step, but a clue to his meaning is to be seen in the passage which follows. The difference, he says, between conqueror and conquered has nothing to do with intrinsic moral worth, and so honour which is based upon that difference is valueless. In any case all alike are subject to property-tax, all alike have access to knowledge; even the title of senator is meaningless since many who hold it have never seen the imperial city in which they are supposed to function. It seems then that St Augustine welcomed the enactment of Caracalla because it swept away distinctions which in fact rested upon nothing else than the historical fact that some men were the victors and others the vanquished, and which perpetuated an 'empty pride' in things which were not only meaningless but harmful to the relation of man to man; such pride was the great obstacle to the realisation of the *civitas Dei*.

Extract 21

The chapter on the virtues of a Christian Emperor is of more importance than would appear at first sight. It has behind it a long history of philosophical reflection, of political thought and propagandist announcement. It has in front of it a long history of speculation upon the nature of

[1] Notably Rostovtzeff in his *Social and Economic History of the Roman Empire*.

monarchy, upon the divine right of kings, upon the relation of Emperor and Pope and of political and ecclesiastical power. If it is possible to say that at one point more than at any other the bridge between the old and the new world is apparent, it is to be found in the *dcD* and this chapter is a good illustration.

It is important to notice the phraseology. St Augustine uses the word *felix,* not *beatus,* when speaking of the happiness of Emperors. *Felix* has a long history behind it as a title applied to generals and Emperors as well as to gods and legions and places. As early as about 146 B.C. temples to a goddess Felicitas begin to make their appearance, and at Cumae there was an annual 'supplication' to the *Felicitas*—'success' or 'prosperity'—of the Emperor.[1] In A.D. 68 Felicitas appears in a list of goddesses in an 'imperial' inscription along with Jupiter, Juno, Minerva, Rome and Augustus.[2] Taken as a name by victorious generals, notably Sulla, Felix becomes a regular element in the imperial title after A.D. 200; it is seen both in inscriptions and on coins.[3] In his laudatory address to Trajan Pliny declares that he cannot do better than echo the universal cry of the Senate, 'O te felicem.' In later times 'Felicitas tua' becomes a periphrase standing for the direct 'tu' addressed to the Emperor. The same fashion prescribed similar phrases with reference to Bishops. Marcellinus, for example, writes to St Augustine as 'Beatitudo tua', 'Sanctitas tua', 'Venerabilitas tua', and many other titles were used. But 'Felicitas' is reserved for Emperors and 'Beatitudo' for Bishops.

We pass now to the ideas contained in the chapter, and here it is difficult to be brief without being obscure. The history of Greek philosophy and statesmanship shows how earnest was the attention and how deep the interest which was devoted to the study of political ideas, of the ideal state and of the ideal monarch. The classical student is, perhaps, apt to imagine that in Greek thought, which he sees through the medium of Periclean or Demosthenic Athens, there was no room for the idea of kingship—that the word 'king' tended to be identified with the King of Persia and that the idea of kingship was morally and politically taboo to the good Athenian. But philosophy took another view. Its cradle was in Asia Minor where kings and satraps and tyrants were familiar enough. Philosophers had stood behind the thrones of the 'tyrants' of Sicily; they had discussed the unity of mankind, the nature of kingship and its relation to the divine ordering of the world with Alexander the Great. They had learned new lessons from the political institutions of republican Rome, and had played no small part in the education of Emperors. From its earliest days Stoicism had pondered upon the political implications of its main doctrines, and

[1] Dess. *I.L.S.* 108.   [2] Op. cit. 233, cf. 2180, 2181, 4833.
[3] The first inscription is dated A.D. 200.

Zeno himself had written an 'Ideal Republic'. While to Epicureanism political activity was inconsistent with the philosophic life, Stoicism drew from certain fundamental dogmas doctrines which covered the field of political speculation and justified the philosopher in actively engaging in public life. Starting from the Universal Reason and Nature as Reason's medium of self-expression, Stoicism passed from the idea of a single Law, operating throughout nature, to the conception of a world-culture and thence to the world-state; and, as the Roman Empire extended the Pax Romana, this venture of faith, encouraged by Alexander's ideals and achievements, seemed to gain valid justification and solid reality. Similarly, Hellenistic philosophy, and particularly Stoicism, with borrowings from other sources, notably Cynicism, started from the idea of the superiority of the good man and arrived at an elaborate theory of the kingship of the 'sage' or the philosopher or the saint as the Emperor of Rome: and this development of theory was due as much to observation of the practical working of institutions as to speculation upon political and moral issues. Emphasis on the personal rule of one man was encouraged by a number of considerations. If the Universal Reason dwells in all men, but pre-eminently in one individual, if all men are by Nature made for a 'political' life, then it is right that political rule should be in the hands of the man most qualified for it, namely the 'wise man'. He will offset any tendency to individualism by his sense of duty to the rest of mankind and will direct the state with full consciousness of a moral purpose such as a republic lacks. Only one man can rule an Empire; he must, it is true, have his 'eyes' and 'ears' posted at vantage points and he will need officials; but officials look always to a superior, and this tendency, when pressed home, means in the long run a king. Further, no other form of constitution can cope with the warfare of individuals or interests or classes; for only an individual can stand above them and reconcile opposing claims; for long centuries, peace and security and order had been the main need of the world and the rule of an Augustus had at last given it what it most desired. The Greek city-state had come to grief when it attempted empire, and any order which was to rise above natural barriers, as Alexander's Empire had given promise of doing, could not be democratic but must be monarchic in character. The 'ecumenical' idea and monarchy became inseparably linked. Hence the monarch is the servant of mankind; he is the possession of the people, whose political needs and hopes he sums up in his person; he satisfies their needs and fulfils their hopes because he is the supreme manifestation of the Reason of God or of Zeus. For Zeus, whose will is the world-law, is often held up as the ideal which the earthly monarch will copy; he is the representative of Zeus on earth. This notion of the king as an emanation of God received much support from the oriental conception

of the king as the 'saviour', but Greek influence always insisted that the 'saving' work of the king should be regarded as having definite form, as a piece of work beneficial to a particular country at a particular time, and not as a vague appellation bestowed by a semi-religious awe.

This very brief and unsatisfying summary will give some hint of the kind of reflection upon monarchy which occupied philosophy from the fourth century B.C. well into the first centuries of our era. The literature devoted to its development was very great. It took the form of treatises, lectures, dialogues and essays; some of it was written in the speculative disinterestedness of the lecture room, some of it took the form of pamphlets of a propagandist nature, as we should now call them; and some was addressed to individual emperors. It was all well known to the educated man of the Roman world, and the ideas which it conveyed were familiar to the age of St Augustine. A great deal of it has been lost, but there still survive whole treatises and fragments of the works of the philosophers, and, in particular, speeches and essays by Dio Chrysostom, Plutarch, Seneca, Pliny and the Latin Panegyrists. Perhaps the best way to give some idea of their contents and tone would be to distinguish the qualities which St Augustine requires in his Christian emperor and to quote parallel passages from Dio Chrysostom and from Plutarch. But no suggestion is made that St Augustine is consciously thinking of these or any other authors; such ideas were current in his day, though to what extent he was influenced by them it is impossible to say. On the other hand the chapter stands in the direct line of the history of thought upon the nature of monarchy as it developed from the days of Greek civilisation to the political theorists of the Middle Ages; and some hint of its antecedents is not out of place.

The happiness of an Emperor is not to be assessed, says St Augustine, in terms of length of reign, or the founding of a dynasty or military victories[1] or successful suppression of rebellion. A pagan Emperor might expect these things; and the mercy of God grants them to a pagan Emperor to prevent a Christian Emperor regarding them as the highest blessings (as he might if they were reserved only to Christian Emperors). In the Christian view the essentials of imperial happiness are righteous rule, disregard of flattery, humility, the employment of power for the extension of the worship of God, fear and reverence and love of God, willingness to share authority; mercy, refusal to gratify personal dislikes, the use of punishment for correction and not for revenge, generosity of mind and action; ascetic self-control. Behind all this must be the right motive—not self-glorification, but love of eternal life, with a sense of sin impelling to

[1] St A. would not approve of the phrase 'Victoria et Felicitas Caesaris' which appears in dedications at Ameria, 50 miles from Rome. Dess. *I. L. S.* 6631 sq.

humility and mercy and prayer. Even then the Emperor is happy only in hope and not in fact.

The following passages, which might be multiplied and elaborated, will show the likeness and the difference between this chapter and the classical ideal of the King.

'If he is of right judgment and loves his fellow men and carefully maintains law in the interest of the security and the advantage of his subjects, if he identifies his own good with that of his subjects and finds the greatest delight and moral satisfaction in their prosperity, then he is pre-eminently happy, and shares his happiness with all, then indeed is he supreme in power and a King indeed.'[1]

'Whose life is safer than the King's whom all guard with equal care? Whose is more serene, more free from anxiety, than his who counts no one his enemy and has nothing with which to reproach himself? Who more happy than he whose goodness is apparent to all? I have spoken in general terms about the good king; and, if anything of what I have said seems to apply to you, blessed indeed are you in the rightness of your judgment and the goodness of your nature, and blessed are we who share in them. And now I wish to describe to you that great and supreme lord and ruler whom all mortals when busy about mortal things ought always to strive to copy, directing themselves as far as possible by his standards and modelling their own characters upon his.' Then follows a long description of Zeus as the Governor of the world.[2]

'So it is with kings who hold their power in trust from Zeus; the king who looks to him and conforms himself to his law and ordinance and rules in justice and uprightness finds his portion in life good and his consummation happy. But whosoever thwarts and dishonours the god who entrusted the gift of kingship to him has had no good of his great authority and power—no more than to be a ruler whose wickedness and vice are obvious to his contemporaries and to his posterity: his lot is that of Phaethon in the story, who in violation of what was fitting set foot upon that mighty and divine chariot of the Sun and was found to be no worthy charioteer.'[3]

'The King above all men should be fond of his friends and relations, for he thinks of them as part of himself. He takes care not only that they should have a share in his so-called happiness, but much more that they should be recognised as worthy to be his partners in government; and he takes all pains to make it clear that this elevation is due not to their kinship to him but to their own high qualities of character.'[4]

'Most rulers have eyes only for their immediate entourage gathered together for no particular reason except that it consists of flatterers; the rest

[1] Dio Chr. 112 R.   [2] *Id.* 55 R.   [3] *Id.* 58 R.   [4] *Id.* 138 R.

they drive away, and particularly the best. But the ideal king makes a careful choice from all persons available to him; he would regard it as absurd to send to Nisaea for his horses as being better than those from Thessaly or to India for his hounds but to employ only those men who happened to be at hand.'[1]

'I cannot tell you whether a man with the power which you describe has really great power or little or none at all. If, for example, he is wise and brave and just and has done all that he has done with sound judgment, I count him strong and think his power very great. But, if he is a coward, senseless and uncontrolled and lawless, attempting everything in a spirit of vainglory, then on the contrary he strikes me as weaker than the most poverty-stricken peasant without a clod of earth to his name, poking about with a pick to find something to eat, let alone digging canals through the highest mountains, as you tell me your kings have done. If a man is unable to control his anger which constantly breaks out over trifles, to curb his desire for vicious pleasures, to thrust grief on one side, especially when there is nothing to grieve about, to endure hardship (even hardship caused by pleasure), to expel from his heart fear which does no good in time of terror but infinite harm—a man like that is no man; he is at the mercy of women and court officials.'[2]

And from Plutarch, 'You would say with greater truth that rulers are God's agents in looking after men's safety and welfare, and are entrusted with the distribution and preservation of God's good gifts to men; . . . apart from law and justice and a ruler it is not possible to enjoy or to make correct use of the generous gifts which the gods bestow. Justice is the aim and fulfilment of the law, law is the work of the ruler, the ruler is the image of God who disposes all things. That image needs no Pheidias or Polyclitus or Myron to sculpt him; he moulds himself to the likeness of God by his own virtues, to become the fairest and most godlike of all the works of man's hands. Even as God has set the sun in the sky as his own most beauteous likeness and has set too the moon, even so in the cities of earth the ruler is the copy of God and his light—the ruler, that is, who of godlike nature upholds right judgments, who has the logos of God as his own mind. . . .'[3]

The same ideas could be illustrated at great length from Latin writers, for example Seneca and Pliny. In the *de Clementia* addressed to Nero, Seneca dilates upon the many forms which clemency should take in an Emperor 'chosen to represent the gods upon earth'. For example, he will punish rarely; if he punishes on his own account, it will be done with all mercy, for autocratic power needs no revenge to console it; if on others' account, it must be only a means to the greater security of the state as a

[1] *Id.* 141 R.   [2] *Id.* 111 R.   [3] *Ad princip. inerud.* 3.

whole. Similarly the positive aspects of mercy are enjoined upon the ruler
—aid to the afflicted, the poor and the victims of misfortune[1]; and indeed
all the moral virtues commended by St Augustine can be found in his
treatise of exhortation. It is not to be expected that any virtues would be
omitted from the list of those attributed to Trajan in Pliny's servile *Panegyric*; accessibility, disregard of flattery, mercy, religion are all noted. But
by his time the Senate was able to assert once again its claim at least to a
share in government; and so the virtue of treating it as a partner is brought
to the attention of the Emperor, and the Senate is exhorted to cooperate
to the full in the enlightened rule of a just Emperor. But in stressing the
point that the Emperor is the regent of the gods Pliny overreached himself—'a state which is devoted to religious duties and which has earned
the everlasting favour of the gods by its piety thinks that no addition can
be made to its happiness except that the gods should imitate the Emperor'.

However ill-suited to the times such a treatise as the *de Clementia* of
Seneca may appear to us to be, it cannot be overlooked as a main link in
the tradition of the ideal ruler. For the writings of Seneca hand on to
mediaeval writers much of the accumulated doctrine of Greek writers such
as we have seen exemplified in Dio Chrysostom and Plutarch; and to the
middle ages this was accessible only through such Latin writers as Cicero
and Seneca.

That ideas of this kind were current in the early centuries A.D. and that
they exercised great influence has recently been demonstrated by Prof.
N. H. Baynes. The Byzantine philosophy of government is that the imperial
power is a terrestrial copy of the rule of God in Heaven. As in Heaven
there is one god, and one divine law, so on earth there must be one ruler
and one single law; that ruler is the Roman Emperor, God's vice-gerent.
The earliest statement of this doctrine is in the Oration composed by
Eusebius on the occasion of the Tricennalia of Constantine, A.D. 336,
where it is set forth with some elaboration. But Eusebius was not an original thinker, and Professor Baynes finds striking parallelisms between
the ideas and the actual language of Eusebius and certain quotations preserved in Stobaeus from earlier philosophers, notably Ecphantus, and
Sthenidas, who were Pythagoreans, and Diotogenes, a Stoic. Thus, Ecphantus says that 'God fashioned him (the king) after himself as the
archetype', and Eusebius speaks of the king as 'modelled upon the archetypal "idea" of the great king'. Similarly, to Diotogenes 'the king stands
to his city as God to creation (κόσμος); he stands to God as the city to
creation. The city composed of many different elements is made to represent the orderly arrangement and harmony of creation: the king, holding
power responsible to none, is himself the living law and is bodied forth as

[1] ii. 6.

a god among men'. Sthenidas is of the opinion that 'the king must be wise; for thus he will be a copy and devotee of the first (that is, archetypal) god'. Ecphantus says the Logos is incarnate in the true king and is the source of his power to save men, whom he saves from sin. And in Eusebius the idea is put as follows: ' . . . the Logos of God from whom and through whom the ruler who is the friend of God bears the image of the Kingdom of Heaven, and, imitating what is higher, directs and steers as a helmsman all that is on earth'. For he cannot say, as Ecphantus says, that the ruler is actually the Logos; to him Constantine is the friend and interpreter of the Logos, Who imparts to His disciples the seeds of true wisdom and gives knowledge of the Father's Kingdom; the Emperor by imitating his Saviour and knowing only how to save actually did save even the godless by teaching them to reverence God ($\epsilon\dot{v}\sigma\epsilon\beta\epsilon\hat{i}\nu$). Using such sources as these Eusebius worked out his theory of kingship; as the state is to the cosmos, so the king is to God; the king should imitate God and remember that kingship is, to use Diotogenes' phrase, a 'God-imitating business' ($\theta\epsilon o\mu\iota\mu\grave{o}\nu$ $\pi\rho\hat{a}\gamma\mu a$); the archetype of the king is in Heaven; the Logos supports the Christian monarch; and so all the virtues required by Hellenistic philosophy—piety, love for men and the rest—can without impropriety be assigned by a Christian bishop to the first Christian Emperor.

THE NINETEENTH BOOK

Analysis
of the Argument of the XIXth Book
THE PROPER ENDS OF THE TWO CITIES

      I. Reply to (B) i–iv, (*a*) and (*a*). Ends and happiness. Eternal life is the supreme good. Ends do not lie in this life and therefore happiness cannot. The reality of evil is ignored by classical moral theory; primary goods are neutral, not good; they may be perverted; virtue implies conflict with evil; e.g. the virtues of *temperantia, prudentia, iustitia, fortitudo* all have to reckon with evil, and the conflict precludes supreme happiness. Final realisation of good is impossible in a world in which the very virtues testify to evil. Happiness can be given only by hope—hope of eternal life free from evil.

c. 5 II. Reply to (B), (*b*) and (*β*). The end includes fellowship. Yet in this life fellowship is full of evil, and therefore cannot offer complete happiness. Consideration of fellowship in

> (*a*) the family; quarrels and treachery; no security. (See also (*c*) iii.)

c. 6
> (*b*) the state; the law-courts are full; the judge must work in ignorance; justice in the cause of injustice; no fellowship here.

c. 7
> (*c*) the world; here evil is 'writ large';
>> (i) difference of language;
>> (ii) wars and fears of wars, foreign and civil; to contemplate wars unmoved is not happiness, but the negation of human feeling;

c. 8
>> (iii) the sorrow of friendship (see (*a*)); estrangement and fear destroy fellowship.

c. 9
> (*d*) the universe; fellowship with angels (or friendly gods, as Varro's). But this is less intimate than the fellowship of men; and angels are good and bad; evil spirits have taught men the worship of false and degraded cults.

Fellowship in all its forms is vitiated by irreducible evil which causes anxiety and fear.

c. 10 Peace is man's aim; in peace the *prima naturae* of body and spirit (see (B) iv) can be realised. Virtue can do its best with our limited good and our inevitable evil, if it refers to an end which is perfect peace or the peace of final perfection.

c. 11 III. The end re-stated. The end has been called eternal life (see (C) I); it has also been called peace (see (C) II). Both definitions by themselves are open to objections, which can be met if the end includes both; the end is peace in eternal life or eternal life in peace.

c. 12 IV. The universality of peace as an end

> (*a*) in war and insurrection; in brigandage;
> (*b*) in the household;
> (*c*) in the most extreme cases of human cruelty and anti-social tyranny—Cacus—
> (*d*) in animal creation; and in man; in man pride may substitute selfish peace for real peace, but it is peace of a kind none the less;
> (*e*) in physical nature.

Peace is dependent upon 'order', the order which runs through the universe.

c. 13 V. Peace in order. Definitions, in terms of 'order', of the peace of (i) the body, (ii) the soul, (iii) body and soul together, (iv) man and God, (v) men, (vi) the household, (vii) the city, (viii) the city of God, (ix) nature. Definition of order. Even misery

178

and evil are not outside or beyond order. Created natures are subject to order, and, whether they are good or bad, are not without
some element of good which implies order. Pain is evidence of
good taken away and good left. Temporal peace and temporal
goods.

c. 14   VI. The new meaning of 'command' given by the new definition of the end. Temporal peace uses eternal peace as its standard
of reference; human frailty and error make such standard necessary. (Summary of the argument that peace is the aim of man's
soul.) Therefore divine overlordship and aid are necessary; peace
with God depends upon ordered obedience to law in faith. The
two chief precepts, 'love God and love your neighbour'; their
implications for a true conception of 'command', a conception
which appears in the definitions given in V. For example, the
peace of the fellowship of the household is 'ordered agreement of
those who live together, whether they command or obey'. To
command (at its best) is to serve, to be a slave to the interests of
the governed. This conception of 'command' is 'natural'.

c. 15   Righteousness (justice) allows men to rule only animals. The
slavery of man to man is due to sin, not to nature. The origin of
the word 'servus'. Penal slavery ultimately due to order. A new
conception of slavery.

c. 16   'Command' is a burden which will gladly be laid aside. Theory
of punishment. The family as an element of the state.

c. 17   VII. The peace of the two cities. The family as a fragment of
the state; it must be so ruled as to bring it into relation with the
law of the state. Comparison of the household living by faith
and the household living without faith. The use of temporal
things is common to both, but the purpose of the use is different.
The two cities have earthly peace as a common aim as far as the
limited purposes of the earthly city allow—hence the need for
obedience to law; but the heavenly city cannot share the laws of
religion; reasons for this. The purposes of the heavenly city
elaborated.

c. 18   VIII. Reply to (B), (c) and (γ). Is certain knowledge possible
or not? On some matters the heavenly city claims sure and positive knowledge; the senses, the mind, the Scriptures, faith. On
some matters agnosticism or suspended judgment is the right
course.

c. 19   IX. Reply to (B), (d) and (δ). Daily life and habits. Reply to
(B), (e) and (ε). The active or the contemplative life. Omitted in
this selection.

c. 20   X. Conclusion of (C) I-IX. The two happinesses compared
(see (A). The discussion started with happiness and comes back
to it). True wisdom (or saintliness) and true virtue. Contrast between the common weal as it is and the hope of things to be.

c. 21   (D) *The Roman common weal*; does it satisfy the definition of classical political theory, especially Cicero's? Fulfilment of the promise made in Book II, 21.

Bk. II, c. 21   Cicero held that the commonwealth had already perished in his day; account of the imaginary discussion in Cicero's *de Republica*. Concord in a city demands justice. Counter-plea that a city cannot be governed without injustice. Scipio's definition; 'the weal of the people'; definition of 'people', (i) 'a gathering of people united in fellowship (*a*) by a common recognition of what is right and (*b*) by a common pursuit of what is to their interest'. By this definition the Roman commonwealth had ceased to be, as Cicero admitted. The deterioration of Roman character was responsible; righteousness (justice) was a sham. True righteousness exists only in the city of God.

Bk. XIX
c. 21 (*cont'd.*)   Scipio's definition, the weal of the people, recalled; the argument of Book II, c. 21, restated (see above). The parts of the definition, (*a*) 'common recognition of what is right'; righteousness and unrighteousness considered, (*b*) 'pursuit of a common interest'; this cannot be a test of a commonwealth, for it leads to worship of self (or of evil spirits) and not to worship of God.

c. 22   Who is the God whom it is claimed the Romans should worship? The nature of that God.

c. 23   (The inconsistencies of Porphyry; omitted in this selection. Sacrifice; the nature of the sacrifice required by God.) Conclusion of the criticism of the first definition (D i).

c. 24   A possible second definition—(ii) 'a people is a gathering of a multitude of rational beings united in fellowship by sharing a common love of the same things'. Many states would satisfy this definition; but all depends on the object of love. Righteousness must be the object.

c. 25   (E) *General conclusion.* Righteousness implies obedience to God; the virtues which make up righteousness must be referred to an external standard which is God.

c. 26   Happiness can then result; happiness implies peace. Both cities use temporal peace, and Christians pray for kings and governments.

c. 27   But the peace of the heavenly city is of a different quality, and righteousness on earth reposes rather in the remission of sins than in perfection of virtues; hence the prayer, 'Forgive us our trespasses.' Evil is a reality. Final peace; peace in happiness and happiness in peace.

c. 28   The unhappiness of those alienated from God; conflict is the cause.

The Proper Ends of the Two Cities

BOOK XIX

CHAPTERS 1-3

(For a synopsis of the argument see page 64)

The first three or four chapters of the nineteenth book may seem tedious and obsolete to the modern reader. They are concerned chiefly with Varro's summary of classical moral theory. Though the full text has not been given in the selections, a synopsis of the argument has been made, for the argument is important.

In the first place, as a glance at the analysis will show, the remaining chapters of the nineteenth book (c. 4 to end) reply to the points raised in the summary of Varro given in chapters 1 to 3, and the reply follows the order of the summary. In short, St Augustine elaborates his own views while criticising those of classical writers, and therefore, at least, an outline of classical theory is necessary. Further, many of the classical doctrines are not obsolete; in one way or another they are held to-day. St Augustine's reply, therefore, is concerned with issues which are alive, even though expressed to-day in different form. Finally, from a historical point of view it is interesting to see the form in which classical theories were handled by a writer in the early fifth century. The *Antiquitates* of Varro (now lost) had already been used by Tertullian (*d. c.* A.D. 240) in his *Ad Nationes*, and by Arnobius (end of third century A.D.) in his *Adversus Nationes*; and now St Augustine uses it in a work directed *Contra Paganos*. About the same time or a little later, Martianus Capella, also an African scholar, composed the *de nuptiis Philologiae* which was based on Varro and had an enormous vogue in the Middle Ages. Later Roman culture depended largely upon 'summaries' of ancient life and thought; the problem of the late Roman Empire and early middle ages was how to present Graeco-Roman culture—for there was no other—in such form that the men of the day could assimilate it. It is due to the 'summarising' work of men like Boethius, Cassiodorus, Isidore that the elements of Graeco-Roman thought were handed on to form our tradition in Mediaeval and Modern Europe. These chapters of St Augustine give an instructive example of the

beginnings of the process. Indeed the authority of St Augustine may have contributed to that process; for the whole purpose of his *de doctrina Christiana* was to stress the importance of secular learning for Scriptural interpretation, and in one passage he urges the amassing of a secular knowledge necessary to Christian wisdom.[1]

St Augustine states that classical moral theory had been concerned to discuss the basis of happiness for man, for it assumed that happiness was the end or one of the ends of human striving. Before discussing the various theories put forward, he explains what is meant by 'end'; the end of our good, he says, is that which makes all other things worth pursuing, while the end itself is desirable only for itself. In this definition he closely follows Aristotle: 'If then, as far as conduct is concerned, there is some one end which we desire for its own sake, desiring everything else only in so far as they contribute to it, and if we do not choose everything for the sake of anything else but it, clearly it must be the good and indeed the chief good.' But, continues St Augustine, though philosophers have varied in their views about the nature of the end, at any rate nature has set a limit to their speculations, so that they have not looked beyond the mind and the body for the 'end'; some have placed it in the mind, others in the body, others in both. He does not say where else it might be looked for; but, outside classical thought, the supreme end has sometimes been held to be such absorption in a divine essence as extinguishes personality, and so destroys both mind and body as man knows them.

Natural man (the argument continues), untutored by any teaching about the nature of morality, strives for positive pleasure, or for negative pleasure, that is, freedom from discomfort, or for both these 'pleasures' combined, or for the satisfaction of certain elementary and primary instincts of the body and the mind which crave free and unhindered satisfaction. The relation of virtue to these objects of striving is ambiguous; sometimes virtue has been regarded as a means to these objects as ends in themselves, sometimes as an end in itself, to the attainment of which the objects of striving are means. These ideas will bear some elaboration.

The word which St Augustine uses for happiness is *beatitudo* which we are most familiar with in 'beatitudes'. The word is first used by Cicero. Speaking about the happy state of the gods he says he does not know which word to use, *beatitas* or *beatitudo*; either word, he adds, is 'utterly harsh, but words have to be softened to the ear by usage'.[2] Seneca, who had much to say about the Stoic view of happiness, avoids the word; his treatise addressed to his brother Gallio he entitled *de vita beata*. But by the time of St Augustine *beatitudo* has become established; the Vulgate,

[1] ii. 16, 24.   [2] Cic. *de natura deorum*. I. 34 (95).

written by St Jerome who was a contemporary of St Augustine, uses the word in Rom. iv. 6 and Gal. iv. 15. It is even taken up into the official language of state-prayers for the Emperor in such a formula as *pro beatitudine felicium temporum*.[1]

The Greek word for 'happiness' is 'eudaimonia' ($\epsilon\dot{v}\delta\alpha\iota\mu o\nu\acute{\iota}\alpha$) which properly means 'under the care of a good Genius'. This is the usual word in all Greek literature. There was another word, or rather two words, for 'happy', 'makar' ($\mu\acute{\alpha}\kappa\alpha\rho$) and 'makarios' ($\mu\alpha\kappa\acute{\alpha}\rho\iota os$). The first of these was used only for the 'happiness' of the gods and of the 'blessed dead'; the second was used of men, but more seldom than 'eudaimon' and perhaps in a more colloquial and flippant way. The interesting point, however, is that 'eudaimonia' and 'eudaimon' are never used in the New Testament. The absence of this word is not difficult to account for. In the first place, 'eudaimonia' was the stock word of the philosophers and the 'happiness' of the Christian was not to be equated with the happiness discussed in Greek philosophy. Secondly, the word itself was objectionable to Christian ears; it seemed to make reference to a daemon, one of those daemons with which Christianity had to wage long warfare in an attempt to expel them from the consciousness of its adherents. It seemed to make 'happiness' depend upon something or some power outside man which controlled the quality of his destiny, whereas to the Christian its source was within, springing up from a right relationship between man and God.

That happiness is the universal object of striving is obvious, as Aristotle said.[2] The history of Greek philosophy makes it clear that philosophers agreed with the plain man in this judgment; but it is no less clear that philosophers were not agreed as to what happiness is and how it is to be obtained. To the Cynics virtue was sufficient for happiness, but for virtue nothing was needed except a negative independence of needs or desires. To the Cyrenaics virtue also was desirable as a means to the sole end which was individual advantage, that is to say pleasures, which is happiness. To the Megarians happiness was to be found in philosophic contemplation. Plato realised that the problem was not so simple. To him happiness has nothing to do with pleasure, but everything to do with morality, which is composed of (*a*) knowledge of those eternal values which alone are real (in his own terminology called 'Ideas'), (*b*) contemplation of those values as they are revealed in the world of sense, (*c*) cultivation of special arts and sciences which satisfy the intellectual and aesthetic needs of life, (*d*) enjoyment of harmless pleasures of the senses.

---

[1] Dess. *I. L. S.* 756, cf. 727.
[2] *Nic. Ethics*, 1102a. Cf. *dcD* xix. 1 (quoting Varro?), *nulla est homini causa philosophandi nisi ut beatus sit.*

To this Aristotle takes exception. First, he criticises Plato's terminology: he insists that happiness is not a state, and that to describe it as a state is to regard it as a state of feeling, and so to reduce it to a superior kind of pleasure: to him happiness is an activity, and is accompanied naturally by pleasure. For this reason virtue cannot be the true end and so be worthy to be equated with happiness; for virtue is compatible with inactivity. And so Aristotle finds the key to the meaning of happiness in function, in the specific function of man. This function which differentiates him from animals is the use of that power in him which enables him to grasp or understand a plan or rule. Happiness is the unimpeded life of this power; it is therefore activity; it is in accordance with virtue, and it must be continuous throughout a man's complete life. Virtue is the source from which good activity is derived; good activity is pleasurable, and a measure of material well-being is a necessary prerequisite to unimpeded activity. The part of virtue is to control desire, to moderate it; the point between excessive control and excessive licence is 'the mean', a point which is decided by the insight of the good man. Happiness, therefore, is the result of a combination of virtues—virtues of intellect and virtues of character.

To the Stoics virtue was the only way of happiness; the good man could be happy in squalor or torment. To the Epicureans pleasure was the supreme end, and in the view of the best of them pleasure included pleasures of the mind; but the happiness of Epicureanism was of a negative kind, meaning freedom from pain or distraction or anxiety or fear; and virtue was a means of avoiding pain of body or mind; positive happiness, it was felt, was beyond the reach of men.

This very brief sketch is perhaps enough to illustrate certain points in the chapters of the *dcD* under consideration. Happiness is assumed in all these philosophies to be the end of man's ambition, though happiness is variously conceived. Virtue is related to pleasure in different ways; sometimes it is a means, sometimes it is an end itself with pleasure as a concomitant. Virtue itself is variously defined, though into that question there is no need to enter.

There remain, however, certain phrases used by St Augustine yet to be discussed more fully.

'Pleasure' (*voluptas*) is the term used for all kinds of pleasurable feeling, whether the gratification of purely animal or gross appetites or the highest form of intellectual or aesthetic or spiritual enjoyment. Some of the Greek philosophers, as for example followers of Epicurus, and some of the Stoics, fell into the error of the hedonistic psychology which assumes that man can desire nothing but pleasure in some form or another—an error which is revealed the moment it is admitted that a distinction can be drawn be-

tween higher and lower pleasures; for, if the higher pleasure is chosen, something other than pleasure is desired and pursued, namely the morally better. But, as the foregoing sketch shows, Greek philosophy as a rule recognised other objects of striving than pleasure.

If *voluptas* stands for the positive and active pleasures, 'quiet' (*quies*, ἀταραξία) is the term used for the pleasure which comes from freedom from disturbing or hampering factors which destroy peace of mind or body—the calm 'pleasure of equilibrium'. Epicurus coupled these two kinds of pleasure, but he assigned greater importance to the second, for in his view the first pleasure removes the pain of an unsatisfied craving and so indirectly ministers to the second, which is a 'harmony of mind and body' brought about by the limitation of desires. Virtue has its place in life as a means of bringing about that equilibrium, for virtue involves asceticism.

The *prima naturae*, 'the primary objects', though not peculiar to Stoicism, are given enhanced importance in its analysis of human nature and the objects of striving; for the doctrine of 'living according to Nature' presupposed some enquiry into the commands of Nature.

By 'primary impulses' the Stoic meant the elementary instincts of self-preservation, self-regard and the maintaining of the body intact in its functions; these instincts man shares with animals. But man also possesses reason, and has therefore an instinct which drives him to use such gifts of mind as he may have and to acquire knowledge. Pleasure is not included among these primary impulses. The old Academy had recognised these instincts, but had regarded them as morally neutral, and early Stoicism adopted the same attitude towards them, regarding them as neither good nor evil. But later Stoicism, perhaps because it laid so much stress on the duty of following Nature, came dangerously near to regarding them as 'goods', for it regarded them as secondary results of the pursuit of virtue, and thus it was easy to regard health, strength, reputation, intellectual efficiency and the fame which sprang from these as things desirable in themselves and so as part of the *summum bonum*. Though in theory the real good of the virtuous man lay in the wise insight displayed in his choice, in practice the objects of the choice easily came to be regarded as desirable objects in themselves.

Virtue is neither pleasure, nor 'quiet', nor both these combined, nor 'primary objects', but may stand in various relations to these. The manner in which virtue stands in relation to the objects of striving forms for Varro the first 'differentia' in his classification of philosophical positions. For desire for virtue, according to Varro's summary, is not one of the desires implanted by Nature, but is something superimposed upon Nature, for virtue is the result of *doctrina*, 'schooling' or 'training'. Thus, we are

brought back to the old problem which vexed the philosophical schools, 'whether virtue can be taught.' The reply of Socrates was that it could be taught, for he thought that virtue was dependent on knowledge, and knowledge could be imparted. Aristotle was more alive to the compelling power of desire and its ability to overcome knowledge. But behind this problem lies the further problem of the 'origin of the moral sentiments', that is to say, whence did man acquire moral values? Many philosophers were familiar with this question. Plato's reply is the most celebrated. He thought that the soul of man had come in contact with moral values in a previous existence; at birth man's consciousness was swept clean of this previous knowledge, but during life he recollected it as he came in contact with the partial and shadowy embodiments of such values impressed upon the material world. The problem is no less familiar to us; nowadays we recognise that moral ideas have developed during the process of evolution and that much of morality can be traced back to elementary 'sanctions' and taboo of primitive man. Yet the tracing of this development, however accurately it may be done, does not dispose of the idea of value itself. That idea cannot be explained away by any description of its growth; it cannot be analysed into terms of an order different from itself. Equally, the fact that ideas of morality have developed from simple forms does not in the least abrogate from the validity of morality itself. What St Augustine has to say on these matters we shall see later.

Varro then goes on to apply four more 'differentiae' to the various possible philosophical positions. The first raises the question whether the end is 'social' or individual, the second concerns the theory of knowledge, the third the manner of life of the philosopher, the fourth the degree to which the practice of philosophy is compatible with an active life. These differentiae are all discussed by St Augustine in turn, as the analysis of the argument shows (see p. 177), and they may be considered as they arise. The application of the five differentiae to the original objects of striving enables Varro to arrive at the imposing total of 288 possible philosophical positions. But Varro is not content with a theoretical classification: he criticises the 'differentiae'. Some he finds irrelevant, and eventually he arrives at his own position, which briefly stated is that happiness is given by a supreme good compounded of goods of the body and goods of the mind; virtue has its own goods and employs the goods of body and mind to its own ends; happiness is social; knowledge is within man's reach; any considerations relating to external habits of life and dress are irrelevant; and both an active and a contemplative life are necessary.

CHAPTER 4

Reply to Classical Theories

Chapter 4 begins the reply of St Augustine to the questions raised in chapters 1-4; it occupies the rest of the nineteenth book. Reference to the 'summary of the argument' will show at what point in the book Varro's various topics are discussed.

The reply comes to the point at once. If the heavenly city were asked to reply to the question about 'ends', it would say that eternal life is the *summum bonum* and eternal death the *summum malum*. To obtain eternal life and to avoid eternal death life must be lived aright. Men do not see their good exposed in front of them; therefore he who wishes to live aright, the righteous man, must live by faith, basing his life on trust or belief; his quest of the *summum bonum* therefore depends upon his having faith. Yet he cannot live his life aright relying on his own resources; aid from outside is necessary to him; he can receive this aid by prayer to the God who gives him the faith to believe that the aid will be given. The ambition of man to make himself happy out of his own resources is amazing folly.

This reply appears remarkably simple and direct; but, partly because of its very simplicity, it raises tremendous issues. It is put forward, in the first place, in opposition to classical moral theories and therefore it is a criticism of them. But it contains also the kernel of St Augustine's criticism of classical thought in general; it marks clearly the contrast between the pagan and the Christian outlook upon life.

At first sight the reply seems to be no reply. Classical moral theory, according to Varro's summary, had used such terms as pleasure, happiness, the 'primary objects', virtue including virtue of character and of intellect: St Augustine retorts in other terms, life, right living, faith, prayer, aid, God. In short, he does not believe that the problem is to be approached primarily by way of the categories of traditional classical theory, which was guilty of defective analysis of human nature; new terms are needed—which we may now consider.

'Life' means to St Augustine the life of the body and the soul regarded as a unity; experience comes to man as single experience to which both body and soul contribute. The body is the instrument of the soul; it is the soul which gives meaning to sensation, and sensation is a stimulation of the senses of such quality as to be recorded in the consciousness. But the life of the soul and the life of the body are essentially the same, and of

the life of both the life of man is made up. Sensation is accompanied by emotion, which takes the form of attraction or repulsion under such names as desire, loathing and fear, pleasure and pain; but all emotions can finally be traced to the love with which each man cherishes his own existence, and love is the power which inevitably draws men to action, good or bad, as his affections are good or bad. But, if love in this sense provides the impulse to action, good or bad, it does not have the last word, for the process is not yet complete. After sense or thought has presented something to consciousness, after desire (or repulsion) has inspired the realisation (or avoidance) of the idea presented to consciousness, the reason, which considers the practicability or the results of such realisation, has yet to agree (or to refuse) to take the necessary steps. The decision to translate consent (or refusal) into action is the task of the will, which is built up upon suggestions to consciousness, upon desire and reason, and is itself an unconstrained but self-determined movement of the mind for the realisation of an object. The will is the distinctive mark of man, and indeed St Augustine goes so far as to say that 'we are nothing but wills; desire and pleasure are simply will consenting to what we wish for; fear and sorrow are simply will refusing consent to what we do not want; . . . and similarly with all the things which we desire or avoid the will is converted into this or that emotion according as it consents or refuses consent'.[1]

Such, in brief, is St Augustine's analysis of the self or of life as the personal life of man.

It is evident that this view of human personality—whether it is a satisfactory analysis or not does not matter at the moment—runs counter to many of the theories of classical thought. Instead of setting the body or sensation in opposition to the mind or thought, St Augustine brings them together, regarding them both as contributors to consciousness and holding that the impulse or urge or energy which may issue in physical appetite is essentially the same as that which issues in moral or intellectual effort. But to him the subjection of the body—and no one knew better than he how strong its desires could be—does not mean the contempt of the body which led much of ancient thought to regard the body as a prison-house enclosing the soul, shutting out the light from it or preventing it from rising to the heights. On the contrary, the dynamic of the physical organism can be sublimated to intellectual or spiritual activity, and thus the line or division drawn by classical theory between body and soul is obliterated. Thus, when one philosophy urges the satisfaction of bodily appetite as the greatest happiness and another recommends its suppression as an evil thing barring the way to happiness, they are both

[1] *dcD* xiv. 6.

wrong; the true philosophy, according to St Augustine, is the harnessing of energy to spiritual ends by desiring the right; the result will be right living.

From another point of view we may say that ancient thought had either exalted feeling and so paved the way to hedonism or cynicism or had enthroned reason and so led to a philosophic idealism which neglected many of the major and most troublesome elements of human nature. To St Augustine such one-sided emphasis in either direction is erroneous because it fails to make a satisfactory analysis of personality. Again, classical thought had little to say about the will, which to St Augustine is the summit of personality; Greek philosophy had always tended to assume, though with varying emphasis, that right conduct issued from right knowledge, and right knowledge depended upon the self-sufficient use of the reason. St Augustine again cuts across this assumption, and maintains that will is the immediate antecedent of action and that good will depends upon the motive power of love for what is good, such love being clarified by the reason.

But St Augustine says that eternal life is the *summum bonum*. Here again the shock to classical thought is obvious. To classical thought the immortality of the soul was either ridiculous or too shadowy an idea to hold the attention for long. Whether Socrates himself regarded it as more than an open question depends on the view taken of the Platonic dialogues, for in the *Apology*, admittedly addressed to an audience of Athenians rather than of disciples, he leaves the alternative of death as a dreamless sleep or the entry into some kind of existence in which it would be possible to converse with Orpheus, Musaeus and the rest.

In the *Phaedo* it is shown that either a soul must be annihilated at the death of the body or it must withdraw. The Socrates of that dialogue prefers the second alternative, relying on the reasonableness of the belief, not the demonstration, that the soul is divine, and from this hypothesis he draws the practical moral that, if life is eternal, the way in which it is lived on earth is of supreme importance; for according to the use we have made of life on earth will be the company which we shall enjoy in heaven. This last theme with its practical example in the death of Socrates is handled with a nobility which has endeared the dialogue to many generations of men; and no doubt it is Plato in this vein which led St Augustine to regard him as approaching nearest of all philosophers to the Christian faith. But Plato was not in the main current of Greek thought, nor was he the influence which carried most weight in the popular ideas of St Augustine's time, nor does the idea of immortality occupy a place in his philosophy corresponding to that of eternal life in the *dcD*. To the best ancient thought, as e.g. to Stoicism, eternal life was a corollary which might or

might not be drawn; to the Christian it was in the forefront of his triumphant faith, and, if it were not true, all else were vain.

The failure of Greek philosophy and religion to consider death and what lies beyond may perhaps account for the popularity of the Orphic mysteries. We know little about them; but there is no doubt that they influenced Greek thought, even the thought of Plato, very considerably. But here again the appeal is of a strictly limited nature; they offered, it is true, the hope of immortality, but they were concerned chiefly with holding out release from the 'sorrowful cycle' of rebirth or reincarnation to initiates who would then receive privileged treatment. Their direct influence was short-lived, but they were absorbed into that amalgam of religions and philosophies and crude superstitions which occupied the Roman world in the early centuries of our era.

Finally, it must be remembered that Greek thought (in contrast with some phases of Hebrew belief) contemplated no resurrection of the body: to Greek philosophy the body was essentially evil and destined to perish. If the soul survived the dissolution of its temporary home, it departed as a disembodied spirit or mind or intelligence, its destiny being either absorption in the supreme Mind or Spirit, or else reincarnation in endless cycles or else a vague existence of a kind beyond even guessing.

To return to St Augustine and eternal life. Eternal life is the *summum bonum*, and eternal death is the *summum malum*. If it be asked how there can be a death which is eternal, the answer is of course that life can be of such quality as to deserve to be described as death—the lasting negation of real life. It is thus implied that eternal life also bears a qualitative sense— the life of such quality as to be permanent, and that quality comes from and is 'adherence to God' (*adhaerere Deo*). All that St Augustine has to say about eternal life and the 'felicity of the Saints' and the winning of everlasting happiness is an elaboration of his phrase 'clinging to God'. This qualitative sense is made familiar to us by many passages in St John's Gospel and Epistles—'search the Scriptures, for in them ye have eternal life',[1] 'this *is* eternal life—to know thee as the only God . . .'[2] 'that ye may know that ye have eternal life'.[3] The life of a believer is of the same quality, as far as it can be, as the life which is really and truly life, the life of God.

Yet the notion of duration is always present; such life is enduring because it is the life of God and those who have such life live for ever, because they have the life of God who is eternal. Now, though St Augustine both in the *dcD* and in his many other writings has much that is profound to say about the qualitative nature of eternal life, in the *dcD* the notion of eternity or of everlastingness appears to receive the greater

[1] v. 39.   [2] 1 John v. 20.   [3] *Ibid.* 13.

emphasis; and this is true whether he is treating of eternal felicity or eternal punishment. This tendency is all the more surprising since St Augustine elsewhere expresses remarkable opinions about the nature of time. Time, he says, is not something which we can measure by the movement of certain bodies, as, for example, the sun. We measure it solely by the effect upon ourselves of all bodies of which we are aware; yet, apart from motions of body, it cannot be thought.[1] Time, therefore, means something different to everybody: and to everybody there is a present of things past (memory), a present of present things (sight) and a present of things future (hope). Hence, if time means to us nothing apart from bodies, time cannot be a starting point from which to begin defining our natures: rather we must start from 'body': and if we are bodies in time, all that is meant is that we are individual creatures in relation to other individual creatures. If this is the law of man's nature, man cannot get outside that law or that nature; and, if time means only being in relation to other creatures, time in this sense, but only in this sense, may be said to be a necessity of our nature. If time, therefore, in the commonly accepted sense is not essential to our nature, time (and the implicit notion of time-limit) is not a necessary concomitant of life (nor is the limit of time, which for the individual is death).

But it must be remembered that the *dcD* besides being a work of Christian philosophy is primarily a tract for the times addressed to the pagans; and of those pagans swarms were at the moment landing in Africa, driven in panic from an Italy menaced by a victorious Alaric. It would not be appropriate here to trace the growth of the belief in Rome as eternal, nor to attempt to describe how shattering to this belief was the capture of Rome by the Goths. The literature bears abundant witness to faith in the unending destiny of Rome. The phrase *urbs aeterna* occurs in Tibullus; Vergil and Horace cherish the notion; Pliny says that prayers are offered for the 'eternity of the empire',[2] and provincials echo them with all sincerity.[3] To confidence in the extension of Rome's dominion 'without limit'[4] had been added faith in her rule as unending. The same idea is reflected in inscriptions found as far apart as Africa, Roumania, Britain and Greece.[5] During the third and fourth centuries the word *aeternus* occurs with increasing frequency, not only in funeral epitaphs in such phrases as *aeterno somno, quieti aeternae*, which may or may not be influenced by Christian ideas, but also in dedications to Emperors. Diocletian, for example, no friend to the Christian, is described as 'the founder of

[1] *dcD* xii. 16.   [2] Plin. *Pan.* 67. 3.
[3] Cf. e.g. Aristides, Ἐις Ῥώμην, *ad fin.* εἴη δ'ἂν οὗτος (sc. ὁ τῆς ἀρχῆς χρόνος) ὁ πᾶς αἰών and his prayer πόλιν τήνδε θάλλειν δι' αἰῶνος . . . ; but in contrast note Commodianus, *Carm. Apol.* 923, *luget in aeternum quae se iactabat aeterna.*
[4] '*imperium sine fine dedi*'.   [5] Dess. *I. L. S.* 3181, 3636, 3657, 3927.

everlasting peace'[1] or 'eternal emperor', Constantius as 'eternal conqueror'; phrases like 'eternal tranquillity'[2] and 'eternal protection' occur
again and again. It may be that words were becoming weaker in meaning
or that extravagant titles for Emperors were being borrowed more openly
from eastern practice.[3] But the general notion conveyed by the inscriptions is that the idea of 'everlastingness' becomes commoner as the
Empire grows older—in fact, that the nearer the Empire approached to its
'fall', the more emphatic became the protestations of its eternity. Behind
such protestations there may have been apprehension; but the result may
well have been—by a process not unintelligible—to embed more firmly
in the minds of the age the very belief whose opposite was half-consciously
feared. To men bred in that belief the siege of Rome came as a shattering
blow. *Romanitas*, the proud tradition painfully and triumphantly built
up for more than a thousand years, was crumbling away before their eyes,
and the future, hitherto filled with the destiny of Rome, was a void, offer-
ing only chaos and uncertainty and perhaps extinction.

To others, who had time and inclination to reflect, the collapse of Rome
would prove conclusively the old theory of 'cyclical history'. Rome was
like all empires before; she rose and waxed and now she was waning. So it
would be with all human endeavour, collective or individual; it would
perish and start again and perish again as time rolled on in ever-recurring
circles, world without end.

To the pagans who had lost their dream of an 'eternal city' St Augustine
presents the conception of a city also eternal, which started with the beginning of human history and not merely from 'the foundation of the city'
and which will abide through the earthly life of man into his endless future
in heaven. Here was eternity which could be counted on never to dis-
appoint its believers. For those who found the notion of infinity too difficult and made its ends meet in the cyclical conception of history St Augustine unrolls the circle, flattening it out again into a straight line and restoring all the difficulties of endless eternity. To St Augustine eternity seemed
to offer no trouble, for, as we have seen, he has views of his own on the
nature of time. But it was inevitable that in performing the task which he
had undertaken in the *dcD* he should seem to overstress the quantitative
and understress the qualitative nature of eternal life. It was inevitable
because he was replying to pagans who had cherished belief in an eternal
city conceived as being wholly upon earth and entirely within time.

'We must live our lives aright to gain the one and to avoid the other,'
that is, to gain eternal life and to avoid eternal death. This is the kind of

---

[1] Dess. *I. L. S.* 618 (A.D. 290), cf. 614.   [2] *Ibid.* 724.
[3] In Plin. *Ep.* x. 83 (87), Trajan is besought by his 'eternity' (the word is reported by
Pliny) to grant a request; the suppliant is an Asiatic city.

phrase which critics of Christian morality seize upon to justify their charge that, to the Christian, morality is based upon a system of rewards and punishments and that therefore it is of a very low order. To do good, they say, for the sake of the reward rather than for the good itself destroys the value of the good action—which indeed ceases to be good if done from such a motive. In actual fact they travesty the Christian point of view and with all justification attack the travesty.

(i) It must be noted that the 'reward', to use for the moment the term employed in the criticism, is of the same order as the means necessary to obtain it. The means *is* the end, and when means and ends are fused they cease to have distinguishable meanings except as different aspects, artificially isolated, of what is essentially one process. The life lived aright is, as far as is possible to human nature, of the same essential quality as the life which is eternal, namely the life of God; this is the truth which the N.T. and particularly St John's Gospel emphasises—'this *is* life eternal'. Thus life of a particular quality is here and now eternal life and nothing can destroy such life. Means and end are the same thing and cannot be separated; the life has, and seeks, no reward except itself.

(ii) The notion of reward seems to be introduced into the matter because the term 'eternal' is stripped of its real meaning and is assumed to mean only 'future', that is, after death; a future life of happiness is then supposed to be the reward or bait which attracts the Christian to live a moral life in this world. But it would not be a great exaggeration to say that the New Testament writers are little concerned with the idea of a future life contrasted with the present life. Rather they assume it and regard life here and life hereafter as of the same piece or texture. Their concern is with the nature of life which was and is and will be life eternal, that is, real life, the life of God in men. The reward does not come afterwards; it is now and will be the life itself.

(iii) The essence of the Christian motive to live the Christian life is love for a personal God. Even on a wholly human plane the motive which is most free from self-seeking comes from spontaneously given affection or reverence for a person. Love and reverence are given to a person independently of the thought of reward or the dread of punishment. The Christian teacher (and St Augustine as much as any) is in no doubt that the basis of Christian morality is love for a personal God—*adhaerere Deo* —and he is equally sure that it seeks no reward outside itself because it can conceive of nothing more rewarding.

(iv) It is by no means certain that the motive of reward is as sordid and as easily eliminated as is sometimes supposed. The schoolmaster who abolishes prizes with the intention of encouraging industry and effort for their own sake nevertheless bestows approval or disapproval on his pupils;

and, though it may be said that the motive so offered is of a higher order than that of the prize, all the same there is reward and the reward is not only the disinterested reward of satisfaction in work well done. In fact, in all processes of education it is necessary to lead up to appreciation of a higher motive through lower motives which are of appeal at the particular stage of training. With men, no less than with children, the experience which at that stage can be encouraged only by the less worthy motive is often the condition upon which appreciation of the more worthy motive depends. Thus the notion of life as a future reward may be for many the necessary antecedent to the notion of life of a particular quality as being itself its own reward.

(v) Again, it is impossible not to be conscious of the distinction between life here and life hereafter; to ask that consciousness of life now should always be accompanied by a consciousness of its being one in texture with life hereafter demands a detachment from daily affairs beyond the power of all but a few. There is, therefore, a natural tendency to put the present in contrast with the future, and this very contrast helps to encourage the idea of eternal life as lying in the future life. From the point of view of conduct this tendency cannot be said to be harmful; the idea of eternal life taken in this sense draws attention to the importance of right conduct in this life, and the notion of reward naturally occurs.

(vi) Finally, with reward is inevitably associated its reverse—punishment; for assessment or judgment may be favourable or unfavourable, and judgment implies justice. To many, the justice of God is necessarily involved if the validity of moral values is to be vindicated, and justice may involve punishment. On the human plane punishment may be inflicted in a spirit of retribution and vindictiveness or as a deterrent or as a means of reformation. In the last book of the *dcD* St Augustine has much to say about eternal punishment and what he says has revolted many of his readers. For he has little to say about punishment as a means of reformation, and his chapters give the impression that he is concerned with a retributive justice of the most primitive kind, upheld primarily as justifiable in itself and secondarily as a deterrent. The reason for this emphasis is that he handles the whole theme from extreme points of view. He regards the good as good, the bad as bad; the lot of the good is eternal life, the lot of the bad must in logic be the reverse, namely, eternal death, which means eternal punishment; the good life *is* eternal life and therefore the bad life must be eternal punishment. The opposite of eternal life is not death or extinction, for to St Augustine as to Plato the soul is indestructible, and retributive justice seems to demand something more than extinction, which to the extinguished can be nothing but a matter of indifference. He does not seem to take into account the possibility that no

one is wholly good or wholly bad and that the presence of some good may destroy the justice of eternal punishment. Hence he neglects the reformatory aspect of punishment which may turn some good into greater good and he appears to concentrate on its retributive character. With vigorous and ruthless logic working upon extreme and exceptional and possibly unreal cases he is carried on to conclusions about eternal felicity and eternal torment which it is difficult to square with the mercy of God. But it may well be that in modern times we have erred in the other direction and have forgotten the inevitable consequences of sin, that we have sought an easy and misguided comfort in the mercy of God interpreted virtually to mean the indifference of God. Without adopting some of St Augustine's extreme conclusions we may be reminded by the rigour of his logic that in believing in the mercy of God we cannot disregard His abhorrence of evil nor forget that the forgiveness of God needs also the self-condemnation of the sinner.

It is only fair to remark that elsewhere[1] St Augustine realises that nothing can be created wholly bad and he asserts that even the devil has elements of good; his badness is due to perversity of will. Yet even in the most perverse will there may yet remain a sense of the loss of goodness. The implications of this admission for the theory of punishment are great; but further consideration is postponed till chapter 13 is reached.

'The righteous man', quotes St Augustine, 'lives by faith.' The sentence which follows contains in highly summarised form the essence of the contrast between the Christian and the classical outlook, and St Augustine intends to emphasise that contrast. It will be remembered that we are still concerned with his reply to pagan moral theory.

St Augustine appeals to Scripture (Habakkuk ii. 4); this in itself is a significant point, as will be seen later, and upon the significant word in the brief quotation—'faith'—the rest of the sentence hangs. Goodness expressed in a good life depends upon faith; the search for the good must be undertaken in a spirit of faith; without faith the resources of man are inadequate to enable him to live the good life; external aid—God's aid—is necessary to him and aid is given only as the result of faith; faith that aid will be given is itself given by God; faith issues in prayer, and prayer has its source in faith.

We are asked, therefore, to consider goodness of life not in terms of nature or reason or pleasure or virtue but in terms of faith, aid, prayer.

Seeing that St Augustine's voluminous works are largely concerned in one way or another with faith, it is rash to attempt to sum up his teaching in a few words; but perhaps a hint may be offered as follows. Graeco-

[1] Ch. 13.

Roman civilisation, as St Augustine knew it after a typical education and a long period of study and reflection, had made the fundamental mistake of attempting to explain the world in terms of the world; principles of interpretation had been sought from within man. This had led to the bankruptcy of ancient thought. The whole intellectual framework of ancient thought had crashed because reason had nothing on which to base itself; it had claimed omnipotence and yet it had been shown in the philosophies of the Greeks and Romans to lead to contradictory conclusions. It had been forced by its own ingenuity into meaningless antitheses, such as form and matter, which it could not reconcile, and in pressing extremes to their logical conclusion it had arrived at varied interpretations of the universe and of man which were poles apart. Reason had sought to establish values when it found them desirable, to deny them when they were inconvenient; mind had been divorced from matter and an unbridgeable gulf set up between the two. Natural science and philosophy had either gone different ways or become indistinguishable; blind law or capricious fortune governed the history of nations and the lot of individual men; Nature was to be despised or worshipped.

Now St Augustine has the profoundest respect for ancient *scientia*, that is, the Graeco-Roman spirit of enquiry and the massive accumulations of knowledge resulting therefrom. But in his view it had failed because it lacked as a starting point a principle operating both within and without the world; the human mind, active within its own world, could find an interpretation neither of itself nor of its world unless it received the aid of a principle operating both in and also beyond itself and its world. The clue to that principle was given by 'faith' which launched itself further than reason unaided. Faith is the readiness to take God at His word—His word being the word of Holy Scripture and the Word, or the Logos, of God. In Scripture is to be found a record of the dealings of God with one nation, and in the record is a guide to the interpretation of history; in the Incarnation is the answer to man's most searching questions about the meaning of existence. Faith is rewarded by 'insight' (*sapientia*). Starting from this new point of departure, namely, Christian insight into values, man has now a clue through the tangles of his accumulated learning (*scientia*). The facts composing that learning are still of importance, but the old self-contradictory and fragmentary interpretations of them, and the systems erected upon those interpretations, will be discarded. Secular learning must be used, and used for the interpretation of Scripture; but the motive of its use will be different. The accumulated data of knowledge will be re-arranged in the light of the new principle of interpretation, and by being seen in a new light will take on a new meaning. Reason is to be as powerful and active as before; but it has to take into account

as one of its basic principles something of which it was unaware before, namely, the insight into the meaning of existence given by an initial act of faith; and faith means taking God at His word as the source of all values.

Though the Latin word for Christian 'insight' and Stoic 'wisdom' is the same, the meaning is very different. The *sapientia* or wisdom of the Stoic was pitched beyond human reach, exalted into the clouds by a merciless and inhuman logic. The picture of man toiling upwards, slipping backwards or plunging deliberately into vices of which he thought he was free, repentant and bracing himself again for further effort, till he rises by struggle and doubt and uncertainty to a goodness with which he is still dissatisfied—this was unintelligible to the Stoic sage. To him virtue is virtue and there are no half measures; it is a complete unity dependent upon a clear and steady understanding of the good. Every act proceeds from a constant virtue and issues with a logical certainty from a stark apprehension of moral values. The sage knows, the rest know nothing; men are good or they are not. No wonder that he was accused of smugness and complacency; as an aloof spectator he watched the misguided world from the cold heights of his detachment, conversing only with the few who shared the rarified levels on which his thought moved. He could reflect upon the weaknesses of mankind; but he offered no remedy, for he was free from the weakness of compassion. Yet his moral sentiments were excellent. They reach the highest stage of pagan reflections upon morality, and the reader of Seneca in selected extracts perforce admires till he reads further and recoils in horror of his self-sufficiency and inhuman humanitarianism. Nor was the sage unconcerned with spiritual things, but the things of the spirit become repellent when handled by a perfect spiritual pride, and men of generous humility turn to a more warm-blooded and human interpretation of life.

Christian *sapientia* is different. The Stoic wise man unfolded before himself a completely traced map of human experience, virtue, intellect, passion, nature. The whole tract of perfection was familiar to him and no situation could surprise him; for he had worked out all from his own resources. The Christian convert groped over the difficult and puzzling country of life, but he was secure in the possession of a clue. The clue was not, in the first place, elaborated by his own efforts, but was granted in response to a conviction that the clue would be given to him. The conviction owed its origin not to his convincing himself, but to the impulse of God urging him to ask for 'insight'. Thus equipped he could find a way through the problems of life, of intellect and morality and action, when they presented themselves. In humble dependence upon external aid, a man among men, he would make his way, and history and knowledge

and human life would take on real meaning apprehended by an insight penetrating ever more deeply into everlasting values.

If 'faith' was an idea little known to classical religion, prayer was more familiar, though Christian thought (unless it descended to non-Christian levels) altered its meaning. The normal attitude of Graeco-Roman religions is conveniently expressed in Cicero's treatise, *On the Nature of the Gods*.[1] 'All men take the view that material goods—vineyards, crops, olive-yards, agricultural produce in plenty, in fact all wealth and prosperity in life, are gifts from the gods. But no one ever put down virtue as 'received' from God. This, of course, is correct. Virtue justly wins for us the praises of others and virtue rightly gives us grounds for self-congratulation, and neither of these things could happen if we held virtue as a gift from the gods and not as an achievement of our own. . . . No one ever thanked the gods for being a good man—only for being rich or famous or out of danger. It is for gifts such as these last—safety, security, riches, affluence—that men call Jupiter by the titles 'Optimus' and 'Maximus', not for justice or self-control or wisdom. . . . To return to the point, it is the universal judgment of mankind that good fortune must be besought from the gods but that wisdom must be won by a man from himself.'

This is the typical point of view, though undoubtedly there are passages in Greek tragedy and in Plato which take much higher ground. So also in Stoicism as represented by Seneca, 'God within man' is a frequent theme. For example, 'The gods are not squeamishly aloof; nor do they grudge themselves; they suffer man to come near and they hold out a helping hand to those who are climbing. Does it surprise you that man goes towards the gods? Why! God comes towards men or rather—more intimately—he comes into men. There is no goodness of mind without God.' Or again: 'You can cancel all your former requests to the gods. Start all over again with others; ask for goodness, for health of the mind and then of the body,' and later, after a protest against unworthy prayers, 'Speak with God as though men could overhear you.'[2]

Even if a higher view is taken of Seneca's sincerity than some critics would allow him, such a passage does not amount to very much; it is a personal and individual expression of opinion and does not square with other utterances of the same author.[3] Moreover, it is not put forward as essential to the main position. But to the Christian (as is clear in the passage of the *dcD* before us), prayer or 'the ascent of the soul to God', as St Augustine elsewhere calls it, is the mainspring of the specifically Christian life. Christian faith, morality and action depend upon it, and St Augustine emphasises it as one of the chief points of contrast between the pagan and

[1] iii. 36 (86).   [2] *Ep.* 73. 15; *Ep.* 10 *ad fin.*   [3] As, e.g., *Ep.* 41. 1; *N. Q.* 2. 37.

the Christian outlook. Speaking generally, the contrast in the two views of prayer lay in this, that the Christian sought to align his will with the will of God and knew that thereby there would follow an irruption of divine energy into human life; the pagan sought to bend God's will to his own, and when, turning philosopher, he realised the absurdity of this aim, he abandoned the idea of prayer as being superstition.

The rest of the long fourth chapter of the nineteenth book (it is not included in the text or translation)[1] is devoted to a review of virtue, and especially the cardinal virtues of temperance, prudence, justice and fortitude of which ancient philosophy made much. None of them, St Augustine contends, can give happiness; their very essence is the frank recognition of evil and they are all attempts to wrestle with evil in different forms, moral or physical; and the constant struggle with an evil which they cannot cast out cannot be called happiness. The virtues themselves have no meaning except in relation to their opposites; if prudence tells us what to choose and what to reject and forewarns us of evil, it takes evil for granted because it must. The virtues are never wholly realised, as they themselves admit; if they are not themselves perfected, they cannot confer happiness, for their irresolvable opposites pulling against them create conflict. Indeed, so great is the evil against which the virtues contend that fortitude, for example, as preached by the Stoics, reached its culmination in suicide; the supreme realisation of this virtue is its own negation. As St Augustine put it with a pun on the word, 'What a curious happiness which seeks the aid of death to achieve its "end"!' Goodness, his argument continues, should lead to life and not to death; goodness leading to everlasting life alone can give happiness, and such life comes from faith. Goodness on earth then is not limited to the earthly life. The goodness which here must be a conflict with evil and therefore cannot give perfect happiness is sustained and fortified by the faith which sees that goodness here is of a piece with eternal goodness, whose perfection is free from inner conflict, and which therefore carries with it perfect happiness. Pagan morality is forced by facts to confess that it does not and cannot make men happy, and one reason is that through lack of faith it sets the limit of human life at death. Christian morality, though it cannot eliminate evil and, therefore, must always be engaged in a struggle, yet knows that its efforts carry their results beyond death, and it gains a strength and a validity and a vindication from the faith that it is in line with eternal goodness. But even so it is offered not happiness but the hope of happiness. Pagan morality being without faith had not even a hope.

That is all St Augustine is concerned with at the moment, namely, that

[1] It is summarised on page 68.

morality, which does not look beyond this life, patently offers not even hope of happiness. He does not go on to discuss two questions which might occur. If our morality is so conditioned by our physical nature and by the physical world and if virtue is a conflict with evil desires and temptations, how can it be said that our goodness is in line with God's goodness? How can it be said that the later of the Ten Commandments have any place in the goodness of God? Secondly, if happiness means the cessation of conflict and yet our morality is unthinkable except in terms of conflict, is it implied that happiness transcends morality and is supermoral or amoral and therefore, to our notions, static; for moral progress means the active overcoming of the morally inferior?

To the first question it may be replied that the objective validity of man's moral judgments is not altered by the consideration that higher beings express their morality in modes other than those in which man gives expression to his. Objectivity means that human judgment as to what is good or bad, as far as men are concerned, is such that every moral intelligence, of whatever order of being, would recognise that for man in his circumstances such and such a standard or course of action is good and is based eventually upon values which are applicable to all moral beings in all circumstances. For example, it would be absurd to suppose that the tenth commandment may be regarded as of no objective moral value on the ground that it cannot constitute any part of the goodness of God. For man it is valid because it expresses, admittedly in negative form, an element of God's goodness, namely love, applied to the special circumstances of human life. Behind it is a positive principle which would be recognised by all moral intelligences as valid in all and not only human circumstances. The second question is closely bound up with the later chapters of the nineteenth book in which the nature of peace is discussed and its consideration is deferred till then.

CHAPTER 5

The Life of Fellowship

With chapter 5 St Augustine passes to the treatment of another aspect of happiness which will occupy him directly to the end of chapter 9 and indirectly to the end of the book. Pagan philosophy, it will be remembered, had sought for happiness in a particular kind of life—a life which, among other things, was directed towards a *summum bonum*. The various kinds of *summum bonum* put forward by classical theory St Augustine has already discussed and he has made his own counter-proposal. But ancient

philosophers had also predicated of the life of happiness that it should be a 'social life', a life of fellowship; the life of the wise man—the man who had the secret of happiness—should be lived with his fellows.

St Augustine says at the outset that he would agree that fellowship is a necessary condition of happiness; for after all he is writing about the city of God and it would be reasonable for him to agree that a city should offer a life of fellowship to its saints. But he denies that any of the forms of social or political relationship known to the pagan world (as, for example, the family or the state) did in fact offer any certainty of happiness. Not much observation was necessary to reveal that within such relationship there was in fact much unhappiness. His argument is that happiness may involve 'society', but society does not necessarily mean happiness; because pagan philosophy had seen the first point, it is not entitled to assume that it can ensure happiness by means of any of the forms of society known to it. Such forms of society he then reviews from the point of view of happiness and finds them wanting.

His statement that the philosophers assumed society to be necessary to happiness needs no lengthy elaboration. The Republic of Plato is founded on the belief that the end of life is virtue and knowledge culminating in wisdom, but that without his fellows the individual cannot attain this end; only as a member of the state can he attain any measure of it. The state, therefore, must train its citizens to reach happiness through virtue and knowledge, and so the state tests everything by this criterion and directs all institutions and all lives to that end. Historically the family contributed to the growth of the state; but, when the state has emerged, the family should lose all separate existence, and children should belong to the state. Plato attempts to reconcile two opposing lines of thought. First, the world is the world of appearance and therefore the most rational man will move in it as little as possible, for the sphere of the Ideas is his real home. Secondly, man is 'social' and needs society in which to achieve perfection, and perfection is the only reality. Therefore reason and society must be combined; the state must embody reason to the utmost and therefore it must be paramount and its interests all-absorbing, and the individual will find himself only as a member of the state.

Aristotle agrees in part and differs in part and the difference is significant. He agrees that the family is historically the origin of the state and that man is a political animal, as is proved by his possession of speech, which would be useless to any but a social being. But origin to Aristotle has nothing to do with the 'nature' of the state. The state is logically prior to the family and the individual, for the state is the end towards which man is striving and in which he fulfils his perfection. But, whereas Plato

had destroyed the family and the individual, Aristotle asserts that both are necessary organisms within an organism and in his view every organism has its own end. The individual and the family are real and have rights and are ends in themselves; the state is the society in which lesser ends, of value in themselves, are absorbed in a larger end.

It may be noted first, that, while both Plato and Aristotle insist that society is necessary to man, neither goes beyond the conception of the Greek city-state. The failure of Aristotle, living when he did, to discuss the development of other forms of political organisation can be due only to the inductive nature of his political theory and is in line with his refusal to sketch an ideal state or to go beyond experience. Secondly, Greek philosophy tended to emphasise more than we should the political aspect of society, probably because it did not move far beyond the city-state. We should be inclined to substitute 'social' or 'sociological' in many contexts where it spoke of 'political'. Thirdly, St Augustine's sympathy is with Aristotle in the preservation of the family as a vital unit of society. His mother's influence on him, the teaching of the Old and New Testaments, his life in Italy, his Roman education and his knowledge of Latin literature, which sets a higher value on the family than perhaps any other, his experience as a bishop and a magistrate—these would bring home to him the supreme value of the family, while at the same time leaving him in no doubt that it was liable to as much discord and unhappiness as any other society of men. If in chapter 5 he emphasises the 'miseries', it is not because he belittles the family as such; he is concerned only to show that it will not by itself achieve happiness for its members.

If, then, the family offers no guarantee of happiness, still less will the state, which is large and contains all the more opportunity for discord. As a symptom of such discord we have only to consider the law-courts, where are revealed not only the wrong-doings of men but the impotence of justice either to discover with any certainty the identity of the wrong-doer or to be just when it is discovered.

CHAPTER 6

The difficulties and perplexities of a judge are feelingly described by St Augustine, and his contempt for the use of torture as a means of eliciting the truth is as outspoken as the doubts of the Roman lawyers themselves. The torture of free men will perhaps surprise the reader familiar only with the judicial procedure of the Republic. During the years of the Republic a free man could not be tortured whether he was in the box or in the dock.

But this rule was broken in the early Empire, and in the late Empire the practice condemned under the Republic appears to be normal; indeed, exemptions from liability to torture are noted in the writings of the lawyers as exceptional. The old rule was changed not by legislation but by the actual practice of the supreme courts, and the change was brought about probably by imperial insistence that nothing should be left undone to bring to light cases of treason (*maiestas*). The proscriptions, of which Augustus himself had not been guiltless, had accustomed people to the extinction of political rivals; and in the following two centuries all depended on the Emperor's attitude to treason and the readiness with which he put a treasonable interpretation upon acts which might have been innocent.

But from the end of the second century a change began. Society tended to be divided into two classes, the *honestiores* and the *humiliores* or *plebeii*, and the legal rights of these classes became more clearly differentiated as time went on. The *honestiores* included men of senatorial and equestrian rank and decurions, that is, members of the councils or senates of townships, and their children. These were exempt from torture as accused persons, and soldiers also had this privilege.[1] But there appear to have been limitations or restrictions; for example, the use of torture was permissible only in trials for treason, the practice of magic (which always had a bearing on treason) and forgery. The treatment of the witness seems to have been brought into line with that of the accused who denied the charge, and many safeguards and modifications are introduced. The first clear appearance of this principle occurs in a lawyer writing in the time of Septimius Severus, and the passage shows that where there is no clear evidence the witness is to be tortured. After Constantine the lower social grades were treated as slaves, whom at all times it was legal to torture when they were giving evidence,[2] and apparently no credence was to be placed in them unless their evidence was so given[3]; the magistrate had some discretion in deciding the kind of person to whom the rule applied and the degree of torture to be inflicted. But in trials for treason no distinction was admitted, according to another text; 'if circumstances demand it, all persons without exception are tortured when their evidence is required.'[4]

On the other hand it is laid down in many of the rescripts of the Emperors that torture, whether of free men or of slaves, was to be used with great care and moderation, and so much restriction was introduced that its legality was much curtailed. The general drift of the restrictions is that

---

[1] Certainly as early as A.D. 183, but if a soldier was a *proditor* his exemption was nullified. Dig. 49. 16. 7.

[2] See R. H. Barrow, *Slavery in the Roman Empire*, pp. 31-5.

[3] Dig. 22. 5. 21. 2, *sine tormentis testimonio eius credendum non est*.

[4] Dig. 48. 18. 10. 1.

torture must be a last resource used under fixed rules and subject to the control of the court and not of interested persons.[1] The lawyers show doubt of its value; for example, it is admitted that evidence given under torture is a 'fragile and dangerous thing, likely to cheat the truth; many men, through sheer fortitude or through becoming hardened to pain, make light of torture and the truth cannot be wrung out of them; others can endure it so little that they will tell lies just as you like rather than endure torture.' 'The evidence of private enemies ought not to be trusted even though given under torture, for they lie readily.'[2] Such admissions go far to concede the argument of St Augustine's chapter.

To bring the matter nearer to St Augustine reference may be made to a letter[3] written by him about A.D. 412. In one of the Donatist disturbances a priest of Hippo had been murdered and Marcellinus tried the ringleaders. He compelled them to confess; but he used no tortures, says St Augustine, such as fire or iron hooks or the rack, but only the scourge which 'is used by teachers of the liberal arts and by parents and often by bishops in administering justice'!

We pass now to the third area of fellowship—the world. To illustrate his point St Augustine takes two causes of the dissociation of nations, namely (i) diversity of language, (ii) war.

CHAPTER 7

The argument that diversity of language alienates nation from nation and man from man is not often heard in Greek and Roman literature. The Greek point of view was briefly that all who did not speak Greek were barbarians and so much the worse for them, and the reluctance of the Greeks to learn other languages has often been noted. The Roman attitude was different; speaking broadly, Greek became the second language of the Empire for literary, commercial and administrative purposes, and Latin or Greek, sometimes both, were the official languages of the provinces. 'Greeks and barbarians', says an unknown author of a panegyric on an unidentified Emperor, 'Greeks and barbarians talk the same language.' But within the Empire scores of languages were actually spoken—Phrygian, Carian, Paphlagonian, Armenian, Aramaic, Arabic and others in the East, Thracian, German and Celtic in the North, Iberian, Berber and Punic in the West; and with their languages scores of tribes kept their customs and religions and all the associations and traditions which lan-

guage enshrines. With these the government did not interfere; and, when the panegyrists of the Roman Empire praise the unity of law and government and loyalty which had been achieved, they do not usually speak of the benefits of unity of language nor do they express regret at its omission. And of course they were right, for the Empire was a unity amid diversity; and, if uniformity was imposed with greater ruthlessness in administrative and economic matters as the Empire grew older, the diversity of language and local habit was beyond the scope of administrative pressure—even if the administration had ever wished it. An interesting passage[1] of the Digest of Justinian, quoting the opinion of Ulpian, lays down that 'trusts (*fidei-commissa*) can be left in any language at all, not only Latin or Greek but in Punic or Gallican, in the language of any other nation', and no doubt this only gave legal sanction to a practice which was too common to be checked.

The Punic and Berber languages were widely spoken in Africa. The stepson of Apuleius (at the end of the second century) could scarcely speak Latin, only Punic.[2] The Emperor Septimius Severus, who was born at Leptis Magna, could not keep his sister at Rome, for she spoke Latin so badly that he was ashamed of her.[3] Punic inscriptions have been found and Punic words sometimes occur embedded in stock Latin formulae; for example, the word nasililim occurs several times in Latin dedications and apparently means a thank-offering to the gods.[4] There is evidence, too, of a Punic literature.[5] But the embarrassment caused by diversity of languages had been felt by St Augustine himself in his capacity as bishop, and this chapter of the *dcD* may well reflect his own experience. For example, he thought it incumbent to appoint as bishop of Fussala, a place not far from Hippo, a man who was proficient in Punic.[6] In one of his sermons he uses a Punic proverb, though he translates it into Latin 'because you do not all know Punic'.[7] When Pelagius went from Africa to Palestine and met in debate the diocesan synod of Jerusalem in A.D. 415, John, the bishop of Jerusalem, spoke only in Greek, while Orosius, Pelagius' critic, spoke Latin. In estimating the reasons for Pelagius' acquittal, which was not unimportant in the history of the Pelagian controversy, St Augustine attributes it partly to the difficulties caused by the use of two languages and the need to use an interpreter, who in fact was not accurate.[8]

St Augustine's plea that a man is more at home in the company of his dog than of a foreigner will be understood by Englishmen; moreover, it

---

[1] 32. 11.   [2] Apul. *Apol.* 98 (cf. edition by H. E. Butler and A. S. Owen).
[3] S. H. A. *Sev.* 15.
[4] e. g. Dessau, *I. L. S.* 4443e *S(aturno) A(ugusto) sacrum Haterii Saturninus et Iulianus nasililim voto susceptum solverunt lib[e]nte animo.*
[5] Aug. *Ep.* xvii.   [6] *Ep.* ccix. 3, cf. lxxxiv. 2.   [7] *Sermo* clxvii. 4.
[8] *De gest. Pel.* 39; Oros. *lib. apol.* vi. 1, *vel prave interpretantem vel plura supprimentem vel alia ex aliis suggerentem.*

reveals a feeling for a dog's companionship which is not very common in ancient literature. Oddly enough, Orosius begins the long history of the world, which he undertook at St Augustine's instigation and dedicated to him, with a passage very similar in feeling. He undertook the history in a spirit of obedience, he says, reinforced by all his will and effort—obedience not unlike that of a dog. 'Of dogs alone can it be said that by instinct they are anxious to hurry on to the task for which they have been trained; of their own nature they so observe the rule of obedience that it requires only the discipline of fear and apprehension to keep them in a state of suspended eagerness until a nod or a signal releases them and sends them off to carry out their errand. They have their own distinctive desires which set them above the rest of animals and bring them close to rational beings —namely, the desire to discriminate, to love and to serve. They distinguish between master and stranger; they do not hate those whom they pursue but they are passionately devoted to those whom they love. In their love of their master and his house they do not stay on guard merely because physically they are adapted to this task; rather they watch over the household because they are moved by a conscientious and anxious love for it.'

That Orosius should have prefaced an otherwise prosaic history with such a passage is remarkable unless St Augustine was a lover of dogs. But these two passages perhaps warrant no more than a fanciful guess![1]

The argument then proceeds with an imaginary reply. Surely the imperial state in maintaining peace imposes not only obedience upon its dependencies but also a common language. At any rate, is the reply, the attempt is made, as the swarms of interpreters testify. But, St Augustine protests, at what a price is peace maintained and imposed—civil wars, wars between allies, foreign wars, and, when wars subside for a moment, fear of their renewed outbreak. Is it any defence to say that a war is just, and that the wise ruler of pagan philosophy will wage only just wars? They will have been forced upon him by the unrighteousness of his enemies. If he is possessed of any human feeling, he will be made miserable by the necessity to wage them and by the reflection that the necessity springs from the wickedness of fellow men. The justice of a war is no comfort to him.

This idea of a just war, which St Augustine does not elaborate, was taken up by the canonists of later centuries. It finds powerful expression in the second book of the *de Monarchia* of Dante. Briefly, his argument is that, since the history of the Roman people was divinely guided, Roman law was in harmony with divine will. The expansion of Roman power was therefore divinely guided and was *de iure*; and, since war was a means

---

[1] But cf. also *de lib. arbit.* i. 16; *de vera rel.* 53; *de Trin.* xii. 2.

of that expansion and a divinely guided people could not use an unlawful means to a lawful end, war itself was *de iure* and, for Rome, was just. It is true that Dante admits that war should be used only as a last resort (he refers to Cicero and Vegetius to support him); he admits, too, that belligerents should be inspired only by 'enthusiasm for justice' and not by hatred or ambition. But he thinks that Rome faithfully observed these conditions, and, when men are gathered together with one accord inspired by a passion for justice, there must God be in their midst. Thus he arrives at his remarkable conclusion that what is obtained by war is obtained *de iure* and what is *de iure* is in accordance with divine will. The contrast with the view of St Augustine needs no demonstration.

CHAPTER 8

This chapter seems at first sight to be an interruption; we expect to pass on to the fourth and last 'range' of fellowship. Perhaps the connection is this: St Augustine has already spoken of the insecurity of the fellowship of one's immediate family and friends; he then passed to the insecurity of human fellowship in the nations. It occurs to him that within each nation there may be a number of men of good will who are bound in ties of kinship or friendship with similar men in other nations. But their presence does not entitle us to see much comfort therein; for the friendship of men so separated is exposed to special fears and worries of its own, and so such fellowship has its own peculiar miseries and can no more be regarded as unmixed happiness than the friendship of men living in the same community. Indeed, such are the unknown dangers which threaten distant friends and such are our fears about them that news of their death, though it may grieve us, often gives us relief, and we congratulate them on their death.

The 'consolations' of which St Augustine speaks are probably the ordinary letters of consolation written by one friend to another or to the relations of a friend. We have several such letters. It is just possible, though less likely, that St Augustine has in mind also the consolatory essays (*consolationes*) which were sometimes written, particularly by philosophers. They were addressed primarily to an individual, a friend or relation, but they had in view a wider number of readers. They contained comforting thoughts upon death and the vanity of human hopes, and gave opportunity for gathering together historical examples of fortitude in adversity. In form they were letters, in fact they were moral treatises.

CHAPTER 9

The fourth range of fellowship is that which stretches from the world to the universe, from the world of sense to the spiritual world. The fellowship of the holy angels is in principle admitted by those philosophers who assume the friendliness of divine beings.[1] It may be said, on the positive side, that such fellowship is not subject to the catastrophes, death and desertion, to which human fellowship is liable. But there is a good deal on the negative side; the fellowship of men with angels is less intimate than that of men with men; but—more important—evil powers may masquerade as good powers and deceive the ignorance of men into thinking them good. Their nature is revealed by the evil nature of the rites which they demand of their worshippers. From their machinations not even the saints are free; but the very strength of the temptations so offered to men makes them desire all the more earnestly the eternal peace and the eternal gifts which peace brings. Such peace is free from conflict; it is in itself final happiness, and in this peace and in this happiness the 'ends' of all virtue find their fulfilment.

The topics which invite consideration are (i) the philosophers to whom St Augustine refers; (ii) the daemons, and their relation to men; (iii) the attitude of Christians to the daemons.

(i) By philosophers St Augustine means the Greek philosophers and in particular the school of Plato and its successors, the Neoplatonists; of these he has specially in mind, besides Plato himself, Speusippus, Plato's nephew, Xenocrates his disciple, and Plotinus, Iamblichus and Porphyry and Apuleius. This is made clear by a passage in *dcD* viii. 12, for in the eighth book he discusses at great length the views of the philosophers on gods and daemons. It may be noted that St Augustine does not make any reference in the *dcD* to Plutarch, whose works (particularly those on 'The failure of oracles' and on 'Isis and Osiris') a modern student would regard as of great importance for the understanding of the daemonology of the second century A.D. Yet Plutarch's works are constantly quoted by the sophists of the fourth century, and they reflect a point of view which was common in St Augustine's time. To Apuleius, on the other hand, St Augustine gives more attention in the *dcD* than we should perhaps think he deserved. But Apuleius was an African, and in Africa no doubt his works had a special currency.

It is impossible here to give a history of the later stages of Platonism or any full account of Neoplatonism. But without a sketch of both it is im-

[1] For 'the city of gods and men' in Stoicism, see Appendix IA.

possible to understand the place of the daemons in the religious thought of the age.

During the five centuries which elapsed between the death of Epicurus (270 B.C.) and the appearance of Neoplatonism, the chief Greek schools, Academic, Peripatetic, Stoic and Epicurean, continued to exist. They produced little that was new or original. Their differences were mitigated and their likenesses were stressed and each borrowed tenets from the other; all with the exception of the Epicurean became eclectic. In one sense this tendency had its merits, for the divisions between school and school were partly due to excessive concentration upon one aspect of a problem to the exclusion of others. From another point of view it was disastrous to the spirit of philosophy, for it tended to encourage the attitude of mind in which vital distinctions are disregarded. During this period, too, there occurred a great revival and development of Pythagoreanism with its symbolism and mystical outlook upon the world, and henceforward Pythagoreanism exercised great influence on philosophy. But, while on the whole the philosophical schools developed minor elements in the thought of the great philosophers or turned over the old problems without making new contributions or engaged themselves in fanciful interpretations of man and the universe, educated men, and uneducated too, became increasingly interested in the religious and pseudo-philosophical ideas which were spread under the conditions of the Roman peace from one end of the Roman world to the other. It is essential to an understanding of the Christian writers and of the relation between Christianity and the society of the day to realise that during the early centuries of our era there was a tremendous upsurge of spiritual energy which sought an outlet in an overwhelming interest in religion and theology. Men of all grades of society sought for some spiritual satisfaction and they were prepared to find it in one or several of the religions or philosophies rapidly being disseminated through the Mediterranean lands. Spiritual demand was great, the supply of religions increased to meet it; the Christians recognised the unprecedented demand and condemned paganism as a means of meeting it.

Passing over Philo of Alexandria and for the moment Plutarch and Apuleius and others, we may make mention of Ammonius Sakkas, born between A.D. 180 and 192, who lectured on philosophy at Alexandria; among his pupils were Origen and Plotinus. Origen is worth noting because it is interesting to find a man who was later to be a Christian philosopher attending the lectures of the founder of Neoplatonism; in succeeding centuries very many Christians, including some of the most famous, were destined to pass through Neoplatonism into Christianity and to bring over elements of their old training into their interpretations of their new faith. Among these was St Augustine himself. Plotinus, the greatest

of the Neoplatonists, travelled to the West and about A.D. 250 lectured to crowded audiences in Rome, urging them 'to return to that dearest country where is the Father and where is all', but living in detachment from the chaotic world which sank into confusion outside his lecture-room. The most influential of his disciples was Porphyry, who migrated to Rome from Sicily—'that Sicilian, whose fame is widespread', 'the best known philosopher of the pagans', as St Augustine described him.[1] For a study of the *dcD* Porphyry is as important as Plotinus. St Augustine had probably read Plotinus in a Latin translation and he bears abundant witness to the great influence exercised upon him by the philosopher in whom, above all others, 'shone forth the face of Plato, the purest and the clearest in all philosophy.' But the works of Porphyry clearly had a greater vogue at the end of the fourth century; he had shown himself the avowed enemy of Christianity in a work in fifteen books, 'Against the Christians,' whereas Plotinus' works contain only veiled and doubtful references to Christianity. In the *dcD* St Augustine devotes many chapters to the refuta-tion of Porphyry's doctrines, and he clearly regards him as one of the main opponents with whom a treatise, with the sub-title *Contra paganos*, should come to grips. To Iamblichus who lived in the reign of Constan-tine the Great the *dcD* makes a few references. St Augustine was not to know that in A.D. 410 was born at Constantinople Proclus, the great systematiser of Neoplatonic teaching and a mainstay of paganism in the East. His is the last great name before the Neoplatonic school at Athens was closed by Justinian in A.D. 529.

(ii) The daemons have a long and varied history in Greek religious thought. For example, the word is used for 'divine agency' in Homer; in Hesiod daemons are the souls of the heroes of past ages, now beneficent agencies; in Aeschylus the dead turn into daemons; in Theognis and Men-ander and elsewhere the daemon is a guardian angel and sometimes the guardian of a family.[2] But the aspect of daemonism which concerns the *dcD* is the development of the idea by the Platonists, or, as we should call them, the Neoplatonists, taking their point of departure from Plato him-self and gathering, as they attracted adherents, all kinds of ideas from Greek and Eastern cults and lore.

In the Symposium of Plato there is a famous passage, put into the mouth of Diotima, which describes the functions of daemons—'All that is daemonic lies between the mortal and the immortal. Its functions are to interpret to men communications from the gods—commandments and favours from the gods in return for men's attentions—and to convey

[1] *Retract.* ii. 31; *dcD* xxii. 3, cf. vii. 25.
[2] E.g. Hom. *Il.* i. 222; iii. 420; Hes. *Op.* 122; Aesch. *Pers.* 628, cf. Eur. *Alc.* 1003; Theognis, 161; Menander, *fr.* 550 Koch.

prayers and offerings from men to the gods. Being thus between men and gods the daemon fills up the gap and so acts as a link joining up the whole. Through it as intermediary pass all forms of divination, all the technique of the priests—sacrifices and rites and spells and divination and sorcery. God does not mix with man; the daemonic is the agency through which intercourse and converse take place between men and gods, whether in waking visions or in dreams.'[1]

This is the most striking reference to daemons in Plato; other passages add little.[2] It is clear that a Platonist of later ages could find in this passage the authority of the master for many forms of philosophic doctrine and theurgic practice suggested to him by existing cult or by the resources of his own speculation. It should be noted that there is here no hint of evil daemons; the gods are good and the inference is that their intermediaries are also good. But the entrance of evil daemons into Platonism was not long delayed; for Xenocrates, a pupil of Plato and president of the Academy from 339 to 314 B.C., elaborated in great detail a daemonology which gave them ample scope. His ideas have to be put together from scattered notices in other writers, notably Plutarch and Stobaeus. Apparently in his view the world-soul (an idea which is Platonic) is placed by the Divine Spirit, itself motionless, in charge of all that is subject to motion and change; it infuses soul into the planets and the sun and moon which are 'daemonic' in nature; at a lower grade it occupies the gods of Olympus and the elements, the lowest plane upon which the Divine Spirit is itself active. At a lower level the separate daemonic powers of Nature and of finite individual existence begin, and it is on this level that good and bad daemons appear, taking up their abode in whatsoever is congenial to them and rendering it happy or unhappy according as the daemon is good or evil. The lower the place held by individual existence in the scale of being, the greater the chance of occupation by an evil being, since the Divine Spirit is so utterly remote. And all this doctrine was linked up with a mathematical conception of the Universe, which owed much, as indeed did Platonism, to Pythagorean ideas; if soul is self-moving number, the Divine Spirit in heaven could be called unity, while the world-soul as the mother of multiformity embodies the principle of duality.

The further away philosophy puts God, the more widely philosophy separates itself from religion, for religion is the attempt to bring man close to God. Yet religion is itself philosophy and cannot avoid being philosophy. Now it has been pointed out earlier that in the centuries with which we are concerned there was a great upsurge of spiritual energy expressing itself in all kinds of religious movements and searchings for the

---

[1] 202d.   [2] *Politicus* 271d, *Phaedo* 107d, 108b, *Tim.* 90a.

knowledge of God; in this restless turmoil of thought the philosophers were themselves involved, and if they did not share it they could not but be fully aware of it. Thus from the side of philosophy they held fast to the rarefied and abstract conceptions of the Deity to which philosophical speculation had led them in its desire to remove God from the world of sense and change and matter; yet they were aware of the need on philosophical grounds to bring into relationship the Creator and creation, form and matter, spirit and body, the Ideas of Plato and the material on which they were 'impressed', the One and the Many.

On the other hand from the side of religion they recognised that a bridge must be built between God and man if the searchings of man for God were to be satisfied. This bridge was provided by varied kinds of intermediate existence—intermediaries between the God of philosophy and mortal finite man—and myth and cult and folklore offered numerous beings to fulfil such a role. But from such a solution of the problem (a problem both philosophical and religious in nature) two results are liable to follow, and did indeed follow. In the first place the interposition of mediate beings intended to bridge the gap may end by making God more remote and inaccessible than ever, till in the minds of his worshippers his place is eventually usurped by the countless beings who were intended to be only his agents. In the second place such intermediaries cease to be mere agents and become invested with independent powers of their own, less in extent and majesty, it is true, than the power of their principal, but for the practical purposes of human kind more immediately important. They must, therefore, be influenced, for they are formidable; they must be flattered and satisfied—in short, they must be 'worked' according to such technique as may be prescribed by the experts. Thus the door is opened to magic of all kinds—clairvoyance, astrology, table-rapping and all the paraphernalia which accompany them. The plain man is thus beset on the one hand by myriad and vague powers influencing every act and every thought of his life in the direction of good or of evil, and on the other hand by competing experts who offer varied rites and procedures to work those powers and to emancipate him from their malign influence or to secure their good will. St Augustine was right when he said that men had entered into partnership with the daemons.

It would be beyond the scope of this book to illustrate at length the extent and the effects of a belief in daemons as shown in the literature of the early centuries of our era. But perhaps it is not irrelevant just to indicate how it entered into the mind of Plutarch. Plutarch was a religious genius rather than a philosopher, though he would have called himself a philosopher. But he differed from most ancient philosophers, except Aristotle, in regarding theology as the crown of philosophy. He was also a

Hellenist with an absorbing interest in the literature, history and religion of the Greeks and so passionate was his love for them that he was unwilling to surrender any part. He recognised the truth of Plato's criticism of the Olympian gods, of oracles and myths and saw the dangers which they presented to real religion and to morality; he realised, too, the need of his day—the need to sort out the rich inheritance of beliefs and cults and fancies which held the imagination of men by their charm and naiveté while repelling sincere allegiance by their inconsistency and remoteness from life. How else can such inheritance be saved except by a clue which will make sense of it all? This clue Plutarch found in a method of interpretation. If only men would penetrate behind the external form, with its infinite variety, in which poets and philosophers had wrapped their best thoughts and ideals, they would find a spiritual reality, good and evil, in the light of which religion and poetic inspiration would become intelligible and the sins and misfortunes of men explicable. And this spiritual reality Plutarch found in the idea of a supreme God and a universe peopled with countless spiritual powers who were his ministers or his opponents. For, if a good agent worked through a cult or an oracle or a poet's imagination, there were evil powers who could corrupt them all or wrap them round with base elements of superstition or immorality or deceit. In works of art or literature and in religious rite and philosophic system men have been true to the vision of the best; but they have failed to see that the best was always twined round with a worst and this double strand in all creation is the work of good and evil powers. It is the task of men who come after to be apprised of this and to welcome the work of the good powers and to reject that of the evil. Thus can the goodness of God be vindicated and a practical guide be placed in the hands of men and the inheritance of literature and religion be saved. All depends on 'trying the spirits', discriminating between the good and the bad daemons which contend for control in the same sphere.

It is a noble idea which is not ruined by Plutarch's failure to provide the criterion. But for him at least the result is that the motions of the heavens, the soul and destiny of man, the history of nations and every individual choice and action which make up human conduct at its highest and most trivial levels are in the hands of the daemons. The effect which one daemon might have on the course of history can be seen from one quotation, 'If the daemon which sent down the soul of Alexander had not recalled it so quickly, one law would have looked down upon all men, and they would be administered according to one common justice as though turning towards one common light.' As for the individual of less exalted destiny, his birth, his death and life after death were under the the control of daemons—and every aspect of the daily round, his crops

and his business, his family, his passions and impulses, his loves and hates. And the daemons might be good or bad.

But besides the philosophical aspect of daemonism, which in the passage of the *dcD* at present under consideration is the relevant aspect, there is another side which in most Christian writers, including St Augustine, is often much more important. Under the heading of daemons were classed all those deities and powers which abounded in all the countries comprising the Roman world—relics of primitive cults which went back to the earliest days of man, fertility and nature powers, heroes now deified, vague worships of some local phenomenon, rites to propitiate some hostile influence, and to promote success, and to heal bodily and mental troubles. These cults had thrived in their thousands, as inscriptions and papyri show, and they persisted no matter what new god might be introduced by fashion or trade or immigrants or the ruling power. In the last centuries B.C. and the early centuries of the Christian era they seem to gain in prominence and power. Naturally our evidence is fuller for these centuries than for the earlier centuries, but it is clear that, while they seem to flourish more abundantly later, they were always in existence, though less conspicuous. But two other causes seem to have given them a new lease. In the first place, philosophy of a popular kind made its way down to the masses to a remarkable degree, and that part of post-Platonic philosophy which taught about daemons was the part most likely to catch the popular imagination. But the movement of philosophy downwards was met by a movement of popular superstition upwards. Many of the local religions had been outgrown intellectually and morally, yet they were dear to their devotees either through habit or love of excitement or some sense of piety and often through simple fear; for there is a state of mind which will not surrender its fears and horrors without a struggle and a feeling of loss. To these cults the popular versions of Neoplatonism seemed to give a new justification. Secondly, the attack of Christianity on the newly entrenched daemons only increased their tenacity: for that attack was directed not only against the daemons themselves but also against the practices and manner of life associated with them. Christianity was interpreted as attempting extermination not only of superstitions but also of settled habits and institutions, which indeed it did attempt; and it was resisted as a kind of nihilism. But the very effort of resistance gave the 'daemons' a new strength. The early Christian writers and preachers matched themselves against the inherited and ingrained sentiments and practices accumulated for hundreds, indeed thousands, of years in the Mediterranean lands and beyond; and their brief and expressive summary for the whole was simply 'daemons'.

(iii) The third question is what position did Christians take up to

counter the prevailing belief in the daemons which, as we have seen, was held in different forms by educated and uneducated alike.

It cannot be emphasised too strongly that the Christians did not deny the existence of daemons—and for good reasons. In the first place the Scriptures are full of them. The Hebrew Scriptures no doubt had early undergone scrupulous revision in the interest of monotheism, but obvious traces of all kinds of daemoniac power remain, and the post-exilic literature abounds with supernatural beings. But the New Testament accepts daemons and principalities and powers as something to be taken for granted; Our Lord's sayings assume the current beliefs and practices and phraseology of the day and St Paul is constant in his exhortation to fight against the powers in the 'heavenly places'. In the second place Christians, including the greatest of the Christian thinkers, had passed through paganism and its daemonology on the journey to the Christian faith. They knew at first hand the 'mysteries' and the beliefs on which they were based; they had laboured with the intricacies of Neoplatonism and had shared its presuppositions. It was impossible altogether to unsay the beliefs of a lifetime, even if it had been demanded, or to think away the whole framework of thought in which they had been brought up and which still supported the rest of the world. Nor was such surrender required. Indeed the more the Christian became convinced of the stark sinfulness of sin and the opposition of good and evil in the world, the more reality he was inclined to attach to the powers responsible for evil. Similarly, the stronger his belief in the Providence of God and His oversight of the world and of the individual, who was called upon to draw close to Him, the more reasonable might appear a belief in ministering angels of good. To St Augustine, as is clear even in the few selected passages of this book, daemons were a reality which could not be denied.

Thirdly, Christians admitted no compromise with daemons, willingly at least. The problem of 'accommodation' had early made itself felt in the affairs of everyday life; there is need only to refer to the first Epistle to the Corinthians where St Paul, while recognising that idols are unreal, points to the daemons who stand behind the idols and urges that Christians must do nothing which suggests fellowship with them, 'I am unwilling that you should be partners with daemons.'[1] As the Church grew in numbers and in confidence, the problem revealed itself with growing intensity at all levels of thought and practice, and the steadfastness with which accommodation was resisted and the lapses from that steadfastness largely make up, from one point of view, the history of the controversies of the first centuries. In the second century an almost friendly appeal was directed to Christians by Celsus, a Platonist and their greatest opponent of that day.

[1] 1 Cor. x. 20.

215

He urged that daemons were ministers of God and that all they asked was a salute—a kiss thrown as you passed a statue[1]; it would be better if Christians would recognise that some conformity to established religion was a duty of those who enjoyed the advantages offered by the state.[2] To this Origen replied that the allegiance of Christians admitted of no compromise and that such allegiance was compatible, unless details were pressed, with loyalty to the civil authority. And so it goes on through the days of the Apologists to Origen and St Augustine—in the realm of theology protests against interpretations of Christianity which incorporated philosophical doctrines and especially Neoplatonism, in the realm of practice repudiations of anything which might be held to be inconsistent with sincere adherence to Christian principles.

Christian apologists, then, neither denied the daemons nor compromised with them; what they did was to expose them for what they were. Retaining the Hebrew and New Testament belief in good angels of God, they classed under the heading of daemons all gods and powers and agencies which found no place in Christianity and labelled them as evil, neither denying their reality nor minimising their power. To expose their malign influence at the very points where the pagan world hailed them as gods and protectors was one of the chief motives for the writing of the *dcD*. In a sense it was Neoplatonism, as voiced by men like Plutarch, which had placed a serviceable weapon in the hands of Christians. For, as will be remembered, Plutarch had sought to explain the evil element in pagan theology by insisting that by the side of each god there sat, as it were, his evil counterpart, corrupting in varied degrees the good and pure myth or rite by distortion or by admixture of gross elements. Such admission, which was made in order to encourage the purifying of religion and so to ensure its survival, was eagerly seized by the Christians. Their reply was, in effect, as follows: on your own admission there are evil powers behind every myth and every manifestation of nature; you minimise that evil and do not realise how deceived you have been; the god is himself the daemon who teaches in the name of religion the iniquities which are the cause of your moral ruin. Some of us admit that the sense of religion which you show is of infinite value if only it were directed to the true God; others of us condemn your paganism root and branch; but all of us regard you and your cults as the victims of the diabolical trickery of evil powers prompting you to evil and persuading you to believe it good. This line of reply can be seen in the age of the Apologists—in Justin and Clement and Minucius Felix and Tertullian and finally in St Augustine,

[1] Cf. Minucius Felix 2.
[2] Celsus' work, Λόγος Ἀληθής, *True Account of Christianity*, is lost; but it is quoted and answered point by point by Origen in his *Contra Celsum*.

and especially in the eighth book of the *dcD* (cc. 14-22). 'Those foul daemons of yours', says Minucius, 'lurk beneath statues and images; by their magic influence they acquire authority as though a god were really present therein; they inspire prophets and dwell in shrines; . . . they rig the casting of lots and manufacture oracles; they are deceived and they deceive; they burden men's minds, pulling them down from heaven and calling them away from the true God to material things; they upset their lives and disturb their sleep; as rarefied essences they creep stealthily into human bodies and imitate diseases; they terrify men's minds and torture their limbs. . . .'[1] No wonder, then, that Tatian (fl. c. A.D. 160) as a convert to Christianity says that in the Scriptures he found an end to the slavery of the world and release from the multitude of rulers.[2] But the Christian attack—for defence was turning to offence—went further—indeed too far. Pagan worship, it was alleged, had been perverted by the daemons into forms which were borrowed from Christianity so that the obvious corruption in pagan religion might in the end be seen to suggest the corresponding corruption in Christianity and both be discredited simultaneously and both brought to ruin. For, as Tertullian said,[3] the daemons were working for the total overthrow of man.

Though the attack on the daemons was the constant preoccupation of all Christian writers of the first centuries of our era, it was St Augustine who elaborated it in the greatest detail. The task which he attempted was nothing less than to review the history of Rome and her institutions in the light of the conception of evil daemons controlling and inspiring her actions and ideals and deceiving her into thinking that evil was good and wrong was right. The magnitude of his effort can be seen only in the full text; but that he should have thought it worth while and necessary to make that effort testifies to the powerful hold which daemonism retained upon the minds of the fifth century. So intimately, in his view, was the Roman world at all levels of thought and society bound up with daemonism that he speaks of a 'fellowship with daemons' and of a 'death-giving partnership of men and daemons', sealed as in a 'treaty', and all such dealings are 'a fornication of the soul'[4]; until the Roman world recognises this, it is doomed to ruin. In the meantime the city of God on earth must wrestle with the temptations to which it is exposed, desiring all the more ardently amid the conflict the peace which is free from conflict.

The Roman world was indeed bound up with daemonism. Originally the pagan gods had been independent of Rome, and Rome had prospered by obeying them. But by now the position is changed, for the 'Eternal City of Rome' has become the leading idea and this greater loyalty has

---

[1] cc. xxvi and xxvii give a long description.　　[2] *adv. Graec.* 29.
[3] *Apol.* 22, *hominum eversio.*　　[4] *de doctr. Christ.* ii. 23; he quotes 1 Cor. x. 20.

thrust the gods into a junior partnership with Rome. The pagan gods are now worshipped, not because they are gods, but because they are the gods of Rome; to attack them is to attack Rome. The pagan gods are therefore as ubiquitous as Rome and as inviolate; no longer do they support, but they are themselves supported by the mighty idea of the everlasting Roman Empire. St Augustine had undertaken no light task.

CHAPTER 10

Not even the Saints, says St Augustine, are free from the anxieties which the temptations and deceit of the daemons impose upon them. But these anxieties have at least one useful purpose; they make men desire with even greater yearning the security in which peace is fullest and most assured, the final peace of God.

And then he casts his mind back to those earlier definitions of the *summum bonum* with which the first chapters of the nineteenth book had been concerned—the 'primary goods of Nature' and the 'virtues' of moral philosophy. It is true that he does not use the actual phrase 'primary goods'; he speaks of the 'gifts of Nature', but his point is that these elementary strivings will be discovered to be implanted by God and that in the final peace those which relate to mind will find their realisation in the healing of the mind by 'insight' and those which relate to the body in the renewed body of the resurrection. In the same way the virtues which, as he said earlier, were in perpetual conflict with evil would find their fulfilment in everlasting peace undisturbed by conflict. This peace would be happiness, the goal of the perfected life.

If this is true of the hereafter, it is true also of the present; for we are called happy when we enjoy the peace, such as it is, which even on earth a good life can give. If a good life secures for us that measure of peace, we can rightly enjoy the blessings of that peace; if we have it not, at any rate goodness will turn to good use even the evil in life. But goodness is most real when it refers all its enjoyment of good and all the use which it makes of good and evil, and indeed its very self, to the end wherein lies our perfect peace.

In this chapter St Augustine passes to a new phase of his argument. At the beginning of chapter 4 he flung down his great challenge to pagan philosophy—that the 'end' for man was to be found in eternal life and in eternal life was his happiness. In the following chapters he has considered different kinds of fellowship, the last of which was fellowship with the saints. But even this fellowship, like the others, was seen in chapter 10 to have defects, partly because, as he says, familiarity with them is difficult,

partly because the daemons obtrude their opposition and their deceit. These defects destroy the peace which all men pursue. Thus it seems that St Augustine has substituted 'peace' for 'eternal life' as the *summum bonum*.

CHAPTER 11

But, as he explains in chapter 11, he does not intend to replace 'eternal life' by 'peace'; the ends of our good may equally well be said to be peace or eternal life; for they are in fact the same thing, though each term has special disadvantages of its own. In ordinary usage peace does not imply eternal life. Nor, again, is eternal life by itself entirely satisfactory as a term, for (i) to one unacquainted with Christian writings eternal life might mean only unending duration of life, though to a Christian it means more, and, therefore, it could be applied to an unending evil life, (ii) in fact, unending duration is the only meaning it has in philosophy and it must be one of its meanings to Christians, since they believe that the wicked will have an unending life in which to endure. Therefore, in order to give the specifically Christian meaning to eternal life, that is to say, life of a particular quality,[1] it is better to combine it with the other aspect of the 'end', namely peace. Thus, says St Augustine, he prefers the phrases 'peace in eternal life' or 'eternal life in peace' to either of the elements of these phrases separately. It is clear that to telescope the terms into 'eternal peace' would not be a compromise satisfactory to St Augustine in this context, for it loses the essential idea of eternal life as life of a particular quality which gives to it its eternity.

The two quotations from Scripture contained in this chapter—Ps. 146 (147) and Rom. vi. 22—give St Augustine opportunity for making play with the various senses of 'end' (*finis*). Since the Latin for 'ends' as goals and 'ends' as boundaries is the same,[2] it was easy for him to cite 'who made thy ends peace' as confirming his own thesis of peace as the end of human endeavour. Similarly with the quotation from Rom. vi. 22, 'you have as your end (that is, *summum bonum*) peace,' though a glance at the previous verse shows that St Paul meant 'consummation' or 'last stage' and not 'end in view'.[3] As for Jerusalem, modern scholarship does not support St Augustine's interpretation 'sight of peace'. It denies that the name has anything to do with peace and would explain it as 'founded by the god Salim'. The older explanations were often based on mistaken philological grounds. Peace, St Augustine goes on, has a meaning for all; it is desired by all and everything that is mortal seeks it and values it above all else.

[1] See p. 190.   [2] See p. 23.
[3] St A.'s quotation is in the same words as the Vulgate. In Greek τέλος bears both meanings, but St Paul never uses it in the sense of 'end in view'.

CHAPTER 12

Chapter 12, which is one of the greatest chapters in the nineteenth book, is devoted to showing that peace is the universal longing of all creation according to a universal law inherent in the 'order' imposed by a Creator who is also an 'Orderer'.

Four terms are brought together in this chapter—order, fellowship, peace, law, all operating throughout Nature or the Universe. Order, it will be remembered, occurred in chapter 4 where 'justice' was said to be the 'just order of Nature'. Fellowship has already engaged attention in chapter 5. Peace was introduced in the last chapter and is the subject of this chapter. Law is mentioned for the first time.

Peace, order, law and fellowship run through the Universe; in animate and in inanimate Nature the order of peace arranges part to part in the whole according to law, and law issues in the fellowship of men and the ordered fellowship of the whole Universe.

The principle that all things ensue peace is illustrated by the consideration of peace as the 'end' of (i) war, (ii) lawlessness, (iii) the most extreme embodiment of anti-social behaviour that it is possible to imagine, (iv) Nature red in tooth and claw, (v) inanimate matter. Even in the supreme examples of perversion of Nature's good the principle remains valid: 'no perversion of good is so great as to destroy the last traces of Nature.'

St Augustine's discussion of (i) and (ii) needs no comment. No age knows better than this age that peace is the declared aim of all belligerents, aggressor or otherwise, and St Augustine recognises, as do all belligerents, that views may differ as to the nature of peace, but such differences do not, of course, affect the argument. What would affect the argument would be to maintain that war is undertaken not to gain an end but for the sheer love of fighting. Possibly St Augustine would reply that, if the instinct of pugnacity were powerful within a man, he could not find any peace within himself unless the instinct were acted upon.

But (iii), (iv) and (v) need comment.

(iii) The legend of Cacus, the son of Vulcan, is well known from the eighth book of the *Aeneid* of Vergil and the first book of the *Fasti* of Ovid as a giant or ogre who lived on a cave on the Aventine Hill and plundered the neighbourhood. He was vanquished and slain by Hercules from whom he had stolen the cattle of Geryoneus. But there was also a tradition that Caca, his sister, had betrayed her brother to Hercules; and in her honour fire was kept burning by the Vestal Virgins and sacrifice was offered.

Cacus appears only in myth and the literary evidence is no older than Vergil. There is, however, reason to take this legend far back into the Etruscan origins of Rome. Cacus has been identified with Caeculus, the founder of Praeneste and the hero-ancestor of the Caecilian *gens*; he, too, was the son of Vulcan, and Cacus and Caca were doubtless primitive fire-gods, one of whose manifestations was the earth-fire bursting from the depths of the earth. The myth of the cult takes the form of a struggle on the site of Rome between the lawless trickery and the Roman quality of 'good faith'; and Altheim would see in the slaying of Cacus 'an expression in picture of Rome's character and historical mission; the idea *debellare superbos* is here expressed on the plane of myth'.[1] If this interpretation is correct, the figure which in Roman tradition expresses the spirit of deceitful lawlessness vanquished by law-loving 'good faith' is the figure used by St Augustine as the supreme example of turbulence and violence unable to resist the power of peace.

(iv) St Augustine points to the parental instinct with its tenderness and affection and to the 'sociable' instinct, which is its accompaniment, to prove that peace is pursued even by the most ferocious animals; and, as has been stressed above, peace implies also law, order, fellowship. The modern social psychologist also starts with the conception of law and society and traces their development back till he also arrives at the parental instinct and the instinct of pugnacity, which he regards as contributing to the origins of law and society. The process may be very briefly indicated thus.

The maternal instinct, which even in animals is accompanied by 'tender' emotion, is easily outraged by threat of harm to the defenceless young, and anger is excited which may break out into the fiercest rage. But in man, perhaps even in some animals, the maternal instinct is capable of great extension, so that the children of others and eventually all weak and defenceless things excite the same tenderness, and their maltreatment causes the same anger. The defence of the weak is one of the earliest sources of law and is still the chief aim of law in a modern society; law in its elementary phases helps to create society and is itself developed in society. But the idea of law is developed also from the instinct of pugnacity, of which the behaviour of the angry mother is only one manifestation, springing from one particular cause. Another kind of pugnacity is that of the male who drives away all rivals including the younger males. As he establishes his patriarchal rule, a kind of 'order' appears in the group; his rivals understand that only on certain conditions can their own impulses be satisfied, and 'prudence' enters into society. The young males are necessary for the defence of the group and eventually may take the lead

[1] F. Altheim, *A History of Roman Religion*, p. 205.

and win the overlordship; but in the meantime the rules and laws of the society are appreciated and acted upon. This primal law is the first step to organised society. When pugnacity becomes systematised, as it is in war-like tribes or states, its contribution to law and order and society is clearer still; for the martial society demands discipline and obedience and com-radeship even on primitive levels and a nation of soldiers is often highly organised. Such in briefest outline is the point of view of Professor McDougal. Thus, while St Augustine sees in wild and fierce animals the presence of order and peace and fellowship and points to them as evidence that these are laws of all creation, the modern psychologist looks in the same place for his origins of society and law and order and eventually peace. The more these two views are considered, the more they appear to be essentially the same.

CHAPTER 12 CONTINUED AND CHAPTER 13

(v) The description of the man hung upside down by a rope, till the life leaves him, and of his body settling down into the ordered process of change which from one point of view is dissolution and from another point of view is the constitution of new forms of matter and the basis of other forms of life—this description is not only an extraordinarily graphic piece of writing, but is of greater philosophical importance than would appear at first sight. In essentials the picture is as follows. A living man is suspended by a rope bound round his feet, so that his head hangs down-wards towards the ground. But his bodily frame was intended to function otherwise, and the topsy-turviness to which it is subjected causes acute discomfort and pain; his mind or spirit, which is what vivifies his flesh, is disturbed in its relations with the body for whose welfare it is naturally anxious, till finally all relation is broken and the spirit departs. Yet even so the limbs remain in ordered relation to each other and the body as a whole obeys physical law and strains against the rope, which prevents it from gravitating towards the earth where it would naturally rest. If the body is taken down and embalmed, the dissolution is arrested; yet the constituent elements remain in relation to one another and the body settles down upon the ground in the manner most convenient to it. If the body is left to itself, it rots away from the rope and settles down into a mass of putrefac-tion; it breaks up into its constituent elements, each of which finds its own place in relation to the surrounding matter. Some find their place as gases, others are absorbed into soil, others become particles of food for minute

organisms or carrion for scavenging animals. The whole process of dissolution occurs according to laws which guarantee 'order' and seem to ensure peace to the infinite variety of constituent elements which make their appearance and fulfil their function. All relevant purposes are fulfilled in an orderly process of change, which employs division and combination and conversion and alteration till the peace of all is brought about.

This description, it will be remembered, is introduced by St Augustine to demonstrate his thesis that throughout Nature and even in the most unlikely places, as for example the beast-man and the decaying corpse, the law of peace reigns supreme. The chapter ought really to be read in conjunction with the series of definitions of peace which follows at the beginning of chapter 13.

But in the meantime it may be noted that the conception of the eternal law of Nature is almost as old as the beginnings of Greek philosophy and it continues throughout the history of thought. The Greeks held that, while sense might be concerned with the changing world, thought could know only what was fixed and changeless, for otherwise nothing could be known. This unchanging 'something' has been conceived either as eternal and immutable law or, at a later stage of speculation, as a changeless matter; and the 'nature' of a thing has been regarded either as the fixed laws of its being (the Platonic and Aristotelian 'forms') without which it would cease to be what it is or as its 'primary' substance, which is the residue when the 'secondary' qualities, which may change, have been stripped away. In the same way Nature as a whole has been regarded as in its essence a system of laws operating eternally and giving existence and individuality to its parts or as essentially nothing but matter, whatever changing shapes it may assume. But Aristotle pointed out that we have and can have no knowledge at all of matter as such, but can know only its 'forms', so that to him the constitution of matter as such was a meaningless problem. St Augustine is a true heir of Plato and Aristotle in maintaining that in the eternal laws governing Nature is to be found the real nature of things; and in his belief in the law of 'order' he carries on the general Greek tradition which sees order everywhere in creation.

CHAPTER 13

The series of definitions with which the chapter opens may be considered under five heads.

(i) 'Ordered' (*ordinata*) is a term common to all the definitions, and 'order' is defined as 'the arrangement which assigns to each thing its own place in relation to other things, whether those things are equal or un-

equal', and 'thing' may apply as much to things mental as to things physical. The ideas of equality and inequality are introduced to show that the 'arrangement' must have regard to relative importance; they emphasise and enlarge the phrase 'its own place'. What is common, therefore, to all the definitions is the idea of 'assigning to each member in a structure or organism or relationship the place therein which is due to it, considering what it is and what is its relation to the whole'. This formula may be read as a preface to each definition: for example, 'if, assigning to each member in a structure or organism or relationship the place therein which is appropriate to it considering what it is and its relation to the whole, you adjust the parts of the body one to the other, the result will be a body at peace;' or again 'if assigning to each member . . . man obeys God in faith under eternal law, the result will be his peace'.

(ii) The ideas of law and fellowship, besides that of order, run through the definitions. 'Fellowship' is obvious in 'agreement' (*concordia*) and in 'unity' (*consensio*) and is implicit in (*a*) the two parts of the soul, in (*b*) the soul and the body, and in (*c*) the relation of man and God. 'Law' is contained in 'order' and is implied in 'adjustment' and in 'agreement' and in the relationship of authority and obedience. Even in 'rest from the appetites' law is not absent, for desires of the irrational part of the soul can relax or be quietened only if they are brought to order by the rational part.

(iii) The series of definitions rises from the lowest to the highest type of peace. But in defining the peace of the body St Augustine does not mean to suggest that the body can be regarded as something separate from the life or the mind or the soul. He is at great pains, as was seen on page 187, to protest against the dualism of classical speculation which tended to separate the two and to forget that the idea of the body is a sheer abstraction, since experience gives us an idea only of the body combined with life or mind or soul. His meaning here is that, in so far as the body can be considered in isolation, its peace consists in the adjustment of its parts; but he quickly leads up to the definition in which the peace of body-and-soul consists in the life and well-being of the living creature as a whole.

Just as the peace of the body is artificially isolated and is thus defined, so the other kinds of peace are isolated from the peace which succeeds them in the series. But the whole point of the series of definitions is that each leads on to the next and is implied in it, or, as St Augustine says in chapter 14, the lower peace is necessary to the higher. Mortal man cannot be isolated from the God of eternal law, nor can the individual man be isolated from his fellows, whether in the fellowship of the race, the family or the state. Nor again can man in his social capacity be isolated from the fellowship, perfect in order and concord, which includes God, man and his fellowman. If in life the attempt is made to treat man as separate from

his fellow or from God, violence is done to the order which runs through Nature, and Nature always reasserts itself; no perversion of good can remove the last trace of Nature. As far as the nature of man is concerned, this is the order of his being, that all aspects of man receive meaning in that all-embracing aspect in which he is seen to be a potential member of the 'city of God'. The order of Nature, which is the continued work of the Divine Orderer, decrees by eternal law that the 'end' of man shall be the city of God. Thus, as the lowest aspects of man are seen to be implicit in the highest, so peace at its highest includes peace at its lowest aspects and peace at its lowest is the pre-requisite of peace at its highest. If order is that which assigns to each member its own place in the pattern of creation, peace involves the special feeling which comes to each member when by his own will he takes that place in the pattern. In so far as he has schemes about a pattern of his own and about his place in it, he will destroy his peace; for he will violate the 'order' of his own nature which was willed for him by the Divine Orderer.

(iv) Peace, whatever else it may do, must involve feeling and therefore is of interest only to what can feel. Now the idea which seems to underlie the varied manifestations of peace at lower and higher levels is that of function which is being fulfilled and which by virtue of its fulfilment is accompanied by higher or lower forms of satisfaction or contentment, the climax being reached in the happiness of the saints. Again, whatever other meaning 'function' may have in other philosophies, in any view of the world in which order with an implication of purpose is an element fulfilment of function is only another way of describing the carrying out of the ordered plan for which the structure or organism is designed. It is clear, therefore, that peace is a process and not a state. Now man can refuse or abuse the function intended for him by his 'nature', though in the long run the 'order' of Nature will vindicate itself. But behave somehow man must; for the 'urge' (ὅρμη) or *nisus*, which in St Augustine's view is the raw material of effort, drives him to it. And in the idea of urge or *nisus* is to be found the explanation of the peace which St Augustine sees in inanimate things. We cannot know that inanimate things have the kind of feeling which man calls peace. But we witness the urge in their constituent elements to bring about changes which observe the order of their natures (as, for example, the chemical changes brought about by decay) and we see 'order' reappearing out of disorder. We know that effort in us which results in ordered process is accompanied by feeling, and we attribute to the same phenomenon in physical nature, namely ordered process, the same feeling which we ourselves experience. This projection, which it is impossible to say is only projection and nothing more, is to St Augustine legitimate because he is so convinced of the truth that order means peace

on the human level that he can nowhere see order without inferring peace.

(v) The last few lines of the chapter take the argument further. God, the wise and just Orderer of all natures, gave to mankind, the ornament of earthly creatures, the power to enjoy 'goods' necessary and suitable to his mortal life and to find a corresponding peace in the enjoyment of them. That gift was given on certain terms, namely that the right use of those goods would lead to the enjoyment of the eternal life and the peace of the city of God, which are unobtainable without that right use. Yet, paradoxically, enjoyment of the goods of mortal life is itself dependent on right use of them and right use is dependent on the 'insight' of the Christian who refers earthly values and earthly peace to eternal values and eternal peace. (This latter point is developed in the next chapter, 14, and is here anticipated.) Thus, if man starts out to enjoy the goods of mortal life, he finds it impossible to gain the enjoyment of them unless he is prepared to go the whole way and to accept 'peace in eternal life' or 'eternal life in peace' as the ultimate goal and the standard of reference in this life.

It may be observed that this line of thought has a bearing on the criticism of Christian morality considered on an earlier page (p. 193) that reward enters too largely into the ethics of a Christian. St Augustine does not ask the Christian to forgo the 'goods' of this life, but to use them rightly; if they are used wrongly they cease to be goods and he loses them. Thus, in one sense, he is a more thorough-going supporter of the 'reward' point of view than perhaps even his critic suspected, for he maintains that the enjoyment of goods is dependent on rightness of use, and so he appears to rest right choice of use upon enjoyment. In another sense he denies that reward enters into the matter at all, for there is no question of forgoing enjoyment here in order that enjoyment may come hereafter; enjoyment of goods both here and later is inseparably bound up with rightness of use. Of course, the implication of the argument is that there can be no enjoyment in wrong use or, more exactly, that men will not find the wrong use of goods to be itself a good. But that is what St Augustine does assert; if, for example, men think stolen sweets are sweetest, they discover them eventually to be not sweet at all.

(vi) It would not be difficult to read too much into St Augustine; yet on the other hand his teaching is not to be estimated below its value. He sees in inanimate nature an 'urge' or *nisus* which expresses itself according to a law of order which is the law of function; he is interested not in matter as such, as were the early Greek philosophers, but in its ordered behaviour. The whole process of change is brought about not by mechanism—for the notion of mechanism as the key to Nature had not yet made its appearance

—but by a *nisus* towards free fulfilment of function; whether on the level or below the level of the conscious, effort implies some kind of purpose. The object of desire is itself influencing the process of change, and change cannot be to St Augustine cyclical in character,[1] whether on the plane of inanimate nature or of human history.

St Augustine certainly does not anticipate modern conceptions which resolve matter into function; but he is considerably closer to contemporary physical theories than to those of the last century. For he was unhampered by the idea of mechanism which modern natural science is abandoning as sufficient explanation of natural process. He asserted the teleology which is now being re-introduced and he emphasised the need to interpret Nature and man in terms of *nisus* and function, function being determined by the law of each thing's nature. Man's function he proclaimed to be the realising of the potentialities inherent in the nature bestowed upon him—man as a physical organism, as a rational creature, as a social being and as capable of enjoying God. And in guiding the urge or *amor* within him towards the fulfilment of these functions man finds his happiness. These are ideas which, so far from being obsolete, are to-day regarded as being recent discoveries.

CHAPTER 13 CONTINUED

That peace is closely related to happiness is clear from the subsequent argument in which it is maintained that even the miserable are not outside and beyond the operation of the law of order. The very fact that they are s eparated or distinguished from the happy is at least a simple indication of order; but, apart from this, even the miserable are not in all respects miserable and, in so far as they are free from unrest, they do adapt themselves to their circumstances and find some peace. The real cause of their misery i s that there is no guarantee against their peace being interrupted by pain or grief. But the life of a created thing simply cannot go on unless there is some measure of fulfilment of function; for utter disturbance of function would destroy life itself and therefore even the miserable have some measure of peace.

From this point the argument is developed that, if all things have a measure of peace, nothing can be utterly and wholly bad, not even the devil. Not even the devil can escape the order in creation, and in punishing the devil for his perversity of will God does not visit punishment upon the good which is inherent in him as a created being, but upon the self-will which has made him what he is. Even pain implies some relic of good, for

[1] See p. 164.

pain is the feeling of the loss of good; it is only what is good that can feel loss of good, and in this sense of loss is to be found the real nature of punishment. Similarly, loss of peace implies some elements of peace remaining. Thus, even in the supreme examples of evil there exist some elements of good and of peace; otherwise punishment would be meaningless.

At this point we may refer back to a previous page (p.194) where it was suggested that St Augustine seemed to overlook the reformatory aspect of punishment. In the passage in front of us he maintains that to take pleasure in the loss of good is evidence of a perverted will; but it is the will of a created being and a created being cannot be wholly bad; therefore there remains some good which feels the loss of good. It might be expected that St Augustine would have gone on to draw the conclusion that punishment derived its justification from the very fact that there remains some element of good not wholly extinguished or indeed able to be extinguished which punishment might be one means of rousing to a greater consciousness of the loss which evil brings about. But he leaves the wicked in torment, though they still possess that element of good which makes them conscious of the loss caused by evil. It does not seem to occur to him that the remaining element of good offers some ground of hope for their reclamation, and that, in so far as that remains, everlasting punishment is an idea difficult to square with the justice of God.

The last few lines of the chapter dealing with the right use of the goods of this life have been discussed on an earlier page (p. 226).

Before we leave the subject of peace it may be noted that Dante also regards peace as the supreme good of man. But, though he was familiar with the *dcD*, he arrives at his conclusion independently of any of the arguments used by St Augustine. He follows Aristotle in regarding the speculative and practical reason as the highest form of activity which distinguishes man from animals; the specific work of man is to make actual the powers of reason. Practical and theoretic reason operate only in conditions of quietness; 'it is obvious therefore that only in the quiet and the tranquillity of peace is the human race able to undertake easily and without hindrance its own distinctive task, a task which is almost divine (witness "Thou hast made him little lower than the angels"). It follows that universal peace is the greatest of blessings for those who are ordained to our blessedness.' This argument is clinched by the recollection that the heavenly choir of angels spoke not of riches or pleasure or honour and the like, but of 'peace on earth to men of good will', and the Saviour Himself greeted His disciples with 'Peace be to you'.[1]

[1] *de mon* i. 3, 4.

CHAPTER 14

This chapter appears to begin by taking the reader once more from one level of peace to the next so as to establish the dependence of the higher levels upon the lower. But the purpose really is rather different.

St Augustine has just dealt with the right use of temporal goods; he opens this chapter by pointing out that in an earthly city—that is to say, if you wish to live only upon an earthly plane—the use of temporal goods is directed towards the enjoyment of earthly peace; if, on the other hand, men aim at living, while on earth, in a heavenly city, the use of temporal goods is directed towards the enjoyment of everlasting peace. Now, if men were irrational creatures, they would want only peace of the body (which he defines) both for its own sake and as contributing to peace of the irrational spirit or life. But man is also rational; all kinds of peace below the 'rational' level he subordinates to the peace of his rational spirit so that he may think and act so as to secure the ordered harmony of thought and action which is the peace of the rational spirit; if peace at lower levels is granted, he is free to use his reason and in the light of the knowledge so gained to direct his life and mould his character. But at this point his limitations become apparent; the human mind, however eager in the pursuit of knowledge, is liable to error, and a non-human guidance is necessary to offer some certitude to follow and some help in following it. The certitude saves him from error, but he is offered only help in following it, for anything more than help (for example, enforcement) would destroy his freedom. His limitation arises from his dwelling in a body, which debars him from direct and full knowledge of truth; all he can do is to launch his faith further than his limited reason will reach and to walk by faith. When he does that, he can refer peace at all lower levels to peace at the highest, which is the peace with God which comes from 'ordered obedience in faith beneath eternal law'. The certitude which is offered as a guide to him is contained in two precepts of love for God and love for neighbour. Now, if a man is commanded to love his neighbour as himself, it is implied that he may love himself and may expect his neighbour to treat him as he would treat himself. Hence arises the 'concord' of mutual love, and, since a man's nearest neighbours are members of his family for whose interests he should provide, we have the beginnings of the family peace which is the 'ordered agreement of those who dwell together, whether they command or obey'. Command, therefore, is exercised in the interest of those who obey; obedience is necessary if the duty of careful forethought laid upon those who command is to be effectively discharged in

the interest of those who obey. In this sense, to be a ruler is to be a slave of one's own subjects.

The chapter thus ends with the important thesis that government is exercised in the service of the governed. The point is made in relation to the family, but in later chapters it will be extended to the larger circle of the state. A long parenthesis on slavery is now inserted which is suggested by the idea of rulers being slaves of their subjects and which interrupts the development of thought; it is therefore better to consider this parenthesis now, and later to join up the last few lines of chapter 14 with the latter part of chapter 16.

CHAPTER 15

The idea that rulers are the slaves of their subjects sends St Augustine off into a digression on the nature of slavery. He states at the outset that it was not the will of his Creator that man should dominate man; but slavery as an institution was introduced by sin. His argument is that slaves are the vanquished in war, who might have been killed but were spared; however just may be the war, it nevertheless creates this situation, whether those who have right on their side win or lose. Slavery in itself is wrong and springs from something evil; but if you admit the existence of that sin, evil follows as a consequence. Even if defeat in war is inflicted on those who are morally in the right, that very defeat, through the humiliation which it brings about, causes them to be conscious of their own wrong-doings.

It is important to realise that St Augustine is not now considering slavery in individual cases. It would be impossible to say that a given man's slavery could justly be attributed to some particular sin committed by him. He urges that the institution of slavery in general is due to sin, or, as we should say, is wrong. Sin brings about its own consequences and those consequences are in a sense a punishment for the sin, though the Creator intended neither the sin nor the consequences.

The sin is lust for domination which in turn is a form of pride (*superbia*) —that sin from which St Augustine derives all others and which means the self-assertion of the individual. He puts the point quite clearly in the *de doctrina Christiana*[1] where he says that 'it is inherent in the sinful mind to crave for ever greater power over men and to claim as his right the obedience which is due to God alone in His right. . . . When he strives after the domination of those who are by nature his equals, that is his fellow-men, he is guilty of insufferable pride'.

[1] i. 23.

The point is then made that a good man may be the slave of a bad master, but the bad master is himself the slave of sin, according to the text of St John.[1] This leads to the reflection that slavery to sin is worse than slavery to a man and that slavery itself may be turned to good moral account by the slave, though this consideration does not justify slavery. But, the argument repeats, the law of order inherent in creation insists that sin shall be followed by its consequences and slavery as an institution is the penal consequence of the sin of pride. That is why the Apostle urges Christian slaves to draw good out of evil if it is impossible for them to gain their freedom, until such time as human overlordship passes away.

CHAPTER 16

The next chapter continues the subject, but looks at it chiefly from the point of view of the Christian master. He will treat all members of his household, whether slave or free, as sons; the task of providing for their interests will be great, so that the burden of the master's responsibility will be less easy than the lot of the slave. On the other hand disobedience in any member will be punished, for it threatens the peace of the household. The purposes of punishment are to bring back the offender to the harmony of the household at the point where he departed from it, to reform him and to deter others. It is a false and culpable clemency which neglects the greater good of the wrong-doer and allows him to fall into worse evil.[2] The chapter ends with the statement that the peace of the household is a fragment of the peace of the state to which it contributes and to which it must always be referred. Hence in governing his own family the head of the household must use the standards and ideals of the state as his guide and so must fit the peace of his household into the peace of the state. But this latter part of the chapter joins up the parenthesis on slavery with the argument dropped at the end of chapter 14, where obedience was seen to be in the best interest of the governed and government to be the service of the governed. At this point we may pause to consider St Augustine's views on slavery.

His derivation of the word *servus* from *servo*, to preserve, is natural enough; it had already been alleged by Donatus, a grammarian who lived in Rome about A.D. 350. But modern philology derives it from *sero* and so *servus* would properly mean 'a man bound to another man'. [3]

---

[1] viii. 34.
[2] These remarks on punishment should be compared with earlier treatment of the same subject, see p. 194.
[3] Isidore borrowed it from St A.(Donatus ad Ter. Ad. i. 28; Isidore, *Orig.* ix. 24); *servus* was originally *seruus*, formed like *ingenuus*.

The treatment of slavery by St Augustine has been found by critics to be lacking in Christian charity and to go no further than enlightened pagan thought as expressed by writers such as Pliny or Seneca. The French historian of slavery, Wallon, clearly shares this view, but he urges that in the *dcD* St Augustine was pardonably tempted to minimise the evils of existing social organisation in order to exalt the idea of Providence before a despairing people who were blinded by recent catastrophe and were ready to attribute their misfortunes to a cruel fate rather than to their own wrong-doings; and he seems to imply that St Augustine shrank from denouncing the moral evil of slavery and advocating its abolition.

On the other hand it may be urged that St Augustine makes perfectly clear that in his mind slavery as such is wrong and that it has its root in sinful lust of power. The neutralising of its evils is within the power of a Christian family and a Christian society, and in this point of view he is at one with St Paul and with the actual history of slavery in modern times. The common humanity of slave and master as equal members of God's household destroys the relationship of slave and master; indeed he says the master's lot is the less enviable. What he does not say, any more than Seneca, is that, if morally slavery is wrong and if in a Christian society its evils would disappear, then legally it should no longer be justified. But that is a step which, though easy to us now, is far too much to expect from a man writing in the circumstances in which St Augustine wrote. Slavery had been interwoven for centuries into the texture of society and its history, though containing much that was revolting and unspeakably cruel, nevertheless showed conclusively that for thousands of slaves slavery had proved to be 'an initiation into a higher culture' and had offered benefits beyond calculation. The abolition of the legal institution of slavery in the fifth century A.D. would have been a far more revolutionary proposal than was the same proposal made thirteen centuries later and opposed by men of undoubted Christian charity. The legal and political aspects were less important in the Roman world of that day than they would appear to us now. St Augustine condemned slavery, but he did not propose its abolition as a legal institution in pagan society, for pagan society did not accept the premisses on which the condemnation was based. In any case the idea could scarcely have occurred to him, so alien was it to ancient ways of thought. Moreover, as we shall see later, St Augustine is not concerned primarily to reform social or legal or political institutions or to write in detail a political theory or to draw up a social charter. He is concerned to show up the root sin from which the state derives what is corrupt within it, and this he has done in relation to slavery. Once he had revealed the moral evils as he saw them, he had done what he set out to do.

CHAPTER 16 CONTINUED

At the end of chapter 14 St Augustine asserted that in a Christian society the authority of the ruler is exercised in the interest of the ruled; the point was made with reference to the family, but it was stated in general terms. In chapter 16 the family is regarded as the origin and as a fragment of the state, and family life should be governed by the head of the household consistently with the ideals of the government of the state. And so the way is made open for a comparison, in chapter 17, of the points in which the earthly state and its aims agree or disagree with the ideals of the city of God.

The points which invite consideration are three: (i) the idea of government as service, (ii) St Augustine's view of authority, (iii) the accommodation of the peace of the family to the peace of the state.

(i) The idea of the ruler as the servant of his subjects was familiar enough in the Greek speculation about the nature of kingship to which reference has already been made. The passages already quoted show some of the qualities of the ideal ruler and many more could be added by even a cursory study of the literature. But the particular elements which St Augustine emphasises are (i) care for the interests of the subject (*consulere*), and (ii) compassionate forethought (*providendi misericordia*). The equivalents for these in Greek thought are 'love of one's fellowmen' (φιλανθρωπία) and 'watchful forethought' (πρόνοια). Both these terms run incessantly through speech and essay and exhortation. 'The kindly and "philanthropic" ruler must not only be liked by his subjects but loved by them. . . . He thinks that his power must bring him not more wealth or pleasure but more trouble and worry, so that his life is more laborious.' 'He gets more pleasure from conferring than receiving benefits, and this is the only pleasure in which he is insatiable.' 'Rule may be defined as the lawful management of men and watchful forethought on men's behalf according to law,' and 'the rule of a king at its best is the rule over a well-governed city or over many nations or over the whole of mankind exercised by a single good man through his outstanding judgement and moral excellence'. These are ideas which go back long before Dio Chrysostom from whom the quotations are taken.[1]

And so in the Roman Empire certain qualities are specially looked for in the Emperor, and whether present or not are extolled as pre-eminent. Such qualities are *Virtus, Constantia, Clementia* and many others, and

---

[1] Dio lived in the first century A.D.; the passages come from his speeches, περὶ βασιλείας i. 50, 51 R; iii. 115 R.

attributes are *Pax, Victoria, Felicitas* and so on. Among them *Providentia* takes a leading place.

Providentia begins by being the power of the gods which takes thought for the state and it acts either directly or through agents; Cicero, for example, saved the state at the time of the Catilinarian conspiracy through his *Providentia* (among other things), but that *Providentia* was due partly to his own cleverness and partly to the inspiration of the gods.[1] In the same way 'Providence' was responsible for the emergence of Augustus, bringing back peace and government. From this time onward *Providentia* appears in 'private' and imperial inscriptions, on coins and in all the literature relating to the Empire. But it gathers to itself certain main connotations. It includes, most obviously, the care of the ruler, as, for example, Trajan, for his subjects, as expressed in works—roads, buildings, corn-supply, security of frontiers, provision for orphaned children, the prosperity of agriculture and so on; but it includes also the capacity for warding off conspiracy and insurrection and for planning for the 'succession'. This last foresight at first meant planning the dynastic succession; but when the elective principle, by which one Emperor chose or nominated his successor, replaced the dynastic principle, *Providentia* signified the wise choice of successor. Into this wise choice there entered also the *Providentia* of the gods who inspired the selection; and so the ruler owed his rule to divine planning and was therefore the agent of the gods.

Though these strands in the idea can be separated, *Providentia* stood for something of emotional rather than intellectual appeal, and the needs of the times determined the precise interpretation put upon it; this is clear if the coins bearing the legend are read in conjunction with contemporary events. With the idea of *Providentia* goes closely that of 'eternity' (*aeternitas*), for the aim of planning and foresight, whether by the gods or by the Emperor, was to ensure the perpetuity of the Roman power; this legend also is of frequent occurrence on coins and inscriptions, as has been seen above.[2]

(ii) The second point is St Augustine's view of authority; it is of great importance for the understanding of the later chapters of this book and will constantly recur.

It has been seen that among the ideas attaching to *Providentia* in the Roman world there must be included the idea that the gods exalted to power as ruler the man who was best able to watch over the welfare of the Roman state and so to ensure its perpetuity. This implies (*a*) a Providence governing the affairs of men or at least of the Romans, (*b*) the divine mission of the ruler and his divine authority. It may naturally be objected that 'men' most certainly meant the Romans and that history

---

[1] *in Catil.* iii (8). 14.   [2] See p. 192.

showed that the gods often made bad mistakes in their choice of a ruler for the Romans, as the Romans were of course aware. But it is important to remember that *Providentia* on the coins and imperial dedications was much more of a prayer than a statement, and it was of all the greater influence because it appealed to the emotions rather than to the reason.

St Augustine's approach is different; his theory of authority is not coloured by hope or wish nor does it appeal to history. It is a categorical statement of ultimate truth. All authority to which obedience need be given is derived from God. The authority of the ruler must be inspired by love of God and love of his fellowmen, by the compassionate care which takes thought for the welfare of his neighbour. Love of neighbour is a precept laid upon man by God. Only authority exercised in this spirit can claim divine sanction; law and government are justified in so far as their motive is the promotion of the good of each man regarded as a neighbour in the Christian sense. Law, therefore, as an instrument of government is not law merely because the ruling power enforces it; authority enforces it because it is law. Law is (as a pseudo-Platonic dialogue puts it) 'a discovery about moral reality'; and, since to the Christian moral reality is an aspect of the reality of God, law is a discovery or a revelation of God. Above the ruler is the law of God and his rule is justified only in so far as it is itself subservient to the law of God.

The other side of authority is obedience, and this aspect of the question St Augustine treats more fully. For, as we shall see in the paragraphs immediately following, his view upon the matter is most intimately bound up with his teaching of the two cities and has had very great influence on political thought ever since.

(iii) Thirdly, St Augustine's statement that the household is the beginning or a fragment (or perhaps we could say 'germ') of the state is of great significance, for he goes on to say that the part must be referred to the whole, and the peace of the household (that is, its fulfilling of function) to the peace of the state. Or, in other words, the 'ordered concord' which a household creates for itself, if authority and obedience fulfil their proper roles, is directed towards, and issues in, a similar concord in the state, in which also authority and obedience play their parts. Therefore the ideals of the family must be consciously adjusted to the ideals of the state; the precepts of the state must be precepts also for the family.

This passage has not always been given its due weight. As is clear from his works, St Augustine attaches the utmost importance to the family and its life; in this passage he asserts that family life should adopt as its own the ideals of the state, that the training of the individual member of the family should be also a training for membership of the state. St Augustine therefore attaches high value to the state and interpretations which make

him disparage the state seem to be beside the mark. The first few lines of the next chapter will make this point even clearer.

CHAPTER 17

For, to paraphrase freely, he urges that the Christian family and the pagan family, in so far as each derives its values from the state, will make the same use of earthly goods and of all that the state can contribute to the necessities of life. To the onlooker the Christian and the pagan family might appear to use those goods in the same way, but the motive and the intentions inspiring that use would be different; the Christian family would thus avoid being captivated by their attractions, for nothing would divert it from the path of duty to God.

The individual therefore, whether Christian or pagan, owes allegiance to the head of the household and to the state; the Christian obeys the state no less than the pagan, but his outlook is different. It is in this outlook and in the spirit determining it that the distinction between the actual state and the city of God lies. The Christian lives in the state and enjoys its goods and contributes to those goods and obeys it; in mind and spirit he lives also in the city of God. He lives one life inside the other, and because he lives as a citizen of the city of God his citizenship of the state is informed with a new spirit. He owes a double allegiance, one allegiance inside the other, to the state and to the city of God.

The argument so far developed might lead us to imagine that for the Christians St Augustine envisages three ranges of fellowship, the family, the state, the city of God—three circles, the largest containing the intermediate which in turn contains the smallest. But such a diagram, though mainly true to his meaning, would not be wholly true to the argument as developed later; for one important exception will be made.

The state (and in this context St Augustine uses the phrase 'earthly city' to mean the state) aims at a 'composition of wills', that is, an interadjustment of wills which brings about the give and take necessary to a society; and it demands that the individual should make concessions in the interest of the continued life of the community. With this aim, as far as it goes, the city of God can wholeheartedly identify itself. The rest of this famous chapter is then devoted to showing how much further the aim of the city of God goes. Because members of this city have a further objective than the citizen of the earthly state, they cannot help being cramped by the limited objective of their pagan fellows. They live a 'captive life' and their gaze is directed towards wider horizons, and so they feel as though they were travellers temporarily putting up before going on to a destiny

pledged to them by their faith. Meantime they loyally cooperate to achieve the limited objective, believing it to be a real good; they obey the law and they are at one with the civil administration, subject to one overriding proviso; they must not be asked to do violence to their conscience or their religion (*salva pietate et religione*).

This is the point at which the paths diverge. The state has its own experts and exponents (*sapientes*) of its own religion, which the Christian must regard as inspired by daemons; he cannot obey, therefore, the state's laws on religion, though he provokes, it is true, hatred and persecution for this reason. And so the city of God gathers together into its membership all those who, of various languages and nations, are of one mind in loyalty to the God of the Christians and who refuse obedience, if need be, to the civil laws inconsistent with such loyalty. But in every other respect it pays no regard to difference of customs, laws and institutions; it seeks neither to abrogate them nor destroy them; rather it preserves and observes them. It protects and strives after all that makes for civil society and the peace which results, but it reserves the right to refer the aims of civil society to an ultimate objective. That objective is membership of a fellowship which exists for 'the enjoyment of God and one's fellow-man in God'; only in such fellowship is to be found peace, which is the realisation of function. 'For the life of a city is, through and through, a life of fellowship.'

And so with this sentence St Augustine rounds off for the moment his treatment of Varro's dictum that the end of life is social. It has occupied him from chapter 5 to the end of chapter 17. It will be necessary later to consider again the double allegiance which the Christian owes. But at the moment certain aspects of the idea of double allegiance may be considered.

The idea was nothing new in the Roman Empire. The great achievement of the Roman Empire might be said, from one point of view, to lie in the success with which she had taught her subjects to be loyal, first, to the township or municipality or district in which they lived, and, secondly to Rome which guarded the peace of the Empire and granted to the townships the very freedom and opportunities which enabled them to win the affection of their citizens. This reconciliation of local and imperial loyalties was Rome's solution of problems which had long exercised her predecessors; and St Augustine's teaching about a double allegiance was addressed to a world thoroughly familiar with the idea and gladly rendering both allegiances.

Again, in her early relations with Christianity, Rome had stressed the identity of allegiance to Rome and allegiance to the religion of Rome. It is true that she allowed the individual to practise (within limits) any private religion of his own[1]; but loyalty to the state none the less involved loyalty

---

[1] Cf., e.g., Tertullian, *Apol.* xxiv, *apud vos quodvis colere ius est praeter verum deum.*

to the gods of the state and in this identification all but the Christians and the Jews were willing to acquiesce. They therefore incurred the suspicion of wishing to establish not so much a state within a state (the two allegiances then might be concentric) as a rival state with an allegiance partly excluding allegiance to the state. The Christians protested that in all but their religion they were loyal subjects of the Empire, but they protested in vain; so ingrained was it in the pagan mind that loyalty to the state carried with it at least perfunctory loyalty to the gods of the state. In short, not only did the Roman world thoroughly appreciate a civic loyalty within an imperial loyalty but also it could not think of an imperial loyalty unaccompanied by a religious loyalty. St Augustine like earlier generations of Christians readily accepted the first idea on behalf of the city of God—the idea of a double allegiance; the second idea, that political allegiance implied religious allegiance, he emphatically rejected.

It must not be supposed, however, that Christians were the first to insist upon a loyalty which was wider and higher than loyalty to the state. Philosophy, Greek and Roman, reserved for the philosopher the right, and indeed the duty, to seek out and to adopt for his own use and to disseminate to such as were able to understand them higher and more comprehensive standards than the prevailing thought or practice contemplated. The philosopher in the Republic of Plato has caught a vision of 'the good as it really is', and he returns to the cave of ordinary contemporary life to do what he can to communicate that vision. But his loyalty is given to 'things as they really are', that is, 'as they should be,' and not to things as they actually are. To him it is given to criticise institutions and laws and practices in the light of his true knowledge. In the same way Diogenes, Epictetus and others who preached a world-state of which men were citizens placed themselves outside existing loyalties and proclaimed their adherence to a wider ideal. But philosophy was not for everyone; philosophers were rare and classical thought recognised that existing allegiances were enough for all but the exceptional. Not so St Augustine; the reservation which he makes he claims as the right of every man. Not only philosophers but every plain man who is a Christian must demand, and must be given, the right to place all that concerns his religion outside the range of the state. The privileged position of the pagan philosopher (who sometimes, it is true, subscribed nominally to the state religion) is to be insisted upon as the right of Christians.

It may be objected that there is nothing new in the point of view elaborated by St Augustine. Christianity from the days of the first martyrs had asserted the justice of it. Yet St Augustine's restatement of it is important and significant for these reasons:

(i) The *dcD* is the first systematic treatise in which due consideration is

given to the state from the Christian angle. The sphere of the state and the sphere of religion are more closely defined and a *modus vivendi* is worked out for the Christian, if concessions are made by the state which enable him with good conscience to be a full and profitable member of it. The limits of state and religion are more clearly drawn, and later ages could actually quote St Augustine as advocating a sharp delimitation of the secular and ecclesiastical spheres, forgetting, of course, that he wrote in a half-pagan world. But at the same time he brings the state and the life of the individual Christian much closer than before, for he shows the Christian that he owes full allegiance to the state (subject to one proviso) and that he can live a Christian life within its limited objective. This was an element in St Augustine's thought which was afterwards neglected.

Christians had not always preached so moderate and reasonable a doctrine. Tertullian, for example, had said quite categorically that there was nothing from which Christians were so far removed in sympathy as from the state[1]; 'we recognise one state only, the world.'[2] Therefore, he said, he withdrew from society, and he would be glad when the world was sad and sad when the world was glad. He was by no means representative, but he was not alone; there were others who took their stand on the text about serving two masters. As for St Augustine, however much he might condemn the vices of the world and of existing states as 'rotting and decaying', he was not secessionist or isolationist, for he was too firmly convinced that society and the state had elements of good in them and that Christianity was a gospel of redemption. On the other hand, he did not believe that the adoption of Christianity as the official religion of the Emperor and the Empire would convert the two allegiances—to religion and to the state—into one allegiance. In a famous chapter which immediately follows the chapter on the virtues of a Christian Emperor he makes it quite clear that rulers who are or pretend to be Christian in order to secure for their rule the prosperity which attended Constantine will be disappointed, as history had shown. St Augustine never asserts that, because the state is professedly Christian, it can demand allegiance of the same kind as the allegiance due to God. For part of its length allegiance to the state may run together with allegiance to God, but they can never be the same and one outdistances the other.

(ii) It is sometimes asserted, mistakenly, that the purpose of the *dcD* was to take advantage of the threatened disruption of the Roman state and to direct the eyes of men away from the crumbling world to a city of the skies. Such chapters as 17 and 18 dispose of this view. St Augustine presupposes that the family is still to go on; it is to take some of its ideals

[1] *Apol.* 38, *nec ulla magis res aliena quam publica.*
[2] In the sense of 'the world, the flesh and the devil'.

from the state and the state is to receive, as far as its limited objective allows, the cooperative support of the Christian. What St Augustine is concerned to do is to show that false ideals due to false religion have brought society to its present moral decadence and threatening collapse. Society can be restored only by the adoption of true ideals based upon true religion. He was too much of a realist, in the sense of recognising the basis of the life of the body as well as of the soul, and too practical in outlook to dispense with the necessity of social organisation. It would be nearer the truth to say that the aim of the *dcD* is to show to society the foundations on which it can rebuild itself.

With this chapter St Augustine concludes his treatment of Varro's dictum that the end of life is social. He goes on now to consider further differentiae of classical philosophy as noted by Varro. But after three chapters he returns to the question of the state.

CHAPTER 18

Varro had found one of his differentiae in the attitude which systems of philosophy adopted towards the theory of knowledge; some held that certain knowledge was possible, as, for example, Platonism and Aristotelianism, others that truth was beyond human reach. The distinction is of course fundamental, for the conclusions of a philosophy both on its theoretical and practical sides depend upon its theory of knowledge. At one period of his life St Augustine had himself been attracted by the tenets of the New Academy; shortly before his baptism he wrote a book to refute them and in the chapter now under discussion he describes, as a kind of madness, the systematic doubt preached in them. Like most of the ancient philosophies and most of the Christian heresies, systematic doubt is a very modern phenomenon and this chapter is therefore worth a little attention.

It has already been seen that the Platonic school suffered many changes after the death of the founder. There were irreconcilable elements in Platonism which gave opportunity for the development of divergent views; some disciples stressed the ethical side of his philosophy, others the cosmological, and the essential metaphysics seems to have dropped away, presumably because there was no one to carry it on till much later. The Academy ceased to offer dogmatic teaching upon anything; it fostered scepticism, which meant enquiry without preconceived notions. In a sense this was in the true Socratic tradition, but the school soon drew away from the Platonic position when it maintained that 'the wise man' would suspend all judgment because as much could be said against as in favour of any line of argument, and the truth could not be ascertained. This doctrine

was begun by Arcesilaus, who died in 240 B.C., and was carried much further by Carneades, one of the ablest critics of antiquity.

The movement apparently began with an attack by Arcesilaus on the 'irresistible impressions' of the Stoics; these impressions were a half-way point between 'knowledge' and 'opinion' and were a common ground in which the 'wise man' and the plain man could meet. We need not pursue his arguments, but it should be observed that scepticism flourished originally as a form of attack on Stoicism and not on Platonism. In his lectures Arcesilaus propounded no positive views of his own; he was occupied entirely with attack and he arrived at the final position that knowledge was impossible; probability was as much as a man could reach and was in any case quite enough for practical purposes.

This point of view was elaborated in detail by Carneades, whose reputation in his own day and later was very high. His doctrine was that we cannot suggest anything which carries the conviction of its own truth; notions which at first sight seem to be true are later found to be false, and there is no criterion inherent in the notion itself by which we can distinguish between truth and falsehood. The senses tell us contrary things about the same objects; reason has to derive its data from the senses, and, though reason may arrange and combine those data, none the less its results, however intricate, are based upon uncertainties. This agnostic attitude was carried, quite reasonably on the premises, into religion and science. If the Stoic based a belief in God on the general agreement (*consensus gentium*), it was easy for the sceptic to show that a belief based upon ignorance, however unanimous, carried no inherent conviction or to argue that evidence for design in the world could be matched by evidence for lack of design or that reason, though perhaps of use to man, could not be predicated of the Universe. Nor could morality be ascribed to God, if he existed; for virtue consists in amending imperfection and, if we are not to attribute imperfection to God, we cannot attribute morality. On the other hand, since man cannot live without action, Carneades taught a theory of probabilities; man must assent to propositions which *seem* to carry the greater probability; some impressions are clearer and suggest verisimilitude more than others and these we can provisionally accept, remembering all the time that they are not certain. He then elaborates a theory of grades or degrees of probability according to the nature of the case; for example, a higher degree of probability may be assigned to an impression which shows some consistency with other impressions. In ethics he attacked the Stoics who thought that the good was 'natural'; he pointed out that they did not accept all that was 'natural' as being good, but exercised selection of some goods as higher than others by means of a criterion which was not itself 'natural'. All the same, though it may have

been inconsistent with thoroughgoing scepticism, he attached high value to moral conduct and was himself of exemplary life.

The foregoing sketch of Carneades' scepticism is derived largely from the philosophical works of Cicero which have come down to us. It was from the works of Cicero that St Augustine derived his knowledge of Greek philosophy after Plato, and it was through the philosophical works of Cicero and the treatises of men like St Augustine that Greek philosophy reached the Middle Ages. In his *Academica*, written in 45 B.C. Cicero reviewed the arguments advanced by the dogmatists who believed in the certainty of knowledge and those of the sceptics. But his sympathies are with agnosticism which in his opinion can successfully defeat any position which bases itself on the evidence of the senses. Similarly a treatise, *de natura deorum*, written about the same time, takes a negative view, theism being attacked with all the ingenuity of the arguments adopted by Carneades. On the other hand, when Cicero deals with the practical problems of ethics, he is much more constructive and positive in outlook; in the *Tusculan Disputations*, for example, and in the *de officiis* he reveals himself as a defender of the Stoic morality, and in the *de finibus* he seems to take up the position of Antiochus (about 78 B.C.) who regarded knowledge as within the reach of man.

With Cicero's philosophical works St Augustine was familiar. It may be remembered that it was to a treatise of Cicero, the *Hortensius* now lost, that he owed his interest in philosophy. In this work Cicero extolled the attractions of philosophy, and as a result of reading it St Augustine's whole outlook was changed, as he himself records in the *Confessions*.[1] From Cicero he went to the Greek philosophers and particularly Plato, studied in translation. For these studies he admitted himself unable fully to express his gratitude. There was indeed a period in his life (about A.D. 383) when in his recoil from Manichaeism he felt strongly inclined to accept an agnostic position such as Carneades had advocated.[2] From these days we must trace his profound and sustained attention to the question of the relation of faith and reason, the senses and authority. After his conversion (A.D. 386) such views were abhorrent to him and he spent part of the following year in writing a refutation of the New Academy in a work called *contra Academicos*. But the real refutation of agnosticism is to be found, not in the one treatise written immediately after his conversion, but in the maturer works of his Christian experience. Chapter 18 of the *dcD* is enough to give an indication of the lines of his reply.

The chapter may be summarised as follows. Systematic doubt, says St Augustine, is madness and the city of God abhors it. The mind and the reason offer to man sure and certain knowledge; such knowledge is limited

[1] iii. 7.   [2] *Confessions* v. 10-12; *deutil ed.* viii (20).

in nature; but, as far as it goes, it is certain, despite the depressing influence of the body, which is corruptible, upon the soul. The Christian believes the senses, which the mind uses as tools; for it is a worse delusion never to believe them than to believe them. The Christian also believes Holy Scripture as the source of that faith by which the righteous man lives; and faith enables him to walk without hesitation. With faith intact he can incur no reproach if he suspends judgment on such matters as lie beyond sense or reason or beyond the range of Holy Scripture or beyond the evidences of witnesses whom it would be absurd to disbelieve.

(i) A short sketch of St Augustine's view of personality was given on an earlier page. There it was noticed that to him there is no dividing line between sense and reason as though reason can dispense with the data furnished by the senses. To him experience, whether coming through the senses or the intellect or the emotions or the desires, is a continuous whole, whatever distinction we may make between higher and lower forms of conscious life, between levels of experience, between the life of animals, which do not reflect upon or systematise their experience, and the life of the human being who orders and arranges his experiences till they make up his science. Such distinctions are convenient only for purposes of description and analysis, and represent no real points of hiatus or discontinuity. Any theory of knowledge, therefore, which disregards or dispenses with any aspect of the continuous and complex experience of man is untrue to the facts. The facts are that man's life is physical and mental, and, since these aspects cannot be divorced except in abstraction, neither can sense-impression, which is one element of experience, be separated except theoretically from another element, as for example the processes of reason. Hence it is not reasonable to doubt the one and to accept the other. Thus St Augustine avoids the Platonic puzzle—how to bring together again mind and matter, reason and sense-data, after the physical world has been shown to lead to nothing but illusion. By St Augustine the divorce was never made, and much vain speculation in later philosophy might have been saved if attention had been paid to the Augustinian psychology and its accompanying theory of knowledge.

(ii) When the senses and the reason have contributed all they can to certain knowledge, there remains, St Augustine says, the province in which faith alone can give knowledge, and faith is derived from Holy Scripture. St Augustine's general treatment of Scripture makes it clear that he welcomes the application of secular knowledge to its interpretation. He has no sympathy with attempts to use Scripture for the divination of the future. He realises that the historical events described in the Old and New Testaments are subject to the same scrutiny to which all historical records are liable, though this is not to say that his conceptions of historical criti-

cism are the same as ours. But, above all, it is clear from his own many volumes devoted to the interpretation of Scripture that he regarded Scripture as the supreme exposition of values, the source of knowledge on matters beyond the reach of reason but within the range of faith.

(iii) When sense, reason and faith have done all that is within their power, there remains much, St Augustine admits, on which man must remain in doubt and must confess ignorance. In such admission there is nothing for which he need incur criticism.

(iv) The order of treatment which this chapter adopts is highly significant. Systematic doubt is madness: there are ample grounds and means of certainty: there remains much that man cannot know by those means. This chapter alone might give pause to those who maintain that the outlook of St Augustine is the same as that of Descartes a thousand years later. This is a matter of some importance, and, though it cannot be fully dealt with here, it cannot be wholly omitted.

Descartes started by rejecting everything that was only probable and regarding as certain only the clear vision of the intellect (which he called intuition); he drew a sharp dividing line between reason on the one hand and perception and imagination on the other. This clear vision of the intellect came not from the 'fluctuating testimony of the senses' nor 'the blundering construction of the imagination' but from 'the conception of an unclouded and attentive mind and springs from the light of reason alone'. He attributes certainty only to the self-evident truths which are seen with the same clarity with which we see that a triangle is bounded by three sides only; all else must be disregarded. Hence Descartes was led to his famous method of doubt; statements which rely on the existence of the senses and concern the outside world which is perpetually changing cannot claim the certainty which he allows only to a mathematical proposition. All of them may be doubted, but doubt implies the existence of a doubter, and therefore the one element of certainty derivable from the making of such statements is the existence of someone who thinks (even though he thinks doubt): hence *cogito ergo sum*.

Now there are several passages in St Augustine which at first sight seem to put forward an argument resembling that of Descartes.[1] There is need to quote only one, but it must be given in its wholeness: it is taken from an earlier book of the *dcD* xi. 26.

'We are and we know that we are and we love the fact and the knowledge that we are. Now in these three propositions which I have just cited no feeling of illusion or mere probability disturbs us. For we do not experience them as we experience externals, that is by bodily sense, as we experience colour by sight, sounds by hearing, odours by smell,

[1] For the chief passages see Notes, p. 282.

flavour by taste, hardness and softness by touch; in these experiences images are presented to us which, though they are immaterial, closely resemble the objects; and these images we can reflect upon and preserve in our memories and we can be excited by them to desire the objects themselves. But without any of the pictures made in the mind by the senses, which may deceive us, I am convinced that I am, that I know my existence and that I love that existence and that knowledge. When these experiences are so true, we have no fear of those who use the objections of the Academics, "But what if you are deceived?" The answer is "if I am deceived, at any rate I do exist, *si fallor, sum*: the man who does not exist simply cannot be deceived. Therefore, since I do exist if I am deceived, how can I be deceived as to my existence when it is certain that I do exist if I am deceived? The fact that I should have to exist as someone if I am to be deceived (supposing I were deceived) puts it beyond all doubt that I am not deceived in the knowledge of my existence. It follows that in being aware of my own knowledge I am not deceived; for, as I know that I am, so I know also that I know. And when I love these two things—my existence and my knowledge of my existence—I add to the things I know a love which makes a third thing of no less value than the other two. . . .'

The two positions—that of Descartes briefly summarised above, that of St Augustine given in two passages from the *dcD* (xi. 26 and xix. 18)—invite comparison.

(*a*) In the first place Descartes starts from doubt and searches for some sure foothold of certainty of existence which he finds in his awareness of his own thought.

St Augustine starts with the conviction that doubt is madness. It is true that at one period in his life he was plunged into an anguish of spirit by a profound scepticism the memory of which he could never efface; and that is one reason why all that he has to say about doubt is of extreme interest. But in his view periods of doubt are periods of abnormality breaking into the normal and necessary disposition of man to believe; the mind is not first deliberately cleared, as with Descartes, of all but self-evident truths owing nothing to the senses or to imagination, for, as we shall see, he regards such a feat as impossible. To St Augustine doubt is neither total nor a starting-point; it can only be partial and it is an episode.

(*b*) Descartes assumes that thought can be entirely independent of objects of thought. He would be right in saying that it is independent of individual objects; but it cannot be independent of objects entirely, as he supposes, or there would be nothing to think about. From this false premiss he contends that the mind is independent of the body, and knows itself with greater certainty than it knows objects, and this conclusion has haunted theories of knowledge ever since. It is true that, as Descartes and

St Augustine and the 'plain man' agree, there can be no knowledge of objects without an existing mind; but it is equally true that there can be no knowledge without existing objects, and it is on this last point that St Augustine is certainly not Cartesian. For, as we have seen, he insists that the mind knows objects more clearly than itself and that its most difficult task is to know itself, for it is itself dependent upon the body.

(c) Thirdly, Descartes is certain of his existence because he is aware of himself as a thinker (or doubter): the certainty of existence is dependent upon the certainty of thinking. St Augustine is certain of his existence, and of his awareness of his existence, and of his love of his existence, because he apprehends these by 'immediate' experience, which carries conviction; he does not need any inference (*ergo*) to establish the certainty. If it should be suggested to him or if at times he should suspect that this awareness is fallacious, his answer is 'I most certainly am, and, if I am in error in being certain that I am, nevertheless I am: for it is necessary to exist, in order to be in error'.

St Augustine gives a far truer description of psychological fact than Descartes. Descartes separates the mind and the body and is certain only of mental activity. Gassendi, a contemporary of Descartes, complained that, since the verb implied a subject, any verb would have done instead of 'I think' and suggested 'I walk'. This criticism misses the mark because Descartes is not really as certain of physical processes as of mental activity, and therefore *cogito* alone carries any certainty. St Augustine, on the other hand, would regard man's consciousness of himself as a physical being as no less real than his consciousness of himself as a thinking being, and would not set up the artificial distinction between body and mind which has been the trouble of idealism since the time of Descartes. This distinction is unreal because the body and the mind are not presented to consciousness as separate phenomena, but are presented in indissoluble combination. Thus, there is a sense in which St Augustine means no more by *si fallor, sum* than Gassendi thought Descartes meant; and St Augustine might have said *si ambulo, sum* in so far as he points out that the subject of a verb exists and that immediate experience is the raw material of reality. But, of course, *si fallor* is vastly more impressive, for it turns doubt of one's existence into a proof of the existence of the doubter, so that not only does the subject of the verb exist but the subject of the verb denoting doubt of existence must also exist, and be aware of his existence, thus destroying the possibility of a thoroughgoing scepticism. *Si fallor, sum* is not *cogito ergo sum* in Descartes' sense.

Chapter 19 is omitted in this selection. It refers back to chapter 2 of the nineteenth book. One of the *differentiae* applied to moral theories by Varro was the implication of any particular theory for habits of daily life, such as

dress; another turned on the distinction between an active and a contemplative life and the relative weight attached to each. See B(*d*) and (δ) of the Analysis, p. 177.

CHAPTER 20

In chapter 20 the argument of the nineteenth book comes back to its beginning. As chapter 1 raised the question of 'ends' and happiness, so chapter 20 rounds off the argument of the intervening chapters and reasserts the conclusion, namely that everlasting and perfected peace is the *summum bonum* of the city of God. Such peace far transcends, as a good, anything that the world can offer. He who pursues it can be said to be happy now, but happy in hope, not in fact.

At this point we must pause to consider a Latin phrase which it is difficult to interpret shortly; yet it is crucial to the transition to the next chapter. The Christian may be said to be happy in that hope (*spe illa*) of Christianity rather than in 'that reality of your pagan world' (*re ista*). The antithesis *spe . . . re* is common enough in St Augustine. *Re* is often contrasted with 'in theory'; it may be strengthened as *re ipsa*; it means 'in actual fact' 'in experience'. But *re ista* is different; *re* means 'the facts or conditions as they are', but *ista* is commonly used by St Augustine to refer to conditions, facts, theories, practices, habits, cults, philosophies of the pagan world as it has been or is, in contrast with Christian faith and practice. *Spes illa*, then, means 'things as they will be according to the hopes of Christians', *res ista* means 'things as they have been and are now in the world and especially the Roman world' or 'life and thought according to non-Christian standards' or 'the existing political, social and moral structure'. Using *res ista* in this sense, St Augustine is reminded of *res publica*, for the existing structure was 'public', and thus he is reminded of his earlier promise to discuss the question whether the Roman commonwealth really aimed at the common weal. This question was suggested to St Augustine by the *de republica* of Cicero and was hastily discussed and quickly postponed in the second book of the *dcD*. Such seems to be the link between chapters 20 and 21; the first words of chapter 21, 'for this reason', show that there is a link.

CHAPTER 21

The *de republica* of Cicero, composed in imitation of the Republic of Plato, even to the extent of concluding with the 'Dream of Scipio' to correspond with the 'Myth of Er', was published in six books about 51 B.C.

In scene it is thrown back to 129 B.C. Scipio Africanus the Younger is the chief speaker in a dialogue which is supposed to cover three days; there were present Quintus Mucius Scaevola, Caius Laelius (consul 140 B.C.), Spurius Mummius, and five others. Though the dream of Scipio had been preserved for us by Macrobius, the treatise as a whole was lost till 1820; in that year Cardinal Angelo Mai discovered in the Vatican library a palimpsest which contained about a third of it, together with St Augustine's Commentary on the Psalms. This Codex Vaticanus 5757 (V) is to be dated to the fifth or sixth centuries. But, if the manuscript is defective, something can be done—as is done in the edition of C. F. W. Mueller[1]—to supply missing passages by inserting the quotations from the original treatise which are preserved in the works of grammarians and excerptors and other writers. These passages are furnished chiefly by Nonius Marcellus, of Tubursicum in Africa, who lived about A.D. 325,[2] Priscian (c. A.D. 500) of Mauretania, Lactantius (c. A.D. 300), also of Africa, Charisius (c. A.D. 350) of Carthage, Tertullian of Carthage, Favonius Eulogius, a pupil of St Augustine, Macrobius, who was a Roman official and writer, proconsul of Africa in A.D. 410, and Aulus Gellius, born about A.D. 130, an Italian who was much influenced as a writer by Fronto, the orator and lawyer of Cirta in Numidia. It would be easy to make too much of what may be coincidence, or may be explicable on other grounds; but the facts just quoted about the place of origin of the writers to whom we owe extracts from the *de republica* seem to point to a particular vogue of the dialogue in African rhetorical schools and literary circles before and after St Augustine's time. However this may be, it is evident that St Augustine, in discussing some of the arguments used in Cicero's *de republica*, was referring his readers to a treatise with which they were familiar.

The subject-matter probably owes a great deal to Panaetius, the Stoic philosopher (180 B.C.-110 B.C.), who had so much influence on the Romans of his day; many of the characters in the dialogue were his friends and pupils, as, for example, Scipio himself, C. Laelius, P. Rutilius Rufus, Q. Mucius Scaevola. Further, it is stated in the dialogue itself that Scipio 'used to discuss politics with Panaetius in company with Polybius, two Greeks who of all Greeks were most gifted in these matters'.[3] And it will be remembered that we have Cicero's own statement, made partly in modest self-depreciation, that his philosophical works were 'copies, and so they cost me all the less trouble to write; I provide merely the words, of which I have no lack'.[4]

---

[1] Teubner text, 1890.
[2] If an inscription (Dess. *I. L. S.* 2943) of that date refers to him.   [3] i. 21, 34.
[4] *ad Att.* xii, 52.

We therefore have St Augustine discussing a treatise on politics written by Cicero, a treatise popular in Africa, owing a great deal to Stoicism seen through Roman experience of government and administration. In course of time St Augustine's treatment of certain passages in that treatise was to be quoted, apart from its context, and used (whether legitimately or not) by very many mediæval writers in their claims on behalf of or against the church or the state. But it cannot be emphasised too strongly, before any attempt is made to consider St Augustine's treatment, that he is concerned with historical criticism, and not with developing a theory of the state, still less a theory of the Christian state. He applies a particular definition of 'a state' to the Roman state and he finds that it does not fit; he quotes a minimum definition which would fit the Roman or any state, but it is a definition, which as he points out, leaves crucial elements within it undefined and therefore it is of little value for constructive political thought. But constructive political theory is not his interest. He is interested in the characters of men, not in the form of states; to him men and families come first; given righteous men, the state will look after itself; religion and morals are antecedent to politics. It is true, as was seen on page 164, that St Augustine attributes value to the state, for it would not accord with his views on Providence and history to deny such value, but the state as such is valuable only as a means of coping with the transmitted havoc caused by the initial mistakes of man and men. He now urges that it is not possible to pass judgment upon any state unless you first know the character of its members; the higher the character of its members, the less is their character due to the state and the less the state can do for them, for that character is derived from their allegiance to the *civitas Dei*.

We may now summarise chapter 21 of the second book which (in this volume) is inserted for convenience in the text of chapter 21 of the nineteenth book. Sallust, in his work on the Catilinarian conspiracy, had condemned the corruption of Rome; Cicero went further and maintained in the *de republica* that in his day there remained only the shadow and not the substance of the Roman Commonwealth. The point was led up to as follows; what harmony is to a choir or orchestra, concord is to a city, and concord is inseparable from justice. The case may indeed be maintained, as by Philus in the dialogue as *advocatus diaboli*, that injustice rather than justice is to the interest of the state; but there are arguments for the reverse of this contention, and such arguments were put forward first by Laelius, then by Scipio. For Scipio maintained that a commonwealth was 'the weal of the people', and in this context 'people' meant 'a gathering of people united in fellowship by agreement as to what was just and by a common pursuit of interest'. If the sovereign power of a commonwealth —king or aristocracy or people—is unjust, there can be no weal of the

people and so no commonwealth. And Cicero, speaking in his own person
in the preface to the fifth book, deplores the disappearance of all standards
through the sheer dearth of men to maintain them; it is through the
wickedness of men that the substance of a commonwealth is lost to Rome.
On Cicero's own admission injustice or unrighteousness had destroyed
the common weal.

St Augustine then goes on to make two points. The first, which is
relevant to the argument of the second book of the *dcD*, is that, if Cicero's
lament had been made in the Christian era instead of before it, the Christians would certainly have been saddled with the blame; as it is, it seems
rather that the Roman gods had failed the Roman state. The second point
is that, so far from Rome having ceased to be a commonwealth, Rome
never was a commonwealth, for true justice never resided there. On
definitions which exclude the criterion of justice she may justify her claim.
But, if justice is included in the definition of a commonwealth, there is
only one place in which justice does reside—call it, if you like, the
commonwealth of Christ (for it is the weal of the people), but commonwealth (*respublica*) carries all kinds of irrelevant associations and we had
better call it 'the city (*civitas*) of God'.

Chapter 21 not only picks up chapter 21 of the second book but also
resumes the political discussion put down at the end of chapter 17 of the
nineteenth book. The first few lines briefly remind the reader of Scipio's
definition, and the rest of the chapter carries on St Augustine's criticism,
which is so swiftly developed that it is best to state it in a series of propositions with comments in brackets.

Res publica, commonwealth, is the same as *res populi*, the weal of the
people. A people is 'a gathering of men united by common agreement as
to what is right and by a common pursuit of interest'. Such is Scipio's
definition. Now agreement in a people about what is right implies that a
commonwealth cannot be carried on without justice (note that *iustitia*
may be justice or righteousness or both). Where there is not true justice
(note the insertion of 'true'), there can be no *ius*. What is done *iure* ('with
right') is done justly (note that *iuste*, justly, crosses over from the legal
sphere of *ius* to the moral sphere). *Iura* ('rights') cannot be said to be un-
fair, for *ius* springs from the fountain of justice (note again the ambiguity).
Where there is not true (note) justice, a people cannot be held together by
agreement about what is *ius*; hence where there is not *ius* and therefore not
justice, there is no weal of the people and therefore no commonwealth.
The argument may now be taken a stage further. Justice is that virtue
which gives to each his due (note the limited 'distributive' sense given to
justice at this point). Man must, in justice, give his Creator his due. Therefore the only commonwealth is the Christian commonwealth, that is the

city of God, which does by definition give God his due (this conclusion is implied at this stage and is made explicit later).

It is clear that throughout this discussion justice is used in a variety of senses, which may be distinguished as follows: (i) the rules and regulations which a state draws up in order to maintain ordered relations among its members; infringement of these rules leads to disorder and the negation of society; they may vary in the degree in which they enshrine moral principles; (ii) moral righteousness, which receives its sanction elsewhere than in the rules of a state, namely in the moral consciousness and in religion— though, if those rules are moral, such sanction may be reinforced by them; (iii) the rendering to each man of what is his due, the content of 'due' being determined by the rules of the state or by morality or by both. But the use of various senses of justice in political or philosophical discussion is by no means peculiar to St Augustine. Further, it is equally clear that, whereas some degree of justice might be attributed to a state, true, that is perfect, justice can be attributed to none known to history; only the city of God can be the repository of real justice, for it is essential to real justice that justice should be done to God. But no pagan state has done justice to God; therefore any definition which will fit a pagan state must be couched in terms which omit all reference to justice. Only the *civitas Dei* can be defined in terms which include the idea of justice.

Hence the questions arise (i) did St Augustine really mean to exclude justice from the definition of all states (as some critics allege), (ii) did he condemn the state as such, (iii) why does he not consider the Christian state instead of assuming that only the extremes, the pagan state and the *civitas Dei*, are to be discussed? These questions may wait a little,[1] for the rest of chapter 21 is concerned with (*a*) reinforcing by additional arguments the previous contention that there can be no justice without obedience to God, (*b*) discussing the second element in Scipio's definition, namely 'a common pursuit of interest'.

The argument continues thus. St Augustine had said that it was unrighteous to become enslaved to evil spirits when God is the sovereign Lord. Objection need not be taken to the rule of God on the ground that all rule is unjust; for in the *de republica* it was shown that enslavement might be for the benefit of the enslaved. The rule of a superior when it is of benefit to the inferior cannot be unjust. Nature supplies analogies; the reason, if ruled by God, rules the evil desires of the mind; the mind, too, rules the body. But the reason and the mind cannot rule righteously unless they are themselves ruled by God; and, if there is not righteousness in individuals, there cannot be righteousness (justice) in the state composed of such individuals. Hence any definition which includes the term

---

[1] They are discussed on p. 258.

righteousness or justice can be applicable only to a commonwealth composed of individuals ruled by God.

At last the conclusion of the discussion has been made explicit. It will be picked up in chapter 24.

In the meantime there remains the second half of Scipio's definition—'common pursuit of interest'. This is easily disposed of. In real fact, pursuit of interest means generally pursuit of one's own lower interests, which leads to bondage to lower desires and so to evil spirits. This was seen clearly throughout Roman history; and it is of no avail to protest that the Roman gods were good, for the review of Roman religion given in the earlier half of the *dcD* proves conclusively that they were not good.

CHAPTER 22

If the objection is made that the credentials of the God whom it is proposed to substitute for the gods of Rome are obscure, then such a reply can only prove the blindness of the objector; for the prophets are God's witnesses testifying to the promise fulfilled in Christ and in the Holy Spirit operating through the Church. Even Varro, the pagan savant, and Porphyry, the enemy of Christianity, recognised His greatness.

CHAPTER 23

This chapter, which exposes at considerable length the inconsistencies of Porphyry, is for the most part omitted in this selection. But the concluding portion of it, which is included, rounds off the criticism of Scipio's definition. It sums up by insisting that, as the individual man is righteous in the devotion to God which in fact issues in love of God and love of neighbour, so only the commonwealth which is composed of such men can be righteous and can satisfy a definition which includes righteousness as a necessary property of the weal of the people.

CHAPTER 24

Chapter 24 is perhaps one of the best known in the *dcD*. But it has often been made to bear a weight of meaning which was never intended by St Augustine.

St Augustine has applied Scipio's definition to the Rome of Roman history; his method has been strictly historical and he has found as a

matter of historical fact that the definition does not fit. What then? The opening words of chapter 24 are of great importance, but they have often been neglected. Literally the translation is, 'But if a people were to be defined not by that definition (of Scipio) but by some other as, for example, if someone were to say, "A people is a multitude of rational beings united in fellowship by sharing a common love of the same things" . . .' St Augustine's meaning and intention, it is suggested, are as follows: 'We have seen', he says, 'that Scipio's definition does not fit historical commonwealths; if you are looking for a definition which would fit, you would have to adopt some other; I will present you with a definition which would fit; I choose it from others as a sample of a defini-tion[1] which would be suitable.' In other words St Augustine is not putting forward a full abstract statement of political theory about the aims or ends of the state, but is finding a minimum definition of a commonwealth which will fit the Roman commonwealth and others. But he goes on at once to show how useless this definition is; for it has been stripped of all qualitative content, and, as he says, it is useless till you have determined first what a people does love and, secondly, whether it loves higher or lower things. It was necessary to strip the definition of all reference to values or moral qualities, such as justice or righteousness, because as long as such terms are left in a definition it can easily be shown that as a fact it did not fit any commonwealth of history; for a state may be good or bad and is in fact both good and bad. St Augustine did not propound a care-fully thought-out contribution to political theory, as many critics seem to have believed. He was not concerned with the ends or aims of the state. All he wished to do was to show (i) that a description of Rome which in-cludes the term justice (*vera iustitia*) is manifestly untrue, as indeed it is of any state except the *civitas Dei*, (ii) a description of the state which is true of Rome or any other state must necessarily leave out all judgments of value and confine itself to neutral terms which have to be given content in the specific historical case to which the description is applied. The only element common to all historical states is 'a common love of something', but the 'something' varies. Since St Augustine's method is purely histori-cal, his argument is not primarily a contribution to political philosophy, if by that term is meant the theory as to what function the state *should* fulfil. In that he has no direct concern or interest. His main aim is to make it clear that the state has not been and cannot be what the city of God is; the reason is that the city of God is by definition the city of righteousness.

Some critics have been shocked to find that St Augustine excluded justice from his definition of the state. If the view put forward in the fore-

[1] Cf. ii. 21 *ad fin.* (p. 116 above), *secundum probabiliores autem definitiones*, which suggests that there, too, he had more than one in mind.

going paragraphs is correct, there was no need to be dismayed at St Augustine's apparent crime. For the critics persist in thinking that St Augustine is concerned with theories about what the state should do, what function it should fulfil and what aims it should set before itself. In that case it would no doubt be shocking to leave out moral values, including justice. If it is realised that St Augustine is here concerned with a piece of historical analysis in order to find a common description of all states which have existed and could exist, good and bad, then there is nothing surprising in his omission of justice, in his sense. For justice, in St Augustine's view, implies love of God and love of neighbour which no society of men manifests except that (partly) historical society or fellowship which St Augustine calls the *civitas Dei*. No state or society which is not the *civitas Dei* can be defined by a definition which includes the differentia of the *civitas Dei*, namely justice or righteousness. Cicero's definition is not a true historical diagnosis of the Roman or of any state, that is, on St Augustine's interpretation of the word 'justice' in the definition.

It is not difficult to see why St Augustine should have described the state as he did, selecting such description from others available. In the first place he sees human personality chiefly as love and will; for him personality depends, as has been seen earlier, upon the things on which a man sets his affection and upon the direction of his will to obtain them. Further, St Augustine insists that the state is composed of individuals and that its character depends on the character of its individual members. Hence its character depends on the things on which it sets its affections. Secondly, it will be remembered that in describing the characteristics of the earthly city and of the city of God St Augustine found the distinction to lie in their 'loves'. One was fashioned by love of self to the contempt of God, the other by love of God to the contempt of self. In short, St Augustine's choice of his sample definition was determined (*a*) by his view of human personality, (*b*) by his previous distinction between the earthly and the heavenly cities.

It is relevant to consider here a famous phrase which occurs in the fourth book, chapter 4—*Remota itaque iustitia quid regna nisi magna latrocinia?* 'And so, set justice aside, what are kingdoms except great robber-gangs?' Famous phrases are often torn from their context and so interpreted. This phrase is almost always quoted without its second word, and yet the word indicates that the meaning is dependent upon the argument of the previous chapter. The result is that the most diverse meanings have been assigned to the question. For instance, Dr Carlyle[1] regards St Augustine as meaning that the feature which distinguishes a kingdom from a band of robbers is that the kingdom possesses justice while the band of robbers does not.

[1] *A History of Medieval Political Theory in the West*, London, 1903.

Mr Christopher Dawson[1] takes the opposite point of view; he maintains that 'the actual tendency of the passage appears to be quite the contrary. St Augustine is arguing that there is no difference between the conqueror and the robber except the scale of their operations, for he continues, "What is banditry but a little kingdom?" and he approves the reply of the pirate to Alexander the Great, "Because I do it with a little ship, I am called a robber, and you, because you do it with a great fleet, are called an Emperor." ' With this interpretation Professor N. H. Baynes agrees.[2] Sir Ernest Barker maintains that to St Augustine the state had its own relative righteousness—'It is not a *magnum latrocinium*; for you *cannot* remove righteousness from it, and St Augustine only said that kingdoms were great bands of robbers *if you remove righteousness*.'[3]

The argument may be summarised thus. In chapter 2 St Augustine announced that he promised to consider what element in the Roman character and what reason moved the true God, in whose hand are all kingdoms, to increase the Roman Empire. He does not redeem this promise till the fifth book, chapter 12 (extract no. 14*a*); for he immediately embarks upon an enquiry (chapter 3) into the imperialism of Rome whose empire was won by war. He is puzzled to know why nations should be enflamed by lust of expansion when as a result they are immersed in war and bloodshed and the uncertainty of conquest; their triumph is ephemeral—bright and brittle; happiness does not lie there. Then, to reinforce his point, he supposes two individuals (note how he invariably goes back to the individual, for every man, he says, is a part even of the greatest city, as a letter of the alphabet is part of a discourse). One individual is poor, virtuous, god-fearing, content and happy; the other is rich, greedy, suspicious, haunted by fear, and miserable. There is no doubt which lot is preferable. So, too, with nations. Hence, if a nation is god-fearing, it is an advantage that the good men who compose it should fling their empire wide—advantageous not to themselves but to their subjects; for them their own righteousness is sufficient. A *regnum* of good men is a blessing to human kind, not merely to themselves; a *regnum* of bad men is a curse to themselves rather than to their subjects, for a man's own wickedness inflicts *real* harm upon himself, while the wickedness of his oppressors does not. The exactions made by the wicked upon the righteous (*iusti*) are not a punishment for wrong-doing but a test of character. If, then, you assume a *regnum* in which power is exercised only by unrighteous men—*remota*[4]

---

[1] *A Monument to St Augustine*, p. 63. On this interpretation it is not easy to see what part the words *remota iustitia* play, since the meaning would appear to be the same if they were omitted.

[2] *The Political Ideas of St Augustine's de civitate Dei*, p. 8.

[3] *Introduction to the City of God, translated by John Healey*, p. xxviii.

[4] On the use of *remota* see note on p. 282.

itaque iustitia—that *regnum* is no different from a band of robbers. (Indeed a band of brigands is a miniature state from one point of view. It is subject to the control of its leader, it is bound together by a compact, it divides the spoil according to a law.) Now suppose this evil band grows by attaching to itself only desperadoes (*tantum perditorum*) and acquires by conquest cities and peoples; it calls itself a *regnum*, not because it has laid aside lust of conquest but because it is outside the reach of punishment. The pirate when captured gave an excellent retort to Alexander when he was asked what he meant by rendering the seas dangerous—'the same that you mean when you make the world dangerous: I do it with one ship and am called a robber; you do it with a great fleet and are called an Emperor.'

The following chapters then go on to describe how Romulus gathered together a motley crew of fugitives from the law and how Ninus embarked upon a career of successful conquest which owed nothing to the help of the pagan gods; and many more chapters expose the futility of pagan worship till finally St Augustine asks what it was in the Roman character which merited the aid of God in the extension of the Roman Empire. Thus we reach the extracts from the fifth book which are given above, pp. 44-61.

The sense of the chapters thus summarised is this: St Augustine is discussing those nations (generally led by one man—Romulus, Ninus, Alexander) which through sheer lust of expansion conquer their neighbours. Their power is precarious, spurious, and it ends in their misery. But, if a nation composed of 'just' men pursues such a career, its expansion may prove a blessing to mankind. If on the other hand you remove righteousness from it—that is, remove the righteous men, suppose it not to contain such men—then such a conquering power is not different from a robber power. Alexander, when he made the world a dangerous place to live in, was like the pirate who made the seas dangerous; neither conferred a blessing on mankind.

In short, *regnum* in this context means 'a conquering power' and has nothing to do with the *respublica* of the second and nineteenth books. *Iustitia* looks back to the *iusti* whose conquests may benefit mankind and has nothing to do with the *iustitia* of Scipio's definition. Alexander is here regarded as a typical conqueror inspired by lust of dominion and he is regarded, for the purposes of this passage, as unrighteous. Having condemned conquest by unrighteous men and approved conquest by righteous men in the interests of humanity St Augustine moves on to consider eventually the place of the Roman imperial expansion in the Providence of God; it had a place therein because there were elements of righteousness within the Roman Empire.

If this is the right interpretation of the famous phrase seen in the light of

its context, all discussion of it, torn from its context, as part of St Augustine's alleged political theory, is beside the mark.

CHAPTER 25

St Augustine does not finish with the people till the end of chapter 26. In chapter 25 the last sentence of the preceding chapter is developed. For the mind to control the body and for the reason to control the baser desires of the mind, the reason and the mind must be subject to God; if not, they will be subject to devils. No matter what particular objective virtues may have in view, they are nothing but vices if they 'refer' to themselves as a standard and a justification rather than to God; they are proud and arrogant, the negation of virtues. Just as life, which is not derived from the flesh but from above it, yet makes flesh active, so what makes man happy comes not from man but from above man—and indeed from every heavenly power and virtue.

This chapter may be regarded as replying to a possible objection. 'Surely the cultivation of the virtues by each individual citizen will produce a people which will not be without righteousness; virtue will enable the mind to control the body and the reason to control evil desires; the result will be a righteous people; there is no need of obedience to God.' To this extremely modern plea St Augustine returns two answers. First, as a matter of fact and experience, the effectiveness of morality without religion is illusory; religion is the basis of morality and is necessary to all effective practice of virtue. Secondly, without such a basis virtues turn into vices; for self-culture, however honourable may be its motives, is still the culture of self, and regard for the self and for nothing else is the source of pride; thus virtues springing from this motive are in the last resort sinful. Goodness, whether on earth or in heaven, must look beyond and above itself; such goodness is alone real and only in real goodness is happiness to be found.

CHAPTER 26

Generalising, then, from the individual to the state, as is his practice, St Augustine argues that a people estranged from God must be the reverse of happy. Yet even such a people loves its own peace, which is by no means to be despised. Indeed, it is to the interest of Christians that pagan states should have such peace as they can create—it is not, of course, peace in the Christian sense—for as long as the city of God and the pagan state are

intermingled and live side by side, Christians may use and enjoy this peace, however unchristian the state providing it. They will use it, however, in full knowledge that it is not their peace; but they can profit by it in their journey through life. Such was the intention of St Paul when he enjoined prayer on behalf of civil powers; he wanted Christians to be able to live a quiet life, ensured to them by the state, and to add to it their own loyalty to God and their own love. And Jeremiah's advice to the Jews carried into captivity was similar.

With this chapter ends St Augustine's reflections upon Scipio's definition and its application to the Roman people. We may pick up the three questions left unanswered on p. 251; they were (i) did St Augustine really exclude justice from the definition of all states? (ii) did he condemn the state as such? (iii) why did he not consider the Christian state instead of assuming that only the extremes, the earthly city and the *civitas Dei*, are to be discussed?

These three questions have already been answered by implication. St Augustine certainly intended to exclude justice from the *definition* of a state which would have to fit all historical states; for he did not see how a state could be defined in terms which included the differentia of the city of God, namely righteousness. But the last thing he intended to do was to deny that some states have exhibited some measure of righteousness (or justice). It would have been inconsistent to deny a measure of justice to a state and yet (i) to regard history as governed by Providence and events as having a real significance contributing to a purpose,[1] (ii) to set a high moral value upon the individual and the family and to consider the family and the state as concentric circles, each circle contributing to the welfare of the other,[2] (iii) to set a high moral value upon the Roman Empire and the virtues which made it, virtues which Christians were bidden to emulate,[3] (iv) to enjoin that Christians should make use of the peace of the state. In short, the *civitas Dei* is the society of those who base themselves on righteousness; other forms of society which could not and would not make this claim exhibit by the Providence of God a measure of justice, some more than others. The 'city' to which he denies righteousness is the 'earthly city', which, as has been seen, is the ideal negation of the *civitas Dei*. Both cities have been and are and will be actual, in the sense that they are made up of real individuals; but neither have been or will be actual as states. In some actual states St Augustine recognises some righteousness to exist. He does not therefore deserve the judgment sometimes passed upon him as a supreme pessimist. Sombre as is his outlook upon the reality of evil, his faith in the perpetual working of Providence in human affairs excludes pessimism as a fundamental element in his view of the world.

[1] See p. 164.   [2] See p. 236 sq.   [3] See p. 163.

Nor does he put beyond the bounds of possibility the Christian state. The virtues of a Christian Emperor have already been reviewed[1] and to the blessings of the reigns of Constantine and Theodosius he gives unsparing recognition. Moreover, he says explicitly[2] that 'if only the Christian teaching about righteousness and uprightness were heard and regarded by the kings of the earth and all peoples, by rulers and all the judges on earth, by young men and maidens, old and young, all of responsible age and of either sex, tax-gatherers and soldiers to whom John the Baptist spoke[3]—then the state would adorn with its own prosperity the lands of this present life and would rise to the pinnacle of eternal life, to reign there in perfect happiness'. But St Augustine's task is not to discuss the Christian state, but to give a glimpse of that fellowship which began before any state and which will endure beyond any and is beyond the reach of any, but whose lineaments must be copied, so far as may be, by any state which aspires to be Christian. St Augustine chose the greater theme, as later ages have testified.

CHAPTER 27

The peace of the Christian is different from temporal peace. Peace with God is obtained in this life by a venture of faith, but hereafter it will be 'by sight'. It is also similar; for both temporal peace and the peace peculiar to Christians are rather a comfort to unhappiness than the joy of happiness.

In the same way Christian happiness consists rather in the remission of sins than in any positive perfection, and the universal prayer of Christians recognises this in 'Forgive us our trespasses'. For the *civitas Dei* realises that reason is not sufficient to enable us to resist temptation, as classical philosophy had taught. However successful the struggle, however heroic the Christian warrior, something always creeps in; it insinuates itself, if not into overt action, at least into word and thought; it causes the word to fall carelessly from our lips and the thought to fly away in forbidden directions; the result is sin. Even victory is insecure and uneasy, and only pride can refuse to ask forgiveness. Christian righteousness therefore consists in obedience, prayer for grace and pardon, thanksgiving, and Christian righteousness can look forward to a final peace in which human nature will be healed; there shall be no wickedness, no conflict or struggle; God will rule man and man will find his pleasure in obedience. Thus will be reached the peace of happiness and the happiness of peace.

And so St Augustine comes back to the opening paragraph of the nineteenth book in which he undertook to reveal in glaring contrast the

[1] See p. 167.   [2] ii. 19.   [3] St Luke, iii. 12.

difference between Christian happiness and the phantoms of happiness which pagan religion and philosophy pursued. And the ideas which have occupied him so much during the nineteenth book recur in this chapter—peace, faith, hope, eternity, 'ends', sin, conflict, immortality, rule, obedience, humility.

CHAPTER 28

Finally, St Augustine, employing that ruthless logic which led him to state without any sign of shrinking or horror the harshest of doctrines, sets out the destiny of the unfaithful. Against a long series of terms applicable to the *civitas Dei* are ranged their opposites—clinging to God)(alienation from God, happiness)(misery, life)(death, peace)(conflict. Yet, though death is opposed to life, death is not the termination of life and so of a life of misery; though there is conflict, there is no victory to put an end to conflict. These are ideas which St Augustine pursues into the following book, where we need not follow him.

CONCLUSION

The world in which St Augustine published his *dcD* was a world disillusioned and bewildered and haunted by fears and uncertainties. It clung passionately to the past, for only the past offered any sure foothold in a changing world. Accepted values were challenged; institutions were tottering; yet the belief rightly dominated men's minds that in the values of the past lay a wealth of effort and achievement which was of vital and permanent significance. With this belief St Augustine was in profound agreement; he did not propose a clean break. But he read history differently. Men had too often taken false standards and had interpreted their private and public affairs in the light of those false standards. Achievement there had been, but in that achievement men had rated as noble what was base and what was base as noble, and too often their point of departure in philosophic speculation had been mistaken. History could be read aright only by the standards of Christian insight into values. Thus read, history gave no support to despair; sure confidence awaited those who had the eyes to see.

To his readers, therefore, he offered no Utopia. He did not draw the outlines of an ideal state nor of a Christian state; he did not parcel out man's world between Church and State. He did not counsel men to escape from the realities of this world into a dream existence or to turn their backs upon the responsibilities of daily life in pursuit of a fugitive otherworldli-

ness. He urged that men should be loyal to themselves and to one another and to the group, family or state, but that they should perform loyally those obligations in love of God and of one another—that they should recognise a higher loyalty which should inform the manner of the discharge of lesser loyalties and that, when higher and lower allegiances conflict, they should cling to the higher. Thus in spite of apparent disaster, no new phenomenon in history, their lives and the lives of all forms of 'fellowship' would be reconstituted; neither the individual nor society need perish if they were based on the 'fellowship of the saints'.

To this it may be replied that in the idea of a double loyalty, one higher than the other and informing it, there was nothing new. Plato had sent his philosophers back into the cave of ordinary human affairs; Zeno, Marcus Aurelius and many more had preached under various names the ideal of devotion to 'the city of Zeus', while being well satisfied if the actual state progressed. Seneca had drawn in language not unlike the language of the *dcD* the outlines of the lesser and the greater allegiance. 'We hold in our thoughts', he says, 'two commonwealths. One of them is extensive and truly common to all, including both gods and men; within it we have no eye for any particular corner, rather the bounds of our citizenship are measured only by the sun. The other is the commonwealth of which we are members by accident of birth. One belongs to the Athenians and Carthaginians and is the concern not of all mankind but of specific groups. Now there are some who can give their interest to both these commonwealths at the same time, some only to the greater, some only to the lesser. The greater commonwealth we can serve even in time of withdrawal from practical affairs (*in otio*), indeed probably better then. We shall be enabled to ask such questions as these: what is virtue, one or many? is it nature or training that makes men good? is this world of seas and lands and all that is included therein the only one of its kind or has God scattered many such worlds in space? is the matter of which everything is composed continuous and compact or is it discrete, with void and solid intermixed? does God sit aloof and watch his creation or does he guide it? Is God outside creation, wrapping it round, or does he indwell the whole? Is the Universe immortal or to be classed as perishable and subject to time? If you ask these questions, what service are you doing God? The answer is that you are ensuring that so great a work of creation shall not go without witness. We commonly say that the highest good is to live according to nature; nature has made us for both purposes—for a life of contemplation and a life of action.'[1]

It may be taken without further elaboration that the idea of a double allegiance was familiar enough to the classical philosophers; the philo-

[1] *de otio*, 31.

sophical works of Cicero are full of it, and largely through his works the idea was well known to St Augustine and to European thought ever since. But the Christian view of that double allegiance was profoundly different from the classical view, and those differences have been perpetuated in two streams of tradition down to our own day.

To St Augustine, as to Christian thinkers in general, the *civitas Dei* is open to all; it requires no passport except the will to enter, for the 'training', of which Seneca speaks, is done within it, as Christian experience testifies. However much classical philosophy might in theory open the 'greater commonwealth' to all, in fact by the very terms in which it was conceived and described it was reserved only for 'philosophers' or 'sages' with an education and an intellectual equipment, to say nothing of an ample portion of leisure, beyond the reach of the normal man. In the Christian view the double allegiance was within the competence of all; for the essence of Christian *sapientia* needed no years of study or contemplation; it needed only faith, and from the initial venture of faith would flow all the possibilities of wisdom of which the ordinary man was capable. He, too, could transfigure all his lesser loyalties in the light of a larger loyalty; he, too, could take back into daily life a philosophy—*nostra philosophia*— more true and more powerful than that of Seneca or Plato or Marcus Aurelius or Cicero. The first of the main points in which the *civitas Dei* and the whole tradition of which it is a part and a source differ from its classical counterparts is its universalism.

The second main difference lies in the view of human nature. Classical philosophy believed that knowledge alone would enable a man to choose the better; vice and virtue alike are within his power, and knowledge is power. This explains the exclusiveness of classical philosophy, but it explains also its fundamental weakness. Its account of human nature was inadequate. The philosopher's aim was 'to know God' and possibly he might love Him; the Christians urged men to love God, for only so could they know Him. If God is love, He is known by love and only under the impulse of love can man give Him service. Will directed by affection is to St Augustine the only ground of action, and a will to do good is the same thing as a love of good reinforced by the will. 'Set your affections on things which are high' and the will can then translate those high ideals into act. The two cities—the city of God and the earthly city—were distinguished by their loves, and the *civitas Dei* was composed of individuals whose wills were nothing more or less than 'good loves'.

The third distinction lies in the contrast between 'clinging to God', (*adhaerere Deo*) and the classical conception of self-sufficiency. As has been seen on earlier pages, assertion of self and reliance on the powers of the self are to St Augustine *superbia*, the source of all sin, and *superbia* is

the product of a bad will or, what is the same thing, a bad love, willing power in all fields for itself and relying on its self-won power. But in St Augustine's view man is not so constituted that he can be independent or can win happiness for himself without admitting dependence upon the author of his being. Of his own resources man cannot overcome the tendency to seek his happiness in his own way and to fail, because without the aid of its Creator his nature has not been given the power to succeed. On the other side lay the classical doctrine inherent in Cicero's statement that 'there is no one in any nation who cannot arrive at virtue when once he has obtained a guide' and the guide is of course Nature. The Reason of God indwells Nature whose child man is, and therefore man has within him reason which will furnish him with all the resources necessary for life and happiness. With the required changes of terminology this is essentially the view of Pelagianism, which is at heart Stoicism and some forms of modern humanism. On this fundamental question man has taken two positions and on each side the stress has fallen on different ideas. On one side faith, grace, prayer, sin and redemption have been emphasised, on the other side free will, choice, individual effort, the resources of personality. Yet one set of ideas is not wholly the property of one side or the other, for the modern humanist may set the utmost store by loyalty, which is faith, may be intensely sensitive to moral evil and wrong-doing, which is sin, and may believe most sincerely that the improvement of the many can come only through the self-sacrifices of the few. Similarly the Christian believes wholeheartedly in the freedom of the will and in individual effort and in the riches which men may, if they will, bring forth from the treasure-house of personality. None the less, though neither side can appropriate the ideas of free will, effort, personality, such emphasis has been laid by each side on different elements and such different meanings have been assigned to them that two utterly opposing philosophies of life have been sharply distinguished.

No one has seen more clearly than St Augustine the radical difference between those philosophies and no work has expressed it more emphatically than the *dcD*. This double tradition has run through the centuries, through philosophy in all its branches and literature in all its aspects and through the affairs of daily life. To-day, as always, the choice has to be made, and some would say that the urgency of right choice is greater to-day than ever before. To gain insight into the alternatives between which it must choose, the twentieth century can go with profit to the *dcD* written in the closing years of the ancient world.

APPENDICES, NOTES
AND INDEX

Appendix I

THE IDEA OF THE 'CITY'

(*A*) Classical conceptions of a 'city'.
(*B*) The origin of the idea of the 'city of God' (*a*) according to St A.
    (*b*) according to modern criticism.

(*A*) *Classical conceptions of a 'city'.*

The idea of a 'city' is by no means unfamiliar to classical thought. It takes various forms—the brotherhood of man, the brotherhood of good men, the city of gods and men. Sometimes it is a philosophical tenet only, sometimes attempts are made to translate it into reality. Some aspects of the idea are presented in the pages which follow without any attempt at completeness.

(*a*) If Dr W. W. Tarn is correct, Alexander the Great was the first man known to us to contemplate the brotherhood of man or the unity of mankind. In Dr Tarn's words, Alexander 'did say that all men were sons of God, that is brothers, but that God made the best ones peculiarly his own; he did aspire to be the harmoniser and reconciler of the world—that part of the world which his arm reached; he did have the intention of uniting the peoples of his empire in fellowship and concord and making them of one mind together; and when, as a beginning, he prayed at Opis for a partnership in rule and Homonoia between Macedonians and Persians, he meant what he said—not partnership in rule only, but true unity between them'.[1] From this brotherhood 'bad' men were excluded, but to Alexander the bad were not the majority, they were 'merely that small residue everywhere which cannot be civilised'.[2] Alexander thus dreamed of the brotherhood of man, based upon a rather vague religious sanction and shared by all men except inveterate law-breakers'; the brotherhood was to be brought about by the efforts of men striving to realise it.

(*b*) In his 'Republic' Zeno, born about 336 B.C., drew a picture of a world state, but it was a state comprising gods and some men—'the best'—and it was a world-state because it drew them from all nations and not because it embraced virtually all men. Indeed 'the best' were in Zeno's opinion remarkably scarce, for they had to have all the virtues; the citizens were very few. There is, it is true, a statement by Plutarch that the 'Republic' of Zeno amounted in short to this 'that we should live not city by city nor deme by deme, each separated from others by its own individual rights, but that we should regard all men as fellow-demesmen and fellow-citizens with one life and one universe around them—something like a herd sharing one pasture and feeding together under common laws. Zeno drew this picture sketching a vision or a phantasy of philosophic good-government and a philosophic state. Alexander turned theory into reality...'[3]

[1] W. W. Tarn, *Alexander and the Unity of Mankind* (Raleigh Lecture), pp. 27, 28.
[2] P. 19; based on Eratosthenes in Strabo, i. 66.
[3] *de Alex. virtute* i. 6, p. 329a. The passage is too long to quote in full.

On this it may be observed (i) that Plutarch does not suggest that Alexander put into practice Zeno's theory, for the dates prevent this, (ii) that the state of gods and some men is not the universal world-state of the passage of Plutarch. As will be seen again later, the universalism of the Stoics and the Cynics either is negative in character—a protest against the parochialism of Greek-city states or of Greeks in relation to the rest of the world—or is a deduction from cosmological theories and is of less importance to the philosophers than those theories.

(c) Chrysippus is stated to have held that ' just as the word "city" can be used in two senses to mean (a) a dwelling-place, (b) the systematic whole made up of residents and true citizens, so the Cosmos may be regarded as a city composed of gods and men, the gods being in authority and men being subject to them. Fellowship subsists between gods and men because they share alike in Reason, which in Nature is Law. Everything else has come into being for their sake. As a corollary it must be held that the god who controls the whole takes forethought for men, since he is anxious to confer benefit and is good and well-disposed to men and is just and possessed of all virtues'.[1] But the passage goes on to give other definitions of Cosmos, some of which are phrased in purely physical terms—air, earth, sea.

(d) Diogenes and the Cynics have little to offer relevant to the idea of the 'city'. Diogenes is said to have claimed to be a citizen of the Cosmos (κοσμοπολίτης). He, too, regards only a certain select class ('the wise', σοφοί) as true members of the 'real city in the Cosmos' (ὀρθὴ πολιτεία ἐν κόσμῳ); all things, he thought, belong to the wise, for all things belong to the gods and the gods are the friends of the wise.[2] But it is clear from the multitude of anecdotes which survive about Diogenes (and which are relevant, even if untrue, as reflecting his attitude) that he is not concerned with the positive and constructive aspect of the 'world-city'; rather he puts it forward with the intention of showing his contempt for local and national institutions and loyalties.

(e) The Utopia of Iambulus, named Heliopolis, which Aristonicus tried to put into effect in 133 B.C. and the actual miniature 'world-state' of Alexarchus on Athos, which was called Ouranopolis (city of Heaven) need no more than a reference here.[3] They assume some kind of brotherhood of man and some affinity of man with the gods, but they can scarcely have had much influence and are interesting rather as testimonies to the influence of the philosophers.

(f) The middle stage of Stoicism, represented by Panaetius and Poseidonius, seems to have disregarded Zeno's distinction between good and bad men and to have extended the world-city to all men. This universality was maintained in Stoicism as voiced by Cicero, Seneca and Marcus Aurelius. But there are certain features in it which invite attention; and, as the references to it are frequently quoted without their contexts and are therefore liable to misinterpretation, it is necessary to quote one or two passages in full.

'Since there is nothing superior to reason and since reason resides both in man and in God the first sharing of reason is between man and God. Where reason is a bond, right reason is also a common possession; and, since right reason is law, we must assume that we are linked with the gods by law also. Further, where there is community of law, there is community of right; those who have community of law and right we must regard as members of the same state (civitatis),

[1] Von Arnim, Stoic. Vet. Fragm. ii. 528.
[2] Diogenes Laertius vi. 63, 72; see D. R. Dudley, A History of Cynicism, p. 35.
[3] Iambulus, Diod. ii. 55-60; see W. Kroll in P.-W. Aristonicus; see C. A. H. ix. p. 104; Alexarchus, Athen iii. 98 D.

and if they obey the same commands and authorities the argument holds even more strongly. Now in fact they are obedient to the heavenly ordinances governing creation and to the divine mind and the all-powerful God, so that the whole universe is to be thought of as a single state (*civitas*) shared by gods and men.' The argument goes on to establish that the religious instinct exists in all men, that virtue enables man to recognise the nature of God and that there is therefore some likeness between God and man; Nature has been created for man's benefit; Nature has destined man for justice and so with Nature as a guide there is no one who cannot attain to virtue.[1]

There are other similar passages in Cicero. For example, 'In the beginning the world was created for gods and for men, and all that is in it was made and invented for the enjoyment of mankind. The world is a kind of house or city shared alike by gods and men.' But the passage continues, 'For gods and men are the only beings to use reason and so to live by right and law. Therefore, as we hold that Athens and Sparta were founded in the interest of the Athenians and Spartans and that everything in these cities belongs rightly to those peoples, so we must hold that everything in the whole world is the property of gods and men.'[2]

Seneca, too, speaks of 'a greater city which includes gods and men' but he says that we 'embrace' it only 'in imagination', and he makes it quite clear that he has in mind the 'world' which the sage, with leisure on his hands, can enter through scientific and philosophical speculation.[3]

To Marcus Aurelius the idea is familiar, but again the context should be noted. 'The end for rational creatures is to follow the Reason and the ordinances of that most ancient city and polity' (that is, the Universe). Again, he speaks of man as 'a citizen of the highest state of which all other states are, as it were, households', but this is set in a context advising careful study of the component elements of Nature if real greatness of mind is to be secured. Again, 'Rational creatures have been made for one another'; . . . therefore do not fret, remember 'the manifold proofs that the Universe is a kind of city'. Finally, 'if then the faculty of mind is common to all, reason also is common and this makes us rational. If reason is common, then that particular kind of reason which tells us what to do and what not to do is common. If that is true, we are citizens; if citizens, we have a share in a city-community; and if that is so, the Universe is a kind of state; for it cannot be said that the whole human race are fellow-members of any other state than this. And from that common city we derive the principles of intellect and reason and law.'[4]

The contexts of the passages quoted above from later Stoicism suggest how the idea of the common city of gods and men was regarded. The Stoics were concerned with Reason as a principle operating in the Universe and expressing itself as law. Man's reason was a fragment of the Universal Reason and by virtue of it man was entitled to a special kind of membership in the Universe. The highest form of membership with which men of that day were familiar was membership of a citizen-body. Moreover, since the Universal Reason expressed itself in law, the natural way for Stoicism to explain to contemporaries the idea of law was to express it in terms of something already understood, namely political

---

[1] Cicero, *de leg.* i. 23-31.
[2] *de nat. deorum* ii. 154; cf. *de fin.* iii (19). 64; *de repub.* i. 19.
[3] *de otio* xxxi; cf. *Ep.* lxviii. 2 and p. 261 above.
[4] *Meditations* ii. 16, iii. 11, iv. 2; iv. 4. Other such passages are xi. 15, xii. 36, iv. 23 (city of Zeus).

law. The Universe is then conceived of as a polity subject to law, but the conception of polity is subordinate to the conceptions of Law and of Reason expressing itself as Law. Undoubtedly the philosophical tendency from Plato onwards to belittle local laws and customs and to enlarge the idea of law to laws of human society, to minimise the differences between men and to emphasise their likenesses, contributed to the idea of a common society. But only a common society of men; the 'city of gods and men' is an idea based upon the abstract doctrines of Universal Reason and Law. Moreover the city is a city of all men by virtue of their reason and is not restricted to the good; the nature of man is the credential of membership, not the moral nature of the individual man.

The subordinate place of the 'city' with the Stoics is shown by their failure to draw implications from it. It is the last term of the argument and leads to nothing more. For man is a member by right and in fact; he need not acquire membership by effort. No religious and no ethical use is made of the idea; it cannot be used retrospectively to interpret human history.

St A.'s conception is entirely different. The 'city' is selective; entry to it is by grace and effort. The idea of the city of God is to him fundamental; on it are built an interpretation of history, a manner of life and an attitude of mind and a sanction for the present life and a hope for the future. The city has a historical existence and is not merely a theoretical corollary from an abstract statement about the Universal Reason. The differences need not be further elaborated, for they are obvious even on a slight acquaintance with the *dcD*. The Stoic and the Augustinian ideas are so far apart that they would never have been compared but for the similarity of phrase; and the purpose of this note is to show the need to put back into their setting sentences sometimes loosely quoted as parallel to or even as sources of St A.'s ideas.

(B) The origin of the idea of the city of God

(a) According to St Augustine

St A. leaves us in no doubt whence he thought he derived the idea of the city of God. Three passages may be quoted.

In *dcD* xiv. 1 he says that the liability to the penalty incurred by sin would have applied to all mankind if it had not been that the 'unowed' grace of God had freed some and put them into another category. Hence, in spite of all the variety of institutions and customs which make cross-divisions among men, there are in the final resort only two *genera* of human fellowship; they are the fellowship of those who live (*a*) according to the flesh and (*b*) according to the spirit in the peace appropriate to their genus. These *genera* we rightly call 'according to our Scriptures' (*secundum Scripturas nostras*) two 'cities'.

In v. 19 (translated on p. 56) it is said that the eternal city is 'called in our sacred literature' the city of God.

In xi. 1 St A. says, 'We mean by the city of God the city to which Scripture bears witness—the Scripture which not through the random activities of human minds but through the ordinances of the supreme Providence has proved superior to the literature of the world, subjecting to itself every work of human genius of whatever description because it surpasses them all in divine authority. In that Scripture it is written "Glorious things are spoken of thee, city of God".' He goes on to quote Psalms xlviii and xlvi and continues, 'By these

and similar evidences, all of which it would be tedious to quote, we have learned that there is a city whose citizens we have longed to be with a longing which its founder has inspired in us.'[1]

In xv. 1 St A. refers to his previous discussions, in course of which he had divided the human race into two classes, one consisting 'of those who live according to man', the other 'of those who live according to God'; 'these divisions we call "mystically" (*mystice*) two "cities".' Mystically can only mean allegorically or metaphorically, and the allegory or metaphor can be taken only from the 'city' of Scripture.

(b) According to modern criticism

A turning-point in the study of the *dcD* was marked by the appearance of H. Reuter's *Augustinische Studien*, Gotha, 1887; for the *dcD* was here studied in the light of the new methods of historical criticism, and the mediaevalism and the 'tendentiousness' of many existing interpretations, especially of the so-called political theory of St A. were exposed. That the 'sources' of the *dcD* invited study had already been indicated in such works as F. Nourisson, *La philosophie de saint Augustin* (vol. ii, pp. 89-146), Paris, 1865; but during the past fifty years more searching enquiries into the origins of St A.'s ideas have been undertaken. The following appendix is intended to give some indication, not a complete survey, of the nature of these enquiries, so far as they relate to the central theme of the *dcD*.

In 1900 T. Hahn published a study (*Tyconius-Studien*, Leipzig) in which he traced the debt of St A. to Tyconius. Tyconius was a lay Donatist of independent view ('not a Donatist, but an Afro-Catholic', Christopher Dawson in *A Monument to St Augustine*, p. 58). St A. had a high regard for him (*uberi eloquio, acri ingenio*) and embodied his 'seven rules' of Scriptural exegesis in the *de doctrina Christiana* (see F. C. Burkitt, *The Rules of Tyconius*; the *liber regularum* was published about A.D. 383).

Tyconius was regarded as inconsistent in remaining true to the (Donatist) Church of his baptism, from which he was excommunicated, while at the same time proclaiming that the Church was beyond national frontiers and the artificial divisions set up by men; it was a world-wide society of the faithful, whose consciences must decide whether they belonged to the body of Christ or the body of the devil. E. Buonaiuti, *Il Christianesimo nell'Africa Romana*, Bari, 1928, pp. 335-40, gives an eloquent and sympathetic treatment of Tyconius; he considers that his influence spread *per osmosi, anzichè per semplice diffusione: attraverso cioè una parete separatoria*, and that St A.'s dependence on him, especially in his view of church and society, is clear. He quotes with approval Hahn's question whether the key to many of the specific ideas of St A. about the church is not found in Tyconius (Buonaiuti, *op. cit.*, p. 340: Hahn, *op. cit.*, 116).

Extracts from Tyconius' commentary on the Apocalypse are quoted by Beatus (a monk of the ninth century). On these Hahn bases his study, which must be read in full if justice is to be done to his argument. Some points of resemblance between Tyconius and St A. are these:

[1] The passages in St A. which refer to the *civitas terrena* as Babylon and to the *civitas Dei* as Jerusalem (as e.g. *dcD* xix. 26, *utimur et nos pace Babylonis*; *Enarr. in Ps.* 86. 6, 64. 2, *nomina duarum istarum civitatum, Babylonis et Jerusalem*) have in mind the contrast in the O.T. between the chosen people and their enemy Babylon and in the N.T. such passages as Rev. xviii. 10.

(*a*) both contrast the *civitas Dei* and the *civitas diaboli* in language which is similar, e.g. *Perspicue patet duas civitates esse et duo regna et duos reges Christum et diabolum et ambo super utrasque civitates regnant. . . . . Hae duae civitates una mundo et una desiderat servire Christo; una in hoc mundo regna cupit tenere et una ab hoc mundo fugere; una tristatur, altera laetatur; una flagellat, altera flagellatur; una occidit, altera occiditur; una ut iustificetur adhuc, altera ut impie agat adhuc. Hae utraeque ita laborant in unum, una ut habeat unde damnetur, altera ut habeat unde salvetur.* Beatus, *Comm. in Apoc.,* 507, 15-33. *Ecce duas civitates, unam Dei et unam diaboli et in utrasque reges terrae ministrant,* 506, 26-30.

(*b*) both have a two-fold view of the Church. St A. is as much in doubt as Tyconius, which is the more important, the 'society of good men' or the hierarchical institution of the Christian Church. (This point, however, might be contested, for a case could be made with reason that St A. is more concerned with the 'society of good men'.)

(*c*) both regard the Church as including sinners.

(*d*) both oppose the Donatist view of the Church as excluding sinners, holding that the final separation will not be till the end of the world. (But the parable of the tares could be a common source.)

The strongest argument seems to be the similar ways in which St A. and Tyconius elaborate the contrast between the two cities; but this consideration does not affect St A.'s claim as to his original source in the Scriptures.

H. Scholz, *Glaube und Unglaube in der Welt-Geschichte*, Leipsig, 1911, p. 78, agrees with Hahn in seeing the influence of Tyconius. V. Stegemann, *Augustins Gottestaat,* Tubingen, 1928, denies such influence, p. 32.

In 1925 Hans Leisegang reviewed the sources of St A.'s conception of the *civitas Dei* in an article, '*Der Ursprung der Lehre Augustins von der Civitas Dei*,' in Archiv für Kulturgeschichte, 16 (1925), pp. 127-58. His intention, he says, is to discover those predecessors of St A. who *had influenced* him, and the stream of thought in which he lay. His main points are as follows:

St A. refers in xv. 2 to Gal. iv. 21 sqq. and argues that, as Hagar is a 'shadow' of Sarah, the earthly Jerusalem of the heavenly Jerusalem, the old covenant of the new, so a *part* of the 'earthly city' is the *imago* of the heavenly city, *non se significando, sed alteram et ideo serviens.* And so Leisegang develops his theory of *three* cities, *civitas caelestis spiritalis, civitas terrena spiritalis, civitas terrena carnalis,* and these stand to each other as original, copy, copy of the copy, Sarah corresponding to the copy, and Hagar to the copy of the copy. Thus, St A. complicates St Paul's simple antithesis.

(The classification of the three cities is accepted by Carl-Victor von Horn in *Dei Staatslehre Augustins nach de civitate Dei* and further elaborated in great detail. The question is discussed in H. Reuter, *op. cit.,* pp. 106-50, V. Stegemann, *op. cit.,* pp. 51 ff. See also Figgis, *op. cit.,* pp. 68 ff.)

Leisegang traces the idea of the Urbild, Abbild, and Abbild der Abbildes to Philo, adding that Philo is the first to put Abel and Cain, Isaac and Ishmael, Esau and Jacob in opposition as representations of two worlds. Yet St A. does not refer to Philo as his source, nor is it likely that he read him. St A. received Philo's ideas through Ambrose, the 'Philo Latinus'. Ambrose taught St A. to interpret the O.T. in a mystical sense (the Manicheans, to whom he belonged in his early days, saw no value in the O.T.), and Ambrose was indebted to Philo. Leisegang then traces in Ambrose the treatment of the allegory of Sarah and Hagar, the idea of *civitas Dei*, the use of such terms as *peregrinus*, the conception of two *sectae, sub duorum fratrum nomine* (i.e. Cain and Abel)

compugnantes invicem et contrariae sibi (*de Cain et Abel* i. 1, 4). He thinks that Ambrose also thought of three cities, the third being above the stars and corresponding to the κόσμος νοητός, *mundus intelligibilis*, of Greek philosophy. H. Scholz, *op. cit.*, finds the antithesis of the two cities in Origen, Lactantius, Ambrose and especially in Tyconius. E. Salin, *Civitas Dei*, Tübingen, 1926, p. 175, thinks that St A. derived the two cities from Tyconius, but that the idea goes back to two roots, the 'vision' of the might and the kingdom of Satan seen by our Lord, and the evil world-soul of Plato's Laws. He urges that this idea of a dualism had spread during the first two centuries and is seen clearly in a passage of the Pseudo-Clementines, ed. Lagarde, xx. 2 sq., where the realm of this world, i.e. of the evil, is opposed to a realm of the other world, i.e. of the good; in this dualism Creation is completed and fulfilled: 'God has ordained two Kingdoms and two Ages; the one is called the Kingdom of Heaven, the other the Kingdom of the Kings of this Age on Earth.' He points, too, to the dualism inherent in Manicheism and to St A.'s early acceptance of it.

The foregoing sketches are perhaps enough to show the kind of 'sources' to which critics have referred St A.'s conception of the *civitas Dei* and its counterpart, though full justice can be done only by a reading of the articles themselves. Some of the critics write as though St A. derived his teaching from the sources enumerated, others regard the sources as influencing the shaping of his ideas. Admittedly a man of the education and experience of St A., of his anxious passion for knowledge and his power of passing the ideas of others through a keenly critical mind, is inevitably influenced in the process.

But the critics, no doubt unintentionally, seem to attach too little importance to St A.'s own statements that the source of his idea of the *civitas Dei* was the Scriptures themselves, and to neglect to trace the elements of the idea to this source. All the elements which make up St A.'s treatment of the *civitas Dei* can be found in the Old or the New Testament, and St A.'s manner of treating and presenting his thought on this matter leaves no doubt that he believed himself to have Scriptural authority for all that he said, however much he owed to the thought and the method of Christian and pagan writers. Moreover, some of the criticism seems to interpret affinity or similarity as indebtedness, and to ignore the consideration that St A. and most of his alleged 'sources' had in front of them the same originals, namely the Scriptures. If X derived a notion from the O.T., St A. may also have derived it from the same source without owing it to X, and he may equally have drawn the same deductions. Full weight should be given to this consideration even while search is made for the influences which may have helped to shape St A.'s interpretation or to account for the emphasis which he may lay upon this or that element.

Appendix II

ST AUGUSTINE'S QUOTATIONS FROM THE BIBLE

Readers familiar with the Vulgate will have noticed that St A.'s quotations from the Bible do not reproduce the text of the Vulgate.

The need for a Latin version of the O.T. and N.T. was perhaps felt most pressingly in the North of Africa. In Rome the Church was more Greek than Roman; the part of the Mediterranean where Greek was least known was Africa, and here a Latin Bible first appeared in the second century. In this version the Latin N.T. is of greater textual importance than the Latin O.T.; for, while the O.T. was translated from the Septuagint, itself a Greek version of the Hebrew, the N.T. was translated from its original Greek. Hence the Latin N.T. is evidence for the early state of the Greek MSS. This Latin version exists in two forms known as the African and the European, and a revised form of the European was known as the Italian. The Italian or *Itala* was the version which St A. used.[1] Cyprian, who died in A.D. 258, used the African.

In A.D. 382 Pope Damasus asked Jerome to produce an authoritative Latin Bible to supersede the many versions in use. 'You urge me to revise the old Latin version, and, as it were, to sit in judgment on the copies of the Scriptures which are now scattered throughout the whole world; and, inasmuch as they differ from one another, you would have me decide which of them agrees with the Greek original.'[2] The Gospels were finished in A.D. 384; the whole Bible in A.D. 405. Naturally, as Jerome expected, the new version, which came to be known as the Vulgate, met with unfavourable criticism. St A. was among the critics,[3] chiefly because he attached high value to the Septuagint version of the O.T.[4] and he disapproved of Jerome's innovation in making direct translation from the Hebrew.

The Italian version of the N.T. does not survive entire, for the Vulgate gradually replaced it. Thirty-eight fragmentary MSS. exist. The old Latin versions and the Vulgate continued in use into the Middle Ages; scribes familiar with one version would unintentionally insert its readings into the other version, till the text of the Vulgate became extremely corrupt. It has been a major task of scholarship to restore the text—a task recently concluded in the edition of J. Wordsworth and H. J. White. [5]

A few examples of the difference between the Italian version as used by St A. and the Vulgate are given below; they are taken from the selection of passages included in this volume.

dcD

v. 15. Mt. vi. 2.

    perceperunt mercedem suam—A.

    receperunt—V.

    ἀπέχουσι τὸν μισθὸν αὐτῶν

[1] Cf. *de doctrina Christ.* ii. 15.
[2] See Kidd, *Documents* ii. No. 138 (Jerome, *praef. in iv Evang.*)
[3] For St A.'s correspondence with Jerome see letters 28, 40, 67, 71, 73, 82, 167.
[4] Cf. e.g. *dcD* xviii. 43.
[5] See F. G. Kenyon, *Our Bible and the Ancient Manuscripts* (new edn. 1945), p. 171.

xix. 8. Mt. xxiv. 12.
   abundavit—A.
   abundabit—V.
   διὰ τὸ πληθυνθῆναι.
xix. 11. Rom. vi. 22.
   A. and V. agree.
xix. 14. 1 Tim. v. 8.
   quisquis autem suis et maxime domesticis non providet, fidem denegat et est
     infideli deterior—A.
   si quis autem suorum, et maxime domesticorum, curam non habet, fidem
     negavit et est infideli deterior—V.
   εἰ δέ τις τῶν ἰδίων καὶ μάλιστα οἰκέιων οὐ προνοεῖ, τὴν πίστιν ἤρνηται
   καὶ ἔστιν ἀπίστου χείρων.
xix. 15. 2 Pet. ii. 19.
   a quo enim quis devictus est, huic et servus addictus est—A.
   a quo enim quis superatus est, huius et servus est—V.
   ᾧ γάρ τις ἥττηται, τούτῳ δεδούλωται.
xix. 26. 1 Tim. ii. 2.
   caritate—A.
   castitate—V.
   σεμνότητι
xix. 27. Mt. vi. 12.
   Dimitte nobis—A. and V. agree.

Notes

I. Some books on:
  (*a*) general background.
  (*b*) general introduction to St A.
  (*c*) texts and translations of the *dcD*

Reference is made to other books in Appendix I(*B*) and in

II. Notes to Extracts and Chapters.

I(*a*)

Sir Samuel Dill, *Roman Society from Nero to Marcus Aurelius*, 5th reprint, London, 1925. (i)

Sir Samuel Dill, *Roman Society in the Last Century of the Western Empire*, 2nd edn., London, 1899. (ii)

T. R. Glover, *The Conflict of Religions under the Roman Empire*, London, 11th edn., 1927.

W. R. Halliday, *The Pagan Background of Early Christianity*, Liverpool, 1925.

G. Boissier, *La Fin du Paganisme*, 1891.

T. R. Glover, *Progress in Religion to the Christian Era*, S.C.M., 1922.

A. D. Nock, *Conversion. The Old and the New in Religion from Alexander the Great to Augustine of Hippo*, Oxford, 1933.

C. N. Cochrane, *Christianity and Classical Culture*, Oxford, 1940.

L. Duchesne, *Early History of the Christian Church*, 3 vols., London, 1924.

B. J. Kidd, *History of the Church to A.D. 461*, 3 vols., Oxford, 1922.

E. Buonaiuti, *Il Cristianesimo nell' Africa Romana*, Bari, 1928.

P. Monceaux, *Histoire littéraire de l'Afrique Chrétienne*, vols. i-vii, Paris. 1901-23.

B. J. Kidd, *Documents Illustrative of the History of the Church*, 2 vols. (vol. i to A.D. 313, vol. ii A.D. 313 to 461), S.P.C.K., 1920.

H. Bettenson, *Documents of the Christian Church* (World's Classics Series), Oxford, 1943.

Pierre de Labriolle, *La réaction païenne*, Paris, 1942.

I(*b*)

E. Gilson, *Introduction à l'étude de Saint Augustin*, Paris, 1st edn., 1928, 2nd edn., 1943. See excellent bibliography: easily the best introduction.

(Essays by ten contributors), *A Monument to St Augustine*, Sheed and Ward, 1930.

H. Pope, O.P., *Saint Augustine of Hippo*, Sands & Co., 1937.

W. J. Sparrow Simpson, *St Augustine's Episcopate*, S.P.C.K., 1944 (slight; contains chapter on *dcD*).

M. E. Keenan, *Life and Times of St Augustine as revealed in his Letters*, Washington D.C., 1935.

F. Cayré, *Initiation à la Philosophie de Saint Augustin*, Paris, 1947.
W. Cunningham, *St Austin and his place in the History of Christian Thought*,
Cambridge, 1886.
See also the books cited in Appendix I(*B*).

I(*c*)

*Sancti Aurelii Augustini Opera Omnia, opera et studio Monachorum Ordinis S.
Benedicti.* The best complete edition of the works is this edition by the Bene-
dictines of St Maur (Paris, 1679-1700). There are later reprints (inferior).

Abbé Migne, *Patrologia Latina: dcD* is in vol. 41. (This is a reprint of the
Benedictine edition: 'the reader ... should use the texts which Migne employed,'
A. Souter.)

Corpus Scriptorum Ecclesiasticorum latinorum, Vienna, since 1866: *dcD* is in
vol. xl.

Sancti Aurelii Augustini Episcopi de civitate Dei, ex rec. B. Dombart quartum
recognovit A. Kalb, 2 vols., Teubner, 1928.

S. Aurelii Augustini de civitate Dei, edited with notes by J. E. C. Welldon,
D.D., 2 vols., S.P.C.K., 1924.

Classiques Garnier, *La Cité de Dieu*. Texte et traduction avec une introduction et des notes, Paris, 1948. Vol. i, ed. by P. de Labriolle, contains Bks. i-v,
vol. ii, ed. by J. Perret, contains Bks. vi-x; the introduction and notes are very
short.

The City of God, by *St Augustine*, translated by John Healey, 1610. A
shortened edition was published by Messrs Dent in 1931 and since reprinted.
It contains an excellent introduction (about 50 pp.) by Sir Ernest Barker.

St Augustine's City of God, translated by Rev. Marcus Dods, D.D., 1871.
(In the Select Library of the Nicene and Post-Nicene Fathers of the Church.)

II.

Introduction

Invasion of Alaric: T. Hodgkin, *Italy and her Invaders*, Oxford; see vol. i (ii)
J. B. Bury, *The Invasion of Europe by the Barbarians*, London, 1928.

The division of the dcD: In a recently edited letter of St. A (Revue bénédictine, 51 (1939), pp. 109-21, C. Lambot, *Lettre inédite de S. Augustin relative
au de civitate Dei*) written to Firmus (cf. *Ep.* 82, 191, 194, etc.), he says it is
'much' to bind up the *dcD* in one volume. If in two volumes, the break should
come after the tenth book; if in more than two, the book should be grouped as
5-5-4-4-4 on the grounds of subject-matter. The *dcD* was published in parts, cf.
e.g. *Ep.* 184*a*, 5-7 (Bks. i-iii by A.D. 414, iv-v by A.D. 415, vi-xi by A.D. 416,
xii-xiv by A.D. 420, xv-xxii by A.D. 426). Lambot argues from the letter that St A.
sent Firmus a *revised* copy of the *whole* of the *dcD* and that the MS. of the *dcD*,
Reims 403, with which the letter is embodied, goes back to this revised copy.

Twenty-two books: E. Salin, *Civitas Dei*, p. 174, propounds the curious hypothesis that the division 10 + 12 is intentionally the same as 10 books of Plato's
Republic + 12 books of the Laws and that thereby St A. intended to show that
he was writing 'theologische Politik, nicht politische Theologie, Staatsgründing,
nicht Geschichtsbetrachtung'!

Civitas: For a consideration of the 'unusual choice' of word, see H. Leisegang
in work cited on p. 272. In some passages *civitas* means 'state', e.g. iv. 3, xviii.
41, *at vero gens illa, ille populus, illa civitas, illa respublica, illi Israelitae:* in others

it is virtually *societas*. The general use von Horn, *op. cit.* p. 14, renders as 'Inbegriff derer, die die Eigenschaft der Zugehörigkeit zu einem irgendwie gearteten diesseitigen oder transzendenten Verband besitzen': and *civitas Dei*, therefore, is 'Inbegriff aller welche die Eigenschaft der Zugehörigkeit zu Gott besitzen'. St A.'s words for 'state' are *respublica, gens, regnum, imperium*.

Extract 1

The explanation of Ps. lxxxvii given in the text assumes the text and order of verses of the R.V. But the Hebrew text and the order of verses are very uncertain, and the general meaning has been variously interpreted. H. Gunker (*Die Psalmen*, Gottingen, 1926) arranges thus: verses 2, 1, 5 second clause, 7, 3, 6, 4 third clause, 4 first and second clauses 5. His interpretation is: 'Jehovah loves the gates of Zion more than all the dwellings of Jacob. His foundation is in the holy mountains and he himself stablished her for ever. Singers and dancers alike say "They all sing thee": Glorious things do they proclaim of thee, thou City of God. Jehovah writes in his book of the people "That man is born here, and that man there (i.e. in widely separated places). I can count Egypt and Babylon among those that know me: there is Philistia itself and Tyre and Ethiopia. Zion I shall call the mother of all, in which all men are born."' For the reading 'mother of all' compare the Septuagint *ad loc.* and 2 Sam. xx. 19. Gunker rejects any idea of the Gentiles coming to Zion; in his view the Psalm refers only to the widespread diffusion of Jews in foreign lands and glories in the unity of Jewry which from all quarters turns its eyes to the centre of its religion, the Holy City; when the Psalmist says, 'Egypt' he means 'Jews in Egypt', much as St Paul uses 'Achaea' and 'Macedonia' in Rom. xv. 26 and 2 Cor. ix. 2. W. O. E. Oesterley (*The Psalms*, London, 1939) regards as the main theme 'Yahweh's recognition of the Gentiles as the children of the Holy City, figuratively represented as their Mother', 'they are recorded as belonging to his family in the heavenly register.' M. Buttenwieser (*The Psalms*, Chicago, 1938) thinks the Psalm glorifies the success of the Jewish propaganda which had resulted in the conversion of large numbers of Gentiles to Judaism.

St A.'s text is *fundamenta eius in montibus sanctis; diligit Dominus portas Sion. Gloriosa dicta sunt de te, civitas Dei. Memor ero Rahab et Babylonis, scientibus me. Etenim alienigenae et Tyrus et populus Aethiopum hi fuerunt ibi. Mater Sion dicet homo; et homo factus est in ea, et ipse fundavit eam Altissimus. Dominus narrabit in Scriptura populorum et principum. Tanquam iucundatorum omnium habitatio in te.* This can be put together from *Enarr. in Psalm.* lxxxvi.

St A.'s 'Messianic' interpretation of the Psalm is illustrated in *dcD* xvii. 14 sqq.; in 17 *Mater Sion* is explained in the same way as in *Enarr. in Psalm. loc. cit.*

For the *Itala* version see Appendix II. See also D. de Brayne, *L'Itala de Saint Augustin*, in Revue Bénédictine, July 1913, pp. 294-314.

Letters of St A.: J. H. Baxter, *Select Letters of St Augustine*, with an English translation, in the Loeb Classical Library.

Donatism was really a separatist movement rooted in nationalism. For it, see P. Monceaux, *op. cit.*, vol. iv for its beginnings, vol. vi. for its literature, vol. vii for St A. and Donatism. J. Tixeront, *Histoire des dogmes*, ii, pp. 222-31. Kidd, vol. i, p. 533 sqq.; ii, 109 sqq., 505 sqq.

For the idea of the *civitas Dei* in other writings of St A., cf. *Confessions.* iv. 15, 26; xii. 11, 12; *de catech. rud.* 31; *Enchirid.* 29; *de ver. relig.* 50; *Enarr. in Ps.*

cxxvi. 3; *de Gen. ad litt.* xi. 20; *Ep.* clv. 9. This list is not complete. The *dcD* is referred to in *Ep.* 184, 5, *ego in quibusdam libris quos de civitate Dei praenotavi, quorum ad vos existimo iam pervenisse notitiam . . .*

Definition of eternal law: ea est qua justum est ut omnia sint ordinatissima: de lib. arb. 1, 15.

Earthly City: H. Hermelink, *Die Civitas Terrena bei Augustin,* in Harnack Festgabe, Mohr, Tubingen, 1921, Salin, *op. cit.,* p. 181; von Horn, *op. cit.,* p. 18 sq.

Extracts 2-6

The Fall: Peter Green, *The Problem of Evil,* 1920 (see also a pamphlet by the same author, *The Premundane Fall,* Mowbray, 1944); N. P. Williams, *The Ideas of the Fall and of Original Sin* (Bampton Lectures), 1927; T. A. Lacey, *Nature, Miracle and Sin,* London, 1916.

Pelagianism: Bettenson, *op. cit.,* p. 73 sqq.; Kidd, *Documents,* ii, nos. 130, 131, 180, 181, 184-6, 189.

Pelagianism as Stoicism: in *Ep.* cxxxiii Jerome traces P. back to Pythagoreanism and Stoicism. Marius Mercator (*P.L.* xlviii. 111) says that in Syria similar views had been expressed, notably by Theodore, Bishop of Mopsuestia, and were brought to Rome by the Syrian Rufinus, who communicated them to Pelagius, who embodied them in his commentary on the Epistle to the Romans. Whether this historical connection existed or not, at any rate the logical connection between Pelagianism and the Nestorian Christology of Theodore is clear; the self-sufficiency of Pelagianism dispenses with the need for a divine Saviour and the result is that Christ is a purely human moral teacher. But it was Augustinianism that provoked Pelagianism, or rather it was Augustinianism that caused classical notions of man to reassert themselves in Christian form.

Definition of Will: voluntas est animi motus, cogente nullo, ad aliquid non amittendum vel adipiscendum; de duabus animabus, x. 14.

To St A. pride is the beginning of sin; it expresses itself in *cupiditas* which is *amor rerum transeuntium,* of which the opposite is *amor rerum amandarum,* i.e. *caritas.*

Extract 8

For early Christian methods of Old Testament exegesis, see A. H. MacNeile, *The Old Testament in the Christian Church.*

For the incorporation of 'just' pagans in the city, see the careful and interesting study by a Chinese Jesuit, *Saint Augustin et les vertus des paens,* by J. Wang Tch'ang-tche, S.J., Paris, 1938. He considers that (i) St A. insists upon 'explicit' faith as a condition of righteousness and therefore excludes non-Christians; if, then, St A. specifically includes Job and others (e.g. Cornelius, see *de praedest. sanct.* vii. 12) it can only be that in his view some special vision was granted to them; (ii) St A. knows nothing of 'implicit' faith (i.e. a loyalty to a high conception of righteousness vouchsafed by God, though independent of the Christian revelation), though there are passages in which he comes close to the 'generous view' and so makes inclusion in the city of God possible to *all* pagans of honest endeavour after righteousness. The case is worked out with great care and earnestness; see esp. pp. 112 to end. But the writer does not seem to do justice to St A.'s insistence on faith as a necessity of 'true' virtue; he attributes this insistence, rightly in some measure, to St A.'s controversy with Pelagius; for to

grant to 'just' pagans the same virtues as to Christians would be to play into Pelagius' hands. The real reason, it may be suggested, is that St A. realises that the inner quality of the externally identical act in pagan and Christian is different, because one is in the last resort self-conscious and self-centred, while the other is self-forgetting and God-centred; the Christian moral act is 'for My sake' and not 'for my sake'.

Extracts 9–12

The Church and the City of God: Appendix H in Welldon, op. cit.; E. Gilson, Introduction . . . pp. 237-9 (with ref.). See also J. N. Figgis, Political Aspects of St Augustine's City of God; E. Salin, Civitas Dei, p. 180.

Extracts 14–20

In the second and eighth books of the Policraticus, John of Salisbury uses the argument and much of the language of dcD v. 1-14; with v. 1-11 cf. Policr. ii. 18-24, 436c sqq.; with v. 12-14 cf. viii. 5, 721a-22a where the Roman's self-sacrifice is discussed.

Extracts 18–20

Constitutio Antoniniana: Dio lxxvii. 9, 5; Dig. 1, 5, 17; Mommsen, Staatsrecht iii. 699, French translation vi (i). 331. The Papyrus is given in H. M. D. Parker, The Roman World from A.D. 138 to 337, London, 1935, p. 334, with the references to the literature on it.

Extract 21

The titles occurring in St A.'s letters are collected in M. E. Keenan, op. cit., pp. 93-7.

Idea of Kingship: J. Kaerst, Geschichte des Hellenismus (esp. ii (2)), Leipsig, 1917; E. R. Goodenough, The Political Philosophy of Hellenistic Kingship; W. W. Tarn, Hellenistic Civilisation; M. P. Charlesworth, Harvard Theological Review xxviii. 1, 1935, with bibliography.

A world-state as Alexander's ideal: W. W. Tarn, Alexander the Great and the Unity of Mankind (Raleigh Lecture), 1933 and, by the same writer, Alexander the Great (Sources and Studies), Appendix 25, 1948. For Eusebius and the Christian idea of kingship in relation to Hellenistic philosophy, see N. H. Baynes, Eusebius and the Christian Empire, in Mélanges Bidez (Annuaire de l'Institut de philologie et d'histoire orientales, Bruxelles), 1934. The passages from Ecphantus, etc., with the references to Stobaeus, may be found there.

BOOK XIX

Chapter 4

C. H. Moore, Ancient Beliefs in the Immortality of the Soul, New York, 1931.

F. Cumont, The Oriental Religions in Roman Paganism (authorised translation), Chicago, 1911.

F. Cumont, After Life in Roman Paganism, New Haven, 1922.

E. Rhode, Psyche (English translation of 8th edition), W. B. Hillis, London, 1925.

F. H. Brabant, *Time and Eternity in Christian Thought*, Bampton Lectures, 1936.

J. Guitton, *Le Temps et l'Eternité chez Plotin et St Augustin*, Paris, 1933 (of greater range than the title might suggest).

Stoicism: E. R. Bevan, *Stoics and Sceptics*, Oxford, 1913; E. V. Arnold, *Roman Stoicism*, Cambridge, 1911; Dill, *op. cit.*, i, Bk. iii, ch. 1 (esp. for *sapiens*).

Chapter 6

Roman Interpreters: W. I. Snellman, *de interpretibus Romanorum*, Leipsig, 1919.

Chapter 7

Just wars: R. Rigout, *La doctrine de la guerre juste*, Paris, 1935.

Languages of Africa: other refs. to Punic in the Letters are 16. 2; 17. 2; 66. 2; 84. 2; 108. 14.

Chapter 8

Consolations: letters of condolence in Latin literature are many, e.g. Cic., *ad fam.* iv. 5; v. 16; vi. 3; *ad Brut.* 9; Sen. *Ep.* 63, 93, 99. They are numerous in English literature as e.g. by Dr Johnson, by Lamb to Coleridge, Cowper to Joseph Hill. A letter by Swift to Mrs Whiteway contains the following sentence which is not unlike in thought to this chapter of St A.: 'I was born to a million disappointments; I had set my heart very much upon that young man, but I find he has no business in so corrupt a world.' For the *consolationes* as a form of literature, see C. Favet, *La Consolation Latine Chrétienne*, Paris, 1937. Seneca, Plutarch, St Ambrose, St Jerome have left *consolationes*: Cicero's *consolatio* on the death of his daughter is lost. The authorship of the *Consolatio ad Liviam* is uncertain. St A. wrote letters of consolation, *Ep.* iii. 244, 263.

Prayer: see Heraclitus, fr. 5 Diels, who despised it; Xen. *Oec.* 5, 19; Plat. *Symp.* 202e, *Legg.* 931c; Persius, *Sat.* 2; M. Aur. v. 7; Sen. *N.Q.* ii. 37, *Ep.* 31. 5, 41. 1; Maximus of Tyre (*Diss.* xi. 2. 7) urges that the only prayer which is answered is the prayer for goodness, peace and hope in death. For the distinction between free and formal prayer, cf. Tert. *Apol.* 30. See, in general, L. R. Farnell, *The Evolution of Religion*, p. 163 sqq.

Chapter 9

T. Whittaker, *The Neoplatonists*, 2nd edn., Cambridge, 1918; C. Bigg, *Neoplatonism*, S.P.C.K., 1895.

Cacus: Munzer, *Cacus der Rinderdieb*, 1911.

Daemons: Nock, *op. cit.*, p. 222 sqq., and for ref. to literature, p. 300; Dill, *op. cit.* (i), p. 425, for philosophical aspect. St A.'s view of daemons is summarised in the following sentence, 'Given true piety the men of God cast out the spiritual (*aeriam*) powers which are the enemies and adversaries of piety; they cast them out not by placating them but by exorcising them; all the temptations arising from their opposition men of God overcome not by praying to the powers themselves but by praying to their God against the powers. For the powers do not overcome or subdue anyone unless because of his partnership in sin.' (*dcD* x. 22.)

Chapter 12

W. McDougall, *Social Psychology*, 7th edn., 1913, cc. x-xii.

Chapter 16

Slavery: the view of H. Wallon quoted in the text is to be found in *Histoire de l'Esclavage dans l'Antiquité* (1879), iii, p. 316. St A.'s general opinion is expressed in such passages as *Enarr. in Psalm.* cxxiv. 7, *sunt domini, sunt et servi; diversa sunt nomina, sed homines et homines paria sunt nomina; de doctr. Christ.* i. 23, *Inest enim vitioso animo id* (i.e. *aliis hominibus dominari*) *magis appetere et sibi tanquam debitum vindicare quod uni proprie debetur Deo . . .Cum vero etiam eis qui sibi naturaliter pares sunt, hoc est, hominibus dominari affectat, intolerabilis omnino superbia est.*

Providentia: see M. P. Charlesworth, *Providentia and Aeternitas*, Harvard Theological Review, vol. xxix, 1936.

Chapter 18

Si fallor, sum: similar passages are *Solil.* ii. 1; *de vera relig.* xxxix. 73; *de Trin.* x. 10, 14; xv. 12, 21; *de beata vita* 7; *dcD* xi. 26; *de lib. arb.* ii. 3, 7. Gilson, *op. cit.*, discusses such passages briefly, but does not indicate the differences between St A. and Descartes. See further, Ch. Boyer, *L'Idée de vérité dans la philosophie de Saint Augustin*, Paris, 1921, pp. 32-41.

Chapter 21

J. N. Figgis, *The Political Aspects of St Augustine's City of God*, 1921.

G. Combés, *La Doctrine politique de Saint Augustin*, Paris, 1927.

N. H. Baynes, *The Political Ideas of St. Augustine's de civitate Dei* (Historical Association Pamphlet, No. 104), Bell, 1936.

Carl-Victor von Horn, *Die Staatslehre Augustins nach de civitate Dei.* Ostdeutsche Verlaganstalt, Breslau, 1934. (Short, but very good; excellent notes.)

M. B. Foster, *Masters of Political Thought* (Plato to Machiavelli), Harrap, 1942, contains a chapter on St A.

H.-X. Arquillière, *L'Augustinisme politique*, Paris, 1934 (influence in Middle Ages).

The literature on this topic is enormous. The bibliographies in Gilson and in Baynes should be consulted.

Chapter 24

It is worth while to draw attention (for the first time?) to the use of 'removeo' in *de Trin.* x. In c. 14, *sed quoniam de natura mentis agitur, removeamus a consideratione nostra;* in c. 17, *remotis igitur paulisper caeteris, quorum mens de se ipsa certa est, tria haec potissimum considerata tractemus,* i.e. 'let us leave out of account for a moment'. This is precisely the same use as *'remota itaque iustitia'.*

Figgis, *op. cit.* does not really discuss the *magna latrocinia* passage. But he agrees that 'St A. did not, as I said earlier, set out to produce a theory of the state', p. 66. On p. 54 he says 'the last thing that he set out to do was to give a theory of the relation of Church and State'. With this view Gilson agrees. Salin, op. cit., p. 188, says, 'Und so bedeutet die Frage: "Was sind Reiche ohne Gerechtigkeit anders als grosse Rauberbanden?" niemals, dass alle Weltstaaten, da ihnen

die wahre Gerechtigkeit ja stets fehlt, Rauberbanden sind, wohl aber, dass nur nach dem Mass der in ihnen vorhandenen Gerechtigkeit sich die Staaten von einer Rauberbande unterschieden.' On p. 243 he urges that the sentence is a condemnation of ancient states only if *iustitia* has a Christian sense involving worship of the true God. The sentence as such is not Christian but 'antik', for from Plato onwards justice is taken to be essential to a state. See also von Horn and the refs. in his notes.

For Alexander as *latro*, see Seneca, *N.Q.* iii, *praef.*, *Alexandri latrocinia*; *de ben.* i. 13, *a pueritia latro.*

Conclusion

'Our Philosophy', cf. *contra Iulianum* iv. 14, 72. '. . . *nostra Christiana quae una est vera philosophia.*'

Index

This index does not refer to the text and translation.